A Matter of Security

Forensic Focus Series

This series, edited by Gwen Adshead, takes the field of Forensic Psychotherapy as its focal point, offering a forum for the presentation of theoretical and clinical issues. It embraces such influential neighbouring disciplines as language, law, literature, criminology, ethics and philosophy, as well as psychiatry and psychology, its established progenitors. Gwen Adshead is Consultant Forensic Psychotherapist and Lecturer in Forensic Psychotherapy at Broadmoor Hospital.

Forensic Focus 25

A Matter of Security
The Application of Attachment Theory to Forensic Psychiatry and Psychotherapy

Edited by Friedemann Pfäfflin and Gwen Adshead

Jessica Kingsley Publishers
London and Philadelphia

First published in the United Kingdom in 2004
by Jessica Kingsley Publishers
116 Pentonville Road
London N1 9JB, UK
and
400 Market Street, Suite 400
Philadelphia PA 19106, USA

www.jkp.com

Copyright © Jessica Kingsley Publishers 2004
Printed digitally since 2007

Library of Congress Cataloging in Publication Data
A CIP catalog record for this book is available from the Library of Congress

British Library Cataloguing in Publication Data
A CIP catalogue record for this book is available from the British Library

ISBN 978 1 84310 177 2

Contents

Foreword

Attachment theory as developed by John Bowlby has since the 1960s stimulated theorizing about the normal and psychopathological development of children, women and men. In an unprecedented way it demonstrated how psychological functioning depends on adequate emphatic interaction from the very beginning of life. The quality of the interaction between the newborn and his or her caregiver, the attachment patterns experienced, the developing process of mentalization of these experiences and the resulting attachment representations are crucial for how an adult will interact with other persons and his or her environment.

Taking this into account, it is not surprising that forensic psychotherapists and psychiatrists enthusiastically engage in attachment research, using its achivements for a better understanding of their clients and for the improvement of the care they offer, both as individual therapists and as protagonists of the systems of detention in secure psychiatric units and in prisons, which have to offer a milieu of security for the sake of society as well as staff and their clients. In both settings one finds an accumulation of failed primary attachment processes that need remedy to interrupt the 'circuit of misery, violence and anxiety' which Sherlock Holmes (Conan Doyle 1895) identified as one of our greatest problems, and which Murray Cox, the founder of the Forensic Focus series, cited in his seminal work, *Mutative Metaphors in Psychotherapy. The Aeolian Mode* (Cox and Alice Theilgaard (1987), London: Jessica Kingsley Publishers.

This volume gathers a body of original work on attachment theory applied to forensic psychiatry and psychotherapy, and also some previously published seminal work from this field.

In the first section on theoretical issues, Peter Fonagy gives a survey of research findings on the developmental roots of violence in the failure of mentalization. He focuses on a time of violence which is predominantly encountered in the lives of forensic psychiatry and psychotherapy patients, and which is embodied as an act of overwhelming rage, and he suggests 'that violent acts are only possible when a decoupling occurs between the representations of subjective states of the self and actions'. Paradoxically, he comes to the conclusion that 'violence is a gesture of hope, a wish for a new beginning, even if in reality it is usually just a tragic end'.

Thomas Ross examines the heterogeneous terminology used in attachment theory and research. According to him, the terms '(attachment) representation', '(attachment) style', and '(attachment) prototype' are usually used adequately and in accordance with the corresponding construct. They denote an intrapsychic mode of handling interpersonal relationship experiences (attachment representation) or relate to manifest behavioural correlates of attachment (attachment style). When the focus is on testing clinical hypotheses and the differentiation of manifest attachment behaviour ('attachment style'), the usage of 'attachment type/prototype' seems appropriate. '(Attachment) pattern' and '(attachment) organisation' are applied in inconsistent ways in the literature. The terms 'attachment status', 'attachment quality', and ' attachment classification' (as a result of a classification process) are not really helpful, or rather useless, as they do not add information beyond what is denoted by the above-mentioned terms. Furthermore, they contain social connotations, which might lead to misunderstandings when discussing human attachment. The same applies to the occasionally used terms 'attachment pathology' and 'attachment difficulty'. They imply social judgments that are not empirically justified.

Drawing on incoherent narratives from the investigation of women who have killed, Franziska Lamott, Elisabeth Fremmer-Bombik and Friedemann Pfäfflin suggest classifying them as 'fragmented attachment representations' (FRAG), thus taking their specificity into account, instead of using the category 'cannot classify' (CC).

In the second section, clinical issues are presented that reflect the application of attachment theory to individual treatment. Paul Renn gives a lucid report of the validity of attachment theory when applied to short-term counseling in a probation setting, which may encourage other clinicians to make use of it.

The third section deals with clinical and institutional aspects of attachment theory within the framework of settings typical for forensic psychiatry and psychotherapy. Gwen Adshead emphasizes the need for psychiatric secure institutions for forensic patients to truly provide a secure base for dealing with intrapsychic as well as interactional conflicts. Anne Aiyegbusi exemplifies the significance of attachment theory for the milieu of forensic institutions, and especially for the work of nurses. Michael Parker and Mark Morris draw on their experience of reflecting on attachment theory for practical purposes in a prison setting.

The fourth section reports attachment research data on specific forensic patient samples. Gwen Adshead investigates the precursors of personality disorders and identifies attachment shortcomings in childhood as a prominent cause of the development of a personality disorder. Thomas Ross and Friedemann Pfäfflin investigate attachment styles, self-regulation and interpersonal problems in a group of 31 imprisoned offenders convicted of at least one violent crime against another person and serving a prison sentence of at least three years. Their data are compared with the data of two comparison groups of non-violent men, prison service trainees and members of a Christian congregation. Finally, Franziska Lamott, Natalie Sammet and Friedemann Pfäfflin report comparative attachment data from samples of women who have killed and been sentenced to either imprisonment or detention in a secure psychiatric hospital, and a group of women who escaped domestic violence by taking refuge in a women's shelter.

In a concluding chapter the editors reflect on the benefits that forensic staff may draw from attachment theory, as well as from attachment research, for their work. Providing a secure basis for patients as well as for staff seems to be essential in order to deal with former deficits of attachment development and to increase security for patients, staff, and society at large.

Friedemann Pfäfflin and Gwen Adshead

Part I

Theory

CHAPTER 1

The Developmental Roots of Violence in the Failure of Mentalization[1]

Peter Fonagy

INTRODUCTION: THE NATURE OF VIOLENCE

This chapter will argue that interpersonal violence is difficult for us to con-template, precisely because it is ultimately an act of humanity (Abrahamsen 1973). We wish to avoid that which is potentially a part of all of us. Both the glamorization and the demonization of violence, strategies which are familiar from the media, serve to distance us from an experience that may not be far from any of us; they help us avoid having to understand violent minds. It is as if contemplating these minds creates such intense fear and helplessness that the mere act of thinking about them becomes impossible. While failing to explore intrapsychic factors may help us to obscure the sim-ilarities between our sense of ourselves and our sense of violent human beings, it also blocks off any insight into how these individuals feel and think. We must enter the violent person's psychic reality, not just in order to be able to offer treatment, but also to better anticipate the nature of the risks they embody both to themselves and to society (Cox 1982). The attempt at explanation does not amount to an exculpation, but understanding is the first step in preventing violence. The answer to the riddle of how an individual can lose restraint over their propensity to injure others must lie in what is ordinary rather than extraordinary: *normal human development.*

There are many ways of categorizing violent acts and it is unlikely that any single set of ideas will be able to explain all the different types. One approach has been to distinguish three types of violent acts. The first consists of violence when it occurs as an act of overwhelming rage. At these times it often appears disorganized as an act, propelled by massive affective outflow or discharge. The second type of violent act appears as a gratification of perverse or psychotic motives. In this context the act appears somewhat more organized and there is a predatory character to the motive state of the violent individual. The unfeeling, prototypically psychopathic character of violent acts may be most obvious here. Finally, violent acts frequently occur in part fulfilment of criminal motives. Such acts of violence may be either organized or disorganized. While single acts of violence often do not match any of these prototypes particularly well, some kind of division of violent acts along these lines has to be accepted. This chapter is mainly concerned with the first type of uncontrolled, affective, disorganized violent act, regardless of the criminality of the motives.

There is an immense multidisciplinary literature on the subject of violence. From these we know that poverty (Laub 1998), access to weapons (Valois and McKewon 1998), exposure to media violence (American Academy of Child and Adolescent Psychiatry 1999), academic failure (Farrington 1989), impersonal schools (Walker, Irvin and Sprague 1997), gangs (Bjerregaard and Lizotte 1995), rejection by peers (Elliot, Hamburg and Williams 1998; Harpold and Band 1998), ineffective parenting (Wells and Rankin 1988), lack of parental monitoring (Patterson, Reid and Dishion 1992), exposure to domestic violence (Elliott *et al.* 1998), and abuse or neglect (Smith and Thornberry 1995) are all associated factors. Commonly in the history of violent individuals we find childhood hyperactivity, attention or concentration deficit and impulsivity (Loeber and Stouthamer-Loeber 1998), or adult psychiatric problems. Perhaps most relevant for our purposes are recent studies that have found a link between narcissism and violence, where violence can be seen as a response to a threat to an exaggerated or grandiose self structure (Bushman and Baumeister 1999).

While such 'facts' of social violence paint a picture of the individual most likely to be at risk, they do not capture the essential nature of the problem. Many with these characteristics do not commit violent crime, and many violent criminals do not fit the descriptions provided particularly well. For example, Eric Harris and Dylan Klebold opened fire in a suburban high school, killing fifteen people, including themselves (Verlinden, Hersen and Thomas 2000). The explosives they brought with them, had they detonated, would have put the death toll into the hundreds. During the attack, the boys excitedly discussed which of their classmates should be allowed to live and who should be killed. They congratulated each other as they fired at pupils at close range. Neither boy came from environments of poverty or neighbourhood disorganization, neither experienced prejudice, nor were they confronted with more media violence than expectable for their group. While they did form an antisocial peer group (the 'Trenchcoat Mafia'), they did not experience academic failure, and isolated themselves by their morbid behaviour, rather than experiencing social exclusion. Their family lives appeared to be within the normal range. Eric's brother was an honours student and star football player, and his father was a decorated pilot. Dylan's parents were concerned about him, and despite evidence of lack of supervision, there is no evidence of abuse, exposure to violence, marital conflict or parental substance abuse. Eric had a psychiatric history of major depression, but Dylan did not. Dylan was temperamentally difficult, and both had a history of aggression, but there is no evidence of medical complications, hyperactivity or substance abuse in their histories.

I do not wish to deny the importance of the above descriptive indicators of violence but simply to say that the psychoanalytic perspective can offer a key additional vector in our understanding of violent behaviour: the intrapsychic. My own psychoanalytic interest in human violence has grown out of the work I have done with borderline personality disordered patients, some with a history of extreme violence. It is my contention that violent individuals have an inadequate capacity to represent mental states – to recognize that their own and others' reactions are driven by thoughts, feelings, beliefs and desires. I will try to show that this lack of a reflective capacity results from the inadequate developmental integration of the two primitive modes of experiencing the internal world. It is consequent upon neglect. In turn, the failure to mentalize creates a kind of psychic version of an auto-immune deficiency state that makes these individuals extremely vulnerable to later brutal social environments. At a certain moment they cease to resist the brutalization, and start sustaining their selves through social violence. As a last resort, and invariably in response to the humiliation that they experience as having the potential to destroy the self, they take up violence as a form of self-defence.

THE SELF IN VIOLENCE: OUR CARTESIAN HERITAGE

At the root of both legal and common sense definitions of violence is the idea of an agentive self – the Jamesian 'I' that causes injury to another's physical being. We consider interpersonal violence to be a consequence of a developmental distortion in the agentive self. While the Jamesian 'Me', the mental representation of self, has been the focus of psychological investigation for much of the century (for a review see Harter 1999), the study of the 'self as agent' has been relatively neglected, in part because of the dominance of the Cartesian assumption that the agentive self emerges automatically from the sensation of the mental activity of the self ('I think, therefore I am'). The influence of Cartesian doctrine has encouraged the belief that the conscious apprehension of our mind states through introspection is a basic, direct, and probably pre-wired mental capacity, leading to the conviction that knowledge of the self as a mental agent (as a 'doer' of things and a 'thinker' of thoughts) is an innate given rather than a developing or constructed capacity. If we understand the acquisition of knowledge of the self as a mental agent to be the result of a developmental process, which can go wrong in certain circumstances, we can gain new perspectives on the origins of interpersonal violence. But in order to gain this new perspective, we must first go back to consider our earliest days.

As a child normally develops, he gradually acquires an understanding of five increasingly complex levels of agency of the self: physical, social, teleological, intentional and representational (Fonagy *et al.* 2002; Gergely 2001). We shall describe the normal developmental stages first, and then speculate about the deviations in the development of the agentive self that might constitute the psychological roots of violence.

The first level of *physical agency* involves an appreciation of the effects of actions on bodies in space. The child begins to understand that he is a physical entity with force that is the source of action, and that he is an agent whose actions can bring about changes in bodies with which he has immediate physical contact (Leslie 1994). Developing alongside this is the child's understanding of himself as a *social agent*. Babies engage from birth in interactions with their caregivers (Meltzoff and Moore 1977; Stern 1985; Trevarthen 1979). In these exchanges the baby's behaviour produces effects on his caregivers' behaviour and emotions. Early understanding of the self as a social agent, therefore, involves at least knowing that one's communicative displays can produce effects at a distance, in the social environment (Neisser 1988).

The types of causal relations that connect actions to their agents on the one hand, and to the world on the other, go far beyond the level of physical description, and we grow to understand much more about both of these relations as we develop. Thus, around eight or nine months of age (Tomasello 1999) infants begin to differentiate actions from their outcomes and to think about actions as means to an end. This is the beginning of their understanding of themselves as teleological agents (Csibra and Gergely 1998; Leslie 1994) who can choose the most efficient way to bring about a goal from a range of alternatives. The limitation of this stage of experiencing the agentive self is one of physicality. Experimental studies of infants towards the end of their first year of life clearly indicate that they expect the actors in their environment to behave reasonably and rationally, given physically apparent goal state and constraints which are also physically evident to the self (Csibra and Gergely 1998; Csibra et al.1999; Gergely and Csibra 1996, 1997, 1998, 2000). Imagine an object which has repeatedly followed a path that included a deviation to get around an obstacle. Then the obstacle disappears. The nine-month-old infant observing this shows surprise if the object continues to follow the deviation around the obstacle that is no longer present. The infant shows no surprise when the object modifies its path to take account of the changed circumstance, the disappearance of the obstacle. In the latter case the object behaved 'rationally', while in the former the infant could not understand why the object was apparently 'inconveniencing itself'.

Sometime during their second year infants develop an understanding of agency that is already mentalistic: they start to understand that they are *intentional agents* whose actions are caused by prior states of mind, such as desires (Wellman and Phillips 2000). At this point, they also understand that their actions can bring about change in minds as well as bodies: for example, they clearly understand that if they point at something, they can make another person change their focus of attention (Corkum and Moore 1995). Developmentally, this point is prototypically marked when the two-year-old child comes to be able to distinguish his own desires from those of the other person. Repacholi and Gopnik (1997) demonstrated that when 18-month-olds were asked to give the experimenter something to eat, they provided her with the particular food item (broccoli vs gold fish crackers) that she had previously expressed a liking for (by saying 'yuk' or 'yummy' when first offered the food item). So, they modulated their own action by considering the specific content of the desire they had attributed to the other previously, even when that desire was different from their own preference. In contrast, 14-month-olds gave the experimenter the item they themselves liked, basing their choice on their own preference, without being able to consider the other's relevant prior intention. The little ones had assumed an identity between their experience of their own desire and the likely experience of the other.

Around three- to- four years of age this understanding of agency in terms of mental causation also begins to include the representation of so called 'epistemic mind states' concerning knowledge about something (such as beliefs; Wimmer and Perner 1983). At this stage, we can say that the young child understands herself as a *representational agent*: that is, her intentional mental states (desires and beliefs) are representational in nature (Perner 1991; Wellman 1990).

Still later, perhaps as late as the sixth year, emerge related advances such as the child's ability to link memories of his intentional activities and experiences into a coherent causal-temporal organization (Povinelli and Eddy 1995), leading to the establishment of the (temporally) 'extended' or 'proper' self (James 1890). Consider this simple variation on the famous 'rouge' studies of mirror self-recognition. A five-year-old child is videoed playing with an experimenter. In the course of the play, the experimenter, unbeknownst to the child, places a sticky label on him. The sticky label remains on when the experimenter and child watch the video together. The child, who has absolutely no difficulty recognizing himself, notices the sticky label but fails to check if it is still on him. When asked to comment, he says: '*That* child has a label on him', and not: 'In the video I have a label on me'. A few months later, aged six, he clearly experiences himself as the same person as the child on the video and immediately removes the sticky label and smiles with the experimenter at the trick perpetrated on him. In other words, the *autobiographical self* has come into being.

As this brief overview indicates, the development of understanding self and agency entails increasing sophistication in awareness about the nature of mental states. A full experience of agency in social interaction can emerge only when actions of the self and other can be understood as initiated and guided by assumptions concerning the emotions, desires and beliefs of both. This complex developmental process must start with the emergence of concepts for each mental state. In order to be able to think about mental states, say fear, we have to develop concepts that correspond to and integrate the actual internal experiences that constitute that state. The concept of 'fear' is a second order representation of fear-related physiological, cognitive and behavioural experiences, just as the concept of 'table' labels and so integrates our actual experiences of tables. Most, perhaps including Freud, have assumed that second order representations of internal states emerged spontaneously. The child suddenly became aware of himself as a thinking being. From the Cartesian perspective, the repeated experience of fear will inevitably give rise to this concept in the child's mind, just as the experience of tables generates the linguistic label. Yet mental states are private and by definition opaque, while physical objects have a socially shared quality. Of course, even concepts concerning the physical world are profoundly socially conditioned. So how do we understand the influence of social experience upon the emergence of mental state concepts? In the Cartesian view that is implicit to much of our thinking, the spontaneous emergence of internal state concepts is rarely questioned. Recent advances in developmental theory suggest a clear role for social experience in the development of mental state concepts.

THE BEGINNINGS OF SELF-AWARENESS: THE CONTINGENCY DETECTION MODULE

Watson's extensive studies of infants (Watson 1979, 1985, 1994) have led Gergely and Watson (Gergely and Watson 1999) to propose that the earliest forms of self-awareness evolve through the workings of an innate mechanism which they call the *contingency detection module*. This mechanism enables the infant to analyse the probability of causal links between his actions and stimulus events. Watson (1994, 1995) proposed that one of the primary functions of the contingency detection module is *self-detection*. While our own actions produce effects that are necessarily perfectly response-contingent (e.g. watching our hands as we move them), stimuli from the external world typically correspond less perfectly to our actions. Detecting how far the stimuli we perceive depend on our actions may be the original criterion that enables us to distinguish ourselves from the external world. Our bodies are by far the most action-contingent aspects of our environments.

Numerous studies have demonstrated that young infants are highly sensitive to the relationship between their physical actions and consequent stimuli (e.g. Bahrick and Watson 1985; Field 1979; Lewis, Allessandri and Sullivan 1990; Lewis and Brooks-Gunn 1979; Papousek and Papousek 1974; Rochat and Morgan 1995; Watson 1972, 1994). For example, Watson (1972) has shown that two-month-olds increase their rate of leg kicking when it results in the movement of a mobile, but not when they experience a similar, but non-contingent event. Sensitivity to contingency thus explains how we learn that we are physical agents whose actions bring about changes in the environment.

In a seminal study Bahrick and Watson (1985; see also Rochat and Morgan 1995; Schmuckler 1996) have demonstrated that infants can use their perception of perfect contingency between actions and their consequences for self-detection and self-orientation as early as three months of age. In a series of experiments, five- and three-month-old infants were seated on a high-chair in front of two monitors so that they could kick freely. One monitor showed a live image of the child's moving legs, providing a visual stimulus that corresponded perfectly. The other monitor showed a previously recorded image of the infant's moving legs, which was unrelated to his present movements. Five-month-olds clearly differentiated between the two displays, looking significantly more at the *non-contingent* image. A number of other preferential looking studies (Lewis and Brooks-Gunn 1979; Papousek and Papousek 1974; Rochat and Morgan 1995; Schmuckler 1996), in which the live image of the self was contrasted with the moving but non-contingent image of another baby, indicate that four- to five-month-old- infants can distinguish themselves from others on the basis of response–stimulus contingencies and prefer to fixate *away* from the self.

Interestingly, Bahrick and Watson found that among three-month-olds some preferred the perfectly contingent image, while others were more interested in the non-contingent image. Field (1979) also reported that her sample of three-month-olds were more inclined to look at the images of themselves. Piaget's (1936) observation that during the first months of life babies perform the same actions on themselves over and over again also suggests that babies are initially preoccupied with perfect contingency. Gergely and Watson (1999; see also Watson 1994, 1995) have therefore proposed that during the first two to three months of life the contingency detection module is genetically set to seek out and explore perfectly response-contingent stimulation. Watson hypothesizes that this initial bias enables the infant to develop *a primary representation of his bodily self* as a distinct object in the environment, by identifying what he has perfect control over. Watson (1995) suggests that an initial phase of self-seeking behaviour may be necessary to prepare the baby to cope with the environment. At around three months the target value of the contingency analyzer in normal infants is 'switched' to prefer *high-but-imperfect contingencies* – the kind of responses that are characteristic of children's caregivers. This change re-orients the infant after three months, away from self-exploration (perfect contingencies) and towards *the exploration and representation of the social world*, beginning with the parents, who provide stimuli that are highly but not perfectly contingent on her responses. Just as the early contingency detector alerts the infant to aspects of her own body by identifying parts of the world that move simultaneously with her actions, the detection of high-but-imperfect contingencies directs attention to the reactions of others and begins the process of helping her define delimiters to her subjective experience. How might this happen?

EARLY UNDERSTANDING OF THE SELF AS A SOCIAL AGENT

A large body of evidence indicates that from the beginning of life babies can tell people apart (Stern 1985). From a very early age they are sensitive to facial expressions (Fantz 1963; Morton and Johnson 1991); they get used to their mothers' voice *in utero* and recognize it after birth (DeCasper and Fifer 1980); and can imitate facial gestures from birth (Meltzoff and Moore 1977, 1989). Young babies' interactions with their caregivers have a 'protoconversational' turn-taking structure (Beebe *et al.* 1985; Brazelton, Kowslowski and Main 1974; Brazelton and Tronick 1980; Jaffe *et al.* 2001; Stern 1985; Trevarthen 1979; Tronick 1989). The currently dominant biosocial view of emotional development holds that mother and infant are engaged in affective communication from the beginning of life (Bowlby 1969; Brazelton *et al.* 1974; Hobson 1993; Sander 1970; Stern 1977, 1985; Trevarthen 1979; Tronick 1989) in which the mother plays a vital role in modulating the infant's emotional states to make them more manageable.

Mothers are generally very good at telling what their babies are feeling, and sensitive mothers tend to attune their responses to modulate their children's emotional states (Malatesta *et al.* 1989; Tronick 1989). During these interactions, the mother will often facially or vocally mimic her baby's displays of emotion with the apparent intention to modulate or regulate the infant's feelings (Gergely and Watson 1996, 1999; Malatesta and Izard 1984; Papousek and Papousek 1987; Stern 1985). The caregiver's mirroring of the infant's subjective experience has been recognized by a wide range of psychoanalytic developmental theorists as a key phase in the development of the child's self (e.g. Kernberg 1984; Kohut 1971; Pines 1982; Tyson and Tyson 1990; Winnicott 1967) as well as developmental psychologists (Legerstee and Varghese 2001; Meltzoff 1990; Mitchell 1993; Schneider-Rosen and Cicchetti 1991). But why should the mere replication of the outward manifestation of the infant's putative internal experience lead to a moderation of affect expression, and how does it lead to the creation of a sense of self?

GERGELY AND WATSON'S SOCIAL BIOFEEDBACK THEORY OF PARENTAL AFFECT-MIRRORING

Contrary to the classical Cartesian view, Gergely and Watson's 'social biofeedback theory of parental affect-mirroring' (Gergely and Watson 1996, 1999) assumes that at first we are not introspectively aware of our different emotion states. They suggest that our representations of these emotions are primarily based on stimuli received from the external world. Babies learn to differentiate the internal patterns of physiological and visceral stimulation that accompany different emotions through observing their caregivers' facial or vocal mirroring responses to these. Social biofeedback in the form of parental affect-mirroring enables the infant to develop a second order symbolic representational system for his mind states. The internalization of the mother's mirroring response to the infant's distress (caregiving behaviour) comes to represent an internal state. The infant internalizes the mother's empathic expression by developing a secondary representation of his emotional state, with the mother's empathic face as the signifier and his own emotional arousal as the signified. The mother's expression tempers emotion to the extent that it is separate and different from the primary experience, although crucially it is not recognized as the mother's experience, but as an organizer of a self-state. It is this 'inter-subjectivity' which is the bedrock of the intimate connection between attachment and self-regulation.

If the mother's mirroring is to effectively modulate her baby's emotions, and provide the beginnings of a symbolic system by means of which the capacity for self-regulation can be further extended, it is important that, as well as accurately reflecting the emotion the child is feeling, she signals in some way that what he is seeing is a reflection of his own feelings; otherwise it is possible that he will misattribute the feeling to his mother. Misattributing the expressed emotion would be especially problematic in cases where the mother is reflecting the infant's *negative* emotion states, say, fear or anger. If the child thinks that the mother *has* the feelings she is displaying, then his own negative emotion state, instead of being regulated in a downward direction, is likely to escalate, as the sight of a fearful or angry parent is clearly cause for alarm.

This attribution problem is solved by a specific perceptual feature of the parent's mirroring displays, which, following Gergely and Watson, we refer to as their '*markedness*'. Marking is typically achieved by producing an *exaggerated version* of the parent's realistic emotion expression, similar to the marked 'as if' manner of emotion displays that are characteristically produced in pretend play. To be sensitive to markedness the child moves away from interpreting reality 'as is' and imposes an alternative construction upon it. This constitutes a move away from the immediacy of physical reality. The marked display, nevertheless, is close enough to the parent's usual expression of that emotion for the infant to recognize its dispositional content. However, the markedness of the display inhibits the attribution of the perceived emotion to the parent: because it is contingent on the infant's behaviour, she therefore assumes that it applies to herself.

Parents who, because of their own emotional difficulties and conflicts, find their infant's negative affect-expressions overwhelming, struggle to mirror their baby's emotions in this marked way. They are likely to react to their infant's negative emotions by reflecting them accurately, but in an *unmarked, realistic* manner. When this happens, the mirroring affect-display will be attributed to the parent as his or her real emotion, and it will not become anchored to the infant either. Consequently, the secondary representation of the baby's primary emotion state will not be established, leading to a corresponding deficiency in self-perception and self-control of affect. Since the infant will attribute the mirrored affect to the parent, he will experience his own negative affect 'out there' as belonging to the other, rather than to himself. Instead of regulating the infant's negative affect, the perception of a corresponding realistic negative emotion in the parent will escalate the baby's negative state, leading to traumatization rather than containment (Main and Hesse 1990). This constellation corresponds to the clinical characterization of *projective identification* as a pathological defence mechanism characteristic of a borderline level of personality functioning (Kernberg 1976; Klein 1946; Sandler 1987; Segal 1964). The features of impoverished affect regulation, excessive focus on physical rather than psychic reality, and oversensitivity to the apparent emotional reaction of the other are clearly features that mark the mental functioning of certain individuals prone to violent acts, and these might be traced back to these patterns of early mirroring. We hypothesize that sustained experience of accurate but unmarked parental mirroring in infancy might play an important causal role in establishing projective identification as the dominant form of emotional experience in personality development characteristic of some violent individuals.

In infancy the contingent responding of the attachment figure is thus far more than the provision of reassurance about a protective presence. It is the principal means by which we acquire an understanding of our own internal states, which is an intermediate step in the acquisition of an understanding of others as psychological entities. In the first year, the infant only has primary awareness of being in a particular, internal, emotional state. Such awareness is non-causal or epiphenomenal in that it is not put to any functional use by the system. It is in the process of social biofeedback that these internal experiences are more closely attended to and evolve a functional role (a signal value) and a role in modulating or inhibiting action. Thus it is the primary attachment relationship that can ensure the move from primary awareness of internal states to a functional awareness. In functional awareness a concept corresponding to the feeling of anger (the *idea of anger* rather than the *experience of anger*) may be used to simulate and so to infer the other's corresponding mental state. It may also be used to serve a signal value to direct action. The robust establishment of these capacities may ensure that the individual can not only moderate his anger through self-regulation but also use it to initiate actions that are likely to effectively deal with the cause. In the absence of functional awareness, anger (once aroused) might be experienced as overwhelming, and the individual will be at considerable disadvantage in the creation of effective strategies to address the cause of the dissatisfaction that generated this emotion. It should be noted that this is not the same as reflective awareness of emotion, where the individual can make a causal mind state the object of attention before, or without, causing action. Whereas functional awareness is intrinsically coupled with action, reflective awareness is separate from it. It has the capacity to move away from physical reality and may be felt to be 'not for real'.

Many studies provide evidence consistent with the social biofeedback model. For example, an unpublished study carried out in our laboratory showed that the rapid soothing of distressed six-month-olds could be predicted on the basis of ratings of emotional content of the mother's facial expression during the process of soothing: mothers of rapid responders showed somewhat more fear, somewhat less joy, but most typically a range of other affects in addition to fear and sadness. Mothers of rapid responders were far more likely to manifest multiple affect states (complex affects). We interpreted these results as supporting Gergely and Watson's notion of the mother's face being a secondary representation of the infant's experience – the same and yet not the same. This is functional awareness with the capacity to modulate affect states.

We can assume that infants' discovery of their high degree of contingent control over their caregivers' reactions positively arouses them and gives them feelings of causal efficacy. They are also likely to experience the pleasurable changes in their affective states that the parents' affect-modulating soothing interactions bring about (and become associated with; see Gergely and Watson 1996, 1999). Since such attuned interactions often involve affect-mirroring, infants may come to associate the control they have over their parents' mirroring displays with the ensuing positive change in their affect state, leading to an experience of the self as a self-regulating agent (Gergeley, Koós and Watson in press; Gergely and Watson 1996, 1999). The establishment of second order representations of emotions creates the basis for affect regulation and impulse control, and provides an essential building block for the child's later development of the crucial capacity of mentalization. If the caregiver mirrors the baby's emotions inaccurately or neglects to perform this function at all, the baby's feelings will be unlabelled, confusing, and experienced as unsymbolized and therefore hard to regulate.

THE TWO PRIMITIVE MODES OF REPRESENTING INTERNAL EXPERIENCE: PSYCHIC EQUIVALENCE AND THE PRETEND MODE

The caregiver who is able to give form and meaning to the young child's affective and intentional states through facial and vocal mirroring and playful interactions, provides the child with representations that will form the very core of his developing sense of selfhood. For normal development the child needs to experience a mind that has *his* mind in mind and is able to reflect his feelings and intentions accurately, yet in a way that does not overwhelm him (for example, when acknowledging negative affective states). This is an experience that a psychologically neglected child may never have, even if there is no doubt about the provision of adequate physical care.

The parent who cannot think about the child's mental experience deprives her of the basis for a viable sense of herself (Fonagy 1995). This idea is a familiar one to us in psychoanalysis (e.g. Bion 1962; McDougall 1989; Winnicott 1956). The child who has not experienced the caregiver's integrative mirroring of his affective states cannot create representations of them, and may later struggle to differentiate reality from fantasy, and physical from psychic reality. This leaves the individual vulnerable to modes of representing subjectivity and the agentive self which are not fully representational or reflective (see below). As we have argued elsewhere (Fonagy and Target 1996), the child of two or three years initially probably experiences his mind pretty much as if his internal states and external reality corresponded exactly. Mary Target and I call this mode '*psychic equivalence*', to emphasize that for the young child mental events are equivalent, in terms of power, causality and implications, to events in the physical world. Not only will the small child equate appearance with reality (how it seems is how it is), but thoughts and feelings, distorted by phantasy, will also be projected onto external reality, unmodulated by any awareness of this distortion, and will possess the full force of actual experience. The child feels that everything that exists in physical reality has a direct representation in his mind and, by extension, everything that is in his mind must exist in the outside world.

Perhaps because it can be terrifying for thoughts and feelings to be experienced as concretely 'real', the small child develops an alternative way of construing mental states. In *'pretend mode'*, the child experiences feelings and ideas as totally representational, or symbolic, with no implications for the world outside. His play forms no bridge between inner and outer reality. Only gradually, and through the safe and attentive closeness of an other mind who can simultaneously hold together the child's pretend and serious perspectives, does the integration of these two modes give rise to a psychic reality in which feelings and ideas are known as internal, yet related to what is outside (Dunn 1996). A recent study with colleagues in Kansas demonstrates the point. The facial expression of six- to ten-year-old children with or without behavioural disorder was measured as they watched violent scenes from several movies. Children with behaviour disorder showed more intense expressions of fear and anger while watching these movie extracts but showed no greater reactions to control clips. The finding supported the prediction that the children with behavioural disorder are less able to differentiate 'pretend' from 'real' and therefore experience the violent movie scenes as 'more real', reacting to these with more intense affect than the children in the control group.

We believe that vulnerability to a regression to the state of psychic equivalence, where internal is equated with external, is an essential precondition for violence. Mentalization (see below), knowing that a thought is just a thought, normally insulates us from the harshness of the social world. This knowledge can only develop out of an attachment relationship where the adult is reflective enough to help the child to play with ideas previously felt to be as concrete, and sometimes as terrifying, as physical reality. By contrast, psychic equivalence exaggerates the threat of other minds. If even children in relatively secure attachment relationships go through a developmental stage where they are exposed to the terrors of this mode of relating, imagine the impact of real brutal intentions, especially if prolonged and severe. Psychic equivalence also facilitates the initiation of violence. Violence is normally triggered when an idea, a feeling, a prejudice, a suspicion, is mistaken for physical reality. The act of violence reflects the

complementary confusion – the erroneous belief that a physical act can
eradicate a mental state.

MENTALIZATION AND REFLECTIVE FUNCTION

Mentalization – the capacity to think about mental states as separate from,
yet potentially causing, actions – we assumed to arise as part of the process
of integrating the pretend and psychic equivalent modes of functioning.
This happens optimally in the context of a playful parent–child relationship.
In such a relationship feelings and thoughts, wishes and beliefs can be experienced by the child as significant and respected on the one hand, but on the
other as being of an order different from physical reality. Both the pretend
mode and the psychic equivalent modes of functioning are modified by the
interaction with the parent in what Winnicott (1971) incomparably termed
a 'transitional space'. While mentalization as a concept has arguably been
part of psychoanalytic thinking since its inception, and as a major line of
theorization in France at least for the last forty years (Lecours and Bouchard
1997), this line of thinking received an undoubted boost from progress in
philosophy of mind and development pertaining to the 'intentional stance'
and 'the theory of mind' (Fonagy 1991, 2000; Fonagy and Target 1997;
Fonagy, Target and Gergely 2000). During the last decades philosophers
(Bogdan 1997; Dennett 1987; Fodor 1987, 1992) and cognitive
developmentalists (Astington, Harris and Olsen 1988; Baron-Cohen,
Tager-Flusberg and Cohen 1993, 2000; Hirschfeld and Gelman 1994;
Perner 1991; Wellman 1990; Whiten 1991) have focused on the nature and
developmental origins of our capacity to attribute causal mental states to
others. Initially, it was Dennett (1987) who argued that applying such a
mentalistic interpretational strategy, which he called the 'intentional
stance', was a significant evolutionary adaptation that enabled us to predict
others' behaviour.

   In opposition to the currently dominant cognitive developmental view,
which holds that even young children can attribute intentional mental states
(such as goals, emotions, desires and beliefs) to others as the causes of their
actions, from a psychodynamic perspective we argue that the capacity for
mentalization is a developmental achievement greatly facilitated by secure
attachment (Fonagy 1991, 1997a). Evidence such as young children's performance on false belief tasks supports this argument. Wimmer and Perner

(1983) were the first to demonstrate that three-year-olds who witness a person leaving an object in container A before leaving the room, and who see the object being transferred to container B in that person's absence, make the (reality-based) error of predicting that she will search in container B (where the object actually is), rather than in container A (where she left the object) when she comes back. By the age of four or five, children do not commit this error any more: they tend to correctly predict that the person will look in container A, because they are able to attribute a false belief to her.

The acquisition of this capacity has come to be known as the development of a theory of mind. 'Theory of mind' is an interconnected set of beliefs and desires, attributed to explain a person's behaviour. Baron-Cohen and Swettenham (1996) appropriately ask '...how on earth can young children master such abstract concepts as belief (and false belief) with such ease, and roughly at the same time the world over?' (p.158). In current models of theory of mind development, the child tends to be seen as an isolated processor of information, constructing a theory of mind using biological mechanisms which, where the child's endowment is less than optimal, have an expectable failure rate. From the viewpoint of developmental psychopathology and its psychosocial treatment, this is a barren picture, which ignores the central role of the child's emotional relationship with the parents in developing the child's ability to understand interactions in psychological terms. The development of children's understanding of mental states is embedded within the social world of the family, with its network of complex and often intensely emotionally charged relationships, which are, after all, much of what early reflection needs to comprehend. Therefore it should not surprise us that the nature of family interactions, the quality of parental control (Dunn et al. 1991), parental talk about emotions (Denham, Zoller and Couchoud 1994) and the depth of parental discussion involving affect (Dunn, Brown and Beardsall 1991), are all strongly associated with the acquisition of the intentional stance in observational studies. The family's involvement in the child's acquisition of a theory of mind is further highlighted by the robust finding that the presence of older siblings in the family appears to improve the child's performance on a range of false-belief tasks (Jenkins and Astington 1996; Perner, Ruffman and Leekman 1994; Ruffman et al. 1998). The ability to give meaning to our own psychological experiences develops as a result of our discovery of the minds beyond others' actions.

For research purposes we have operationalized the ability to apply a mentalistic interpretational strategy as reflective function (Fonagy, Target, Steele and Steele 1998) as the plausible interpretation of one's own and others' behaviour in terms of underlying mental states. This implies awareness that experiences give rise to certain beliefs and emotions, that particular beliefs and desires tend to result in certain kinds of behaviour, that there are transactional relationships between beliefs and emotions, and that particular developmental phases or relationships are associated with certain feelings and beliefs. We do not expect an individual to articulate this theoretically, but to demonstrate it in the way they interpret events within attachment relationships, when asked to do so. Individuals differ in the extent to which they are able to go beyond observable phenomena to give an account of their own or others' actions in terms of beliefs, desires, plans and so on. This cognitive capacity is an important determinant of individual differences in self-organization, as it is intimately involved with many defining features of selfhood, such as self consciousness, autonomy, freedom and responsibility (Bolton and Hill 1996; Cassam 1994). The intentional stance, in the broad sense considered here (i.e. including apparently irrational unconscious acts), creates the continuity of self-experience which is the underpinning of a coherent self structure.

ATTACHMENT AND REFLECTIVE FUNCTION (RF)

Reflective function is assessed and measured by scoring transcripts of the Adult Attachment Interview (AAI) according to guidelines laid out in the Reflective Function (RF) manual (Fonagy et al. 1998). The characteristics of attachment narratives that raters look for as evidence of high RF include awareness of the nature of mental states (such as the opaqueness of mental states), explicit efforts to tease out the mental states underlying behaviour, recognition of the developmental aspects of mental states, and showing awareness of mental states in relation to the interviewer. There was a strong relationship between scores on the RF scale and the Strange Situation behaviour of infants (Ainsworth et al. 1978) whose mothers and fathers had been assessed using the AAI before the birth of the child (Fonagy et al. 1991). In a subsequent study on the same sample, we found that RF was particularly predictive of secure attachments with mothers, in cases where mothers independently reported significant deprivation in childhood (Fonagy *et al*. 1994).

A growing body of evidence links mindfulness with attachment. The caregiver's mindfulness about the child's mental states appears to be a significant predictor of the likelihood of secure attachment. Recent evidence by Slade and her colleagues provided an important clue about the puzzle of intergenerational transmission of attachment security. They demonstrated that autonomous (secure) mothers on the AAI represented their relationship with their toddlers in a more coherent way, conveying more joy and pleasure in the relationship, than did dismissing and preoccupied mothers (Slade *et al*. 1999). That the mother's representation of each child is the critical determinant of attachment status is consistent with the relatively low concordance in the attachment classification of siblings (van IJzendoorn *et al*. 2000). We believe that the parent's capacity to adopt the intentional stance towards a not yet intentional infant, to think about the infant in terms of thoughts, feelings and desires in the infant's mind, and in their own mind in relation to the infant and his/her mental state, is the key mediator of the transmission of attachment and accounts for classical observations concerning the influence of caregiver sensitivity (Fonagy *et al*. 1995). Those with a strong capacity to reflect on their own and their childhood caregiver's mental states in the context of the AAI were far more likely to have secure attachments with their own children – a finding which we have linked to the parent's capacity to foster the child's self-development (Fonagy *et al*. 1993).

A more direct test of this hypothesis was provided by Elizabeth Meins and colleagues (Meins *et al*. 2001). They analyzed the content of speech of mothers in interaction with their six-month-old children and coded the number of comments the mother made on the infant's mental states (knowledge, desires, thought, interest), on the infant's emotional engagement (e.g. assertions about the infant being bored), comments on the infant's mental processes ('Are you thinking?'), and comments about what the infant might think the mother thinks, or attempts on the infant's part to manipulate the mother's mental state ('Are you just teasing me?'). The comments were further coded as appropriate if an independent coder agreed that the mother was reading the child's mental state correctly, in line with the immediate history of the interaction, and was not cutting across the child's apparent intentions with assertions about putative mental states that were incongruous with the infant's current state of mind. The proportion of such 'appropriate mind-related comments' was highly significantly associated with attachment security in the child six months later, and significantly contributed to the prediction even when traditional measures of maternal sensitivity were controlled for.

The above series of studies demonstrated that high levels of reflective function are associated with good outcomes in terms of secure attachment in the child. Security of attachment on the Adult Attachment Interview (AAI) in 131 moderately at-risk adolescents (Allen et al. 1998) predicted low risk for Conduct Disorder (CD) and delinquency and was associated with peer competence, lower levels of internalizing behaviours, and low levels of deviant behaviour. The converse of this association is naturally that low levels of reflective function generate insecure and perhaps disorganized attachment. The latter category of attachment in infancy is most likely to be associated with aggressive and potentially violent behaviour later in development. A good proportion of toddlers who go on to manifest conduct problems show disorganized attachment patterns in infancy (Lyons-Ruth 1996; Lyons-Ruth and Jacobovitz 1999). The nature and origin of this attachment pattern, characterized by fear of the caregiver and a lack of coherent attachment strategy (Main and Solomon 1986), is as yet poorly understood (Solomon and George 1999). Some evidence is available that links it with frightening or dissociated behaviour on the part of the caregiver (Lyons-Ruth, Bronfman and Atwood 1999; Schuengel et al. 1999). Some attachment theorists have linked it with an approach-avoidance conflict on the part of the infant (Main and Hesse 1992), while others consider it reflective of a hostile–helpless state of mind in the caregiver (Lyons-Ruth, Bronfman and Atwood 1999) or an indicator of inadequate self-organization (ibid.; Fonagy and Target 1997). The suggestion here is that poor reflective function undermines attachment processes and these in their turn might in some way generate behavioural difficulties. It is the impact of attachment disorganization upon an agentive self that might be most important for us in understanding violent behaviour. We shall return to this issue after considering another aspect of the mentalization attachment relationship: where secure attachment can be seen to lead to superior mentalization.

ATTACHMENT, REFLECTIVE FUNCTION AND VIOLENCE

Our longitudinal study of attachment clearly demonstrated that secure attachment in infancy was likely to be associated with superior mentalizing skills four or five years after the assessment of attachment security (Fonagy 1997a). If secure attachment advances mentalizing capacities and the development of an agentive self structure, is there any evidence that insecure attachment status is associated with marked deficits in mentalizing capacities in groups of violent criminals? A study conducted by Alice Levinson and Peter Fonagy (Levinson and Fonagy, submitted), which coded and compared the RF of 22 prisoners with 22 psychiatric patients matched for personality disorder but without a criminal record, and 22 normal controls, showed that the prisoners had experienced more abuse and neglect than the patients, yet were more likely to be coded apparently resolved with respect to their experience of trauma according to the Main and Goldwyn (1994) classification system. Prisoners were more likely to be dismissive in their attachment patterns, and the prisoners' RF was more impaired than that of the patients. Violent offenders showed the greatest deficits. This led the researchers to argue that prisoners' developmental path of psychopathology is characterized by a disavowal of attachment-related experiences and of the capacity to think about them, in partial response to severe childhood trauma. The impairment of RF removes a critical barrier that might normally inhibit offending, making individuals who have suffered this impairment more liable to act, especially in violent ways.

More recently, using a relatively simple measure of reflective capacity, we have shown similar deficits in behaviour-disordered children. The 'Reading the Mind in the Eyes' test (Baron-Cohen *et al.* 1997; Baron-Cohen *et al.* 2001) is a measure of the extent to which children can accurately infer mental states, including attitudes such as contemplativeness, from facial expressions restricted to the area around the eyes. There is indication that the test is valid in separating those with known deficits of mentalization, such as autism or Asperger's syndrome, from those with comparable IQ deficits but no mentalization deficits. In our study, six- to ten-year-old children rated as behaviour-disordered by parents or clinician were found to perform poorly in this task, regardless of IQ or differences in verbal ability. Another study, which compared 40 preschoolers with conduct problems (assessed by parent report) with a matched control group, also reported deficits on a theory of mind task, an emotion-understanding task and simple executive function tasks (Hughes, Dunn and White 1998).

The relatively impoverished mentalizing capacity of aggressive and violent young people, we believe, is relevant to their disorder in several ways. First, inaccuracy about mental states of others may lead them into social difficulties and interpersonal problems. They may, for example, judge interactions as threatening when they are actually benign (Coie and Dodge 1998; Crick and Dodge 1994; Dodge, Pettit and Bates 1994; Matthys, Cuperus and van Engeland 1999). Thus, these children may be unable to use their aggression in a strategic, goal-oriented way, and they are probably inappropriately conceptualized purely in terms of behavioural difficulties (Pope and Bierman 1999). Second, the diminished empathic capacity might remove key constitutional inhibitions over violence ('the violence inhibiting mechanism') of the kind suggested by James Blair on the basis of work with anti-social personality disorder (Blair 1995; Blair *et al.* 1997; Blair *et al.* 1999). Third, from a psychodynamic developmental psychopathology perspective (Bleiberg 2001), the absence of a mentalizing function is thought to reveal alternative strategies that emerge in place of mentalization, strongly imbued with the modes of functioning that antedate mentalization, namely the externalization of affect, psychic equivalence, and a sense of self which is not capable of experiencing ownership of action (Fonagy 1997b; Fonagy and Target 2000; Fonagy *et al.* 1997a; Fonagy *et al.* 1997b). Before considering what psychosocial experiences might lead to the undermining of mentalization in the history of violent individuals, we would like to consider the aspect of agentive self deficit that might be most closely linked to violent behaviour: a lack of experiential ownership of action.

AGGRESSION AND THE OWNERSHIP OF ACTION

Stern (1985) pointed out that a sense of ownership of one's actions, whether derived from the experience of forming plans, proprioceptive feedback, or the objective consequences of physical actions on the environment, contributes significantly to the sense of self-agency. Early in self-development, ownership of action is evidently dependent on the contingent responding of the caregiver to the child's expressions of internal states (Gergely and Watson 1999; Watson 1994, 1995). In our view such agency also crucially depends on the quality and reliability of internal representations of the mental states, as ownership of action is intimately tied to the mental state (beliefs and wishes) that initiated it. It is impossible to conceive of self-agency as fully established by the actual actions of the child, as a large proportion of these will fail to achieve their intended objective, because of the child's immature physical and cognitive capacities. In fact, it could be argued that if the sense of self-agency were uniquely to be based on feedback from immature action systems, deficiency in this sphere would be universal. The recognition of the child's intentional stance by (older) others must, then, be critical in making the thought 'real' for the child. Interpersonal interaction, which permits the registration of perceptions, thoughts and emotions as causes and consequences of action, and the contemplation of these mental states without fear, must constitute an important part of the foundation of self-agency. The earliest foundation is presumably the baby's sense that he brings about the caregiver's mirroring behaviour. Playfully supportive, child-focused *intersubjective interpersonal interactions* enable the infant and young child to register internal states as both causes and consequences of action. The reflective caregiver is required to make sense of the young child's wishes, express her understanding of these, and help him to complete the action, if the two-way connection between intentions and action is to be established.

The caregiver who is able to do this for the child in this way affirms that his mental representation 'caused' the completed action, strengthening his sense of himself as an agent. Those who experience severe neglect or coercive, rigid, frightening and, at an extreme, abusive parenting will frequently experience their sense of self-agency as massively curtailed, and confined to the more firmly established bodily domain. Neglectful or abusive parenting constitutes a denial by the parent of the child's internal reality as a causal part of his phenomenal world. The contingency normally established between social mirroring and action that creates an awareness of internal states that are responsible for behaviours is simply absent. The social reaction that enhances, or perhaps actually creates, internal experience of mental states is seriously non-contingent and therefore fails to give the same status to the connection between internal experience and action that normally exists for most of us. Further, because the caregiver denies the child's intentional state, and fails to help him complete his action, this action will have limited impact on the external environment, and the essential link between intention and action will be further undermined in the child's mind. Action undertaken by the child, then, in a very real sense, will not be felt as having been forged within the self. The individual, having physical awareness of his bodily self, will 'know' that aggressive or violent action was committed by him. Yet the subjective experience of these acts will not be the same as it is for acts committed by individuals whose agentive self is intact. In individuals who commit aggressive or violent acts, the possibility of disconnecting internal state and action will lead to actions that are not curtailed by mentalization of their implications. They are by no means random acts, and are most frequently motivated by self-interest and more or less accurate cognitive appraisals of social situations. The actions can apparently be disowned because of a deficiency of the agentive self, but as a secondary effect of this deficiency the action is not fully examined for its impact on the object's affective and epistemic states.

Thus the agentive self, the mind that is detected by another mind that is capable of responding contingently with it, discovers its potential for controlling its own and others' actions through mental states. This can only fully occur in the context of attachment relationships. We suggest that violent acts are only possible when a decoupling occurs between the representations of subjective states of the self and actions. Actions are here experienced as 'agentless'. Understanding the developmental roots of violence entails understanding the conditions under which this kind of separation of internal states and self-initiated actions can come about. In the remainder of this essay we shall consider the developmental assumptions that a psychoanalytic model of violence, formulated along these lines, has to make in order to provide a credible explanation of acts of impulsive violence.

NEGLECT AND THE PREDISPOSITION TO VIOLENCE

According to the model proposed, mind-aware interpersonal interaction is essential for the development of robust representations of internal states. In individuals whose caregivers could not facilitate this understanding, primitive modes of psychic reality, the pretend mode and the mode of psychic equivalence persist into adulthood. While extreme physical neglect of the kind that comes to the attention of child protection services will obviously undermine the acquisition of the capacity to mentalize through the mediation of the primary object, much more subtle (what one might call 'middle-class') forms of psychological neglect are equally deleterious to the emergence of mentalization. Neglect associated with increasing financial and social pressures on the modern Western family is widely reviewed (at times in terms verging on moral panic) and will not be considered here. It is clear that single-parent and dual-employment households are increasing in proportion and that the amount of time parents (particularly fathers) spend with children is surprisingly low according to most surveys (e.g. NICHD Early Child Care Research Network 1996). The average father spends just 7.5 minutes per week in one-to-one contact with his child. Although we know that different types of trauma play a significant role in the psycho-genesis of violence (e.g. Johnson, Cohen, Brown, Smailes and Bernstein 1999), we believe that it is the persistence of the mode of psychic equivalence, associated with early psychological neglect, that subsequently makes these individuals vulnerable to such harsh social experiences. Evidence suggests that it is early neglect rather than either physical or sexual abuse which carries the greater risk for the subsequent emergence of social violence (Johnson-Reid and Barth 2000). The brutalization of attachment, of affectional bonds, in childhood or adolescence, and even in young adulthood, appears to be a necessary, but not a sufficient condition for aggravated assault and murder. Weakness in the capacity for mentalization due to non-contingent mirroring and the absence of child-focused, intersubjective, interpersonal interactions undermines the links between internal states and actions and creates subsequent difficulties when the young person's resources to understand are challenged by the hostility and destructiveness of their world.

The persistence of the mode of psychic equivalence, due to the care-giver's failure to provide a relationship in the context of which men-talization and the sense of self as a psychological entity can develop, is a key aspect of the tendency of violent individuals to express and cope with thoughts and feelings through physical action, against their own bodies or in relation to other people. Violent individuals violate themselves as much as or more than they violate others (Gilligan 1997); examples from one of England's high-security prisons include not just self-cutting and swallow-ing razor blades but gouging eyes out and inserting bedsprings into urethras. Not being able to feel 'themselves' (their self states) from within, they are forced to experience the self through action (enactments) from without.

The lack of a stable sense of a representational agentive self is of central importance to our understanding of violent acts. The capacity for symbolic representation of one's own mental states is clearly an essential prerequisite of a sense of identity. Those who lack it are not only deficient in self-love; they will lack an authentic, organic self-image built around internalized representations of mental states. The absence or weakness of a representational agentive self brings to the foreground a non-mentalizing self working on teleological principles, leaving the child, and later the adult, with an inadequate understanding of their own subjectivity and of the interpersonal situations they encounter on a daily basis, and consequently with sometimes intense affect which remains poorly labelled and quite confusing.

A further important complication arises from the processes that generate the failure to achieve a representational agentive self. In early childhood the failure to find another being behaving contingently with one's internal states, and available for the intersubjective processes detailed above that permit the creation of the representational self, can create a desperation for meaning as the self seeks to find itself, its mirror image, in the other. The desperation leads to a distortion of the intersubjective process and leads the individual to take in non-contingent reflections from the object. Unfortunately, as these images do not map onto anything within the child's own experience, they cannot function as totally effective representations of the self. As Winnicott (1967) noted, inaccurate mirroring will lead to the internalization of representations of the parent's state, rather than of a usable version of the child's own experience. This creates what we have termed an *alien experience within the self*: ideas or feelings are experienced as part of the self which do not seem to belong to the self (Fonagy 1995, 2000). The representational agentive self is not effectively established for the neglected child, because the second order representations of self states are distorted by containing representations of the other.

These representations of the other internalized as part of the self probably originate in early infancy when the mother's reflective function at least partially but regularly failed the infant. The infant, trying to find herself in the mother's mind, may find the mother instead, as Winnicott (1967, p.32) so accurately put it. The image of the mother comes to colonize the self. Because the alien self is felt to be part of the self, it destroys any sense of coherence of self or identity, which can only be restored by constant and intense projection. Clinically, the projection is not motivated by guilt, but by the need to re-establish the continuity of self-experience.

The residue of maternal non-responsiveness, this alien other, probably exists in seed form in all our self-representations, as we have all experienced neglect to a greater or lesser extent (Tronick and Gianino 1986). Normally, however, parts of the self-representation which are not rooted in the internalized mirroring of self-states are nevertheless integrated into a singular, coherent self-structure by the capacity for mentalization. The representational agentive self creates an illusion of coherence within our representations of ourselves by attributing agency, accurately or inaccurately assuming that mental states invariably exist to explain experience. Dramatic examples of this have been noted long ago in studies of individuals with neural lesions, such as individuals with surgical bi-sections of the corpus callosum, so-called 'split-brain' patients (Gazzaniga 1985). When presented with emotionally arousing pictures in the hemi-field without access to language, they would find improbable mentalized accounts for their heightened emotional state. They are also material for entertainment in stage hypnosis demonstrations, and a source of scientific controversy when hypnosis is used to assist in the recovery of repressed memories (Dywan and Bowers 1983; Kihlstrom 1994; Spiegel and Scheflin 1994).

The normal process of attributing agency through putative mental states preconsciously works in the background of our minds to lend a coherence and psychological meaning to one's life, one's actions, and one's sense of self. This may indeed be an important psychological function of the fully fledged, autobiographical, agentive representational self. Individuals whose capacity for mentalization is not well developed may need to use controlling and manipulative strategies to restore coherence to their sense of self. The 'alien' aspects of the self may be externalized into an attachment figure. Using processes often described in the clinical literature as projective identification, the attachment figure is manipulated into feeling the emotions that have been internalized as part of the self but are not entirely felt to be 'of the self'. These are not self-protective manoeuvres in the sense of needing to shed feelings which the individual cannot acknowledge, but rather they protect the self from the experience of incongruence or incoherence that has the potential to generate far deeper anxieties (cf. Kernberg 1982, 1983; Kohut 1977). The attachment figure thus performs a 'life-saving' or, more accurately, a 'self-saving' function by ridding the self of the unbearable internal representations. Unfortunately, in performing this function, in becoming (for example) angry and punitive in response to unconscious provocation, the attachment figure is in the worst possible state to help restore the afflicted individual's mentalizing function, because she has lost touch with his mental world. In adults such predisposition to projective identification is likely to mark severe psychological disturbance.

BRUTALIZATION AND THE ACT OF VIOLENCE

The suggestions that follow are rooted in three studies we have undertaken, giving interviews (the Adult Attachment Interview) concerning attachment histories to almost 100 young criminals in psychiatric and non-psychiatric forensic settings.[2] Almost all the individuals in these samples who committed violent crimes, irrespective of other concurrent psychiatric problems, endured coarse and cruel treatment at the hands of others. But importantly, these others were part of their close or intimate social group: they could be family, close friends, or schoolfriends. Brutal treatment appears from our interviews to generate violence *only* when it is perpetrated in the context of a relationship with a quality of intimacy. It is not brutality *per se* that breeds violence, as cognitivists or social learning theorists suggest. Social violence entails a history of the brutalization of an affectional bond.

Permit me to expand on our findings. The prisoners tend to report that they were forced to submit to an authority figure (usually a parent, and most commonly a step-parent) who threatened and then administered excessive force, battering the young person until the latter begged for mercy. In our samples, beating to the point of loss of consciousness was common, and more extreme 'punishments' included crucifixions, bodily mutilations, and systematic burning. There was, however, no relationship between the severity of the reported abuse and the seriousness of the violence later committed by the prisoner. The experience of shame is the invariable and it is replaced by intense rage that is apparently generated to restore the vulnerable sense of self.

The same process of the brutalization of affectional bonds can arise without the experience of physical harm, when the individual is forced to witness an attachment figure undergoing battering. The experience of shame and humiliation, followed by rage and a thirst for revenge, appear strikingly similar, regardless of whether the person is the victim of the battering or a witness. The family is not always involved in the brutalization. In about 70 per cent of our cases the prisoners, as children or adolescents, experienced brutalization by a combination of the family and the adolescent's intimate peer group (or gang).

The absence of the capacity for mentalization and the re-emergence of psychic equivalence make individuals with a history of psychological neglect exceptionally vulnerable to brutalization in these contexts. The attacks cannot be attenuated by mentalization of the pain engendered by the dehumanization of attachment. Unmentalized shame is not an 'as if' experience. It is tantamount to the destruction of the self. It would not be an exaggeration to label this emotion 'ego-destructive shame'. The coherence of the self-representation, identity itself, is under attack. The more robust the capacity for mentalization, the more easily the person may see both what lies behind the attack and its meaning, and not mistake it for the possibility of a real destruction of the ego. Ultimately, brutalization, if sufficiently severe, will generate ego-destructive shame even in those with exceptional capacities for mentalization. The humiliation is so intense that all things felt to be internal (subjectivity) become experiences to be resisted. In describing their experience of brutalization, prisoners frequently report finding the very act of thinking unbearable. Explicit phrases such as 'I stopped thinking', 'I went numb' or 'I could not bear to think' are quite common antecedents to the point where inevitably victim will turn into victimizer.

Why should the brutalization of affectional bonds be associated with such an intense and destructive sense of self-disgust verging on self-hatred? The shame concerns being treated as a physical object in the very context where special personal recognition is expected. Unbearable shame is generated through the incongruity of having one's humanity negated, exactly when one is legitimately expecting to be cherished. Violence or the threat of violence to the body is literally soul-destroying because it is the ultimate way of communicating the absence of love by the person inflicting the violence, from whom understanding is expected. As Freud (1914) taught us, the self is sustained by the love of the object so that it can become self-love; the sign of a self starved of love is shame, just as cold is the indication of an absence of heat (Gilligan 1997). And just like cold, shame, while painful as an acute experience, when intense and severe is experienced as a feeling of numbness or deadness.

The state of humiliation can only be erased through selective but deep disavowal of the subjectivities of both the object and the self. A prisoner who was incarcerated for aggravated assault recalled his alcoholic father urinating on him and his sister regularly when he returned home late at night from drinking. He reported that his terror of his father coming home changed at a certain point into an explicit wish to maim and disfigure him. At that point, he said, 'the fucking bastard stopped existing for me'. In many criminals a similar dramatic reconfiguration of the self seems to take place. There is a turning point when the normal barrier against intentionally injuring another human is penetrated. From this point, the person appears to feel no remorse for violent acts performed on others. A state that might be mistaken for psychopathy sets in. The word 'functional' might be inserted before 'psychopathy' since the disappearance of interpersonal sensibility is thought to be defensive, temporary and reversible.

So far we have talked about the predisposition to violent crime. This must be distinguished from the act of violence itself. While the predisposition involves the destruction of interpersonal awareness in a specific context, I would suggest that the act of violence itself represents the perverted restoration of a rudimentary mentalizing function.

The act of violence, whether impulsive or calculated, is rarely one of blind rage. Rather, it is a desperate attempt to protect the fragile self against the onslaught of shame, mostly innocently triggered by an other. The experience of humiliation, which the individual tries to contain within the alien part of the self, comes to represent an existential threat and is therefore abruptly externalized. Once outside, and perceived as part of the representation of the victim in the perpetrator's mind, it is seen as possible to destroy, once and for all. In this sense violence is a gesture of hope, a wish for a new beginning, even if in reality it is usually just a tragic end.

It is hard to feel empathy for violent actions. Yet, in a sense, given the reality of shame in the mode of psychic equivalence, we may say that they are committed in self-defence. Violence is a defence against the destructive actuality that humiliation and ego-destructive shame, experienced in the mode of psychic equivalence, generate. Certain individuals may have no resources other than violence to protect their self-representation that is crucially weakened by their impaired mentalizing capacity. Superficially, acts of violence may be perceived as cathartic, but I believe the restoration of equilibrium is less to do with drive discharge than to do with the acquisition of an inner gestalt, the creation of an inner peace – an odd kind of tranquillity.

CONCLUSION: OUR VIOLENT SOCIETY

Individuals whose impaired capacity for mentalization drives them to commit violent acts are victims of a social structure that fails to support families and the parenting function sufficiently to enable us to give adequate care to our young. This social structure provides few alternative structures within which children could arrive at self-recognition through social interchange with a benevolent and dependable figure for attachment. Furthermore, this social structure perhaps cruelly places supreme emphasis upon individuation, individuality and the achievement of selfhood. The failure of the coherent representation of self–other relationships, and the complications within self-organization that become manifest as a consequence, occur with increasing frequency in families regardless of material wealth, because society has relinquished some of its caretaking functions, demolished its institutions for supporting emotional development, and shifted its priorities from the mental and emotional to the material. The collective violence of social groups (Nazism, ethnic cleansing) also draws its motive force from a delusion about the eradication of shame, even if at the level of nationhood or social class. We collectively pay a heavy price for favouring matter (physical well-being) over mind (the coherence of subjectivity). It is the task of psychoanalysis, the pre-eminent academic discipline concerned with subjectivity, to redress this imbalance.

NOTES

1. This chapter was presented to the Annual Meeting of the Royal College of Psychiatrists, 12 July 2001.

2. My collaborators in this work were Alice Levinson MD (forensic psychiatric personality disorder sample n = 22), Andrew Hill-Smith MD, Pippa Hugo MD (young murderers sample n = 22) and Gillian McGauley MD (mixed forensic psychiatric sample n = 50).

REFERENCES

Abrahamsen, D. (1973) *The Murdering Mind.* London: Hogarth Press.

Ainsworth, M.D.S., Blehar, M.C., Waters, E. and Wall, S. (1978) *Patterns of Attachment: A Psychological Study of the Strange Situation.* Hillsdale, NJ: Erlbaum.

Allen, J.P., Moore, C., Kuperminc, G. and Bell, K. (1998) 'Attachment and adolescent psychosocial functioning.' *Child Development 69,* 1406–1419.

American Academy of Child and Adolescent Psychiatry (1999) *Children and Television Violence.* Washington, DC: AACAP.

Astington, J., Harris, P. and Olson, D. (1988) *Developing Theories of Mind.* New York: Cambridge University Press.

Bahrick, L.R. and Watson, J.S. (1985) 'Detection of intermodal proprioceptive-visual contingency as a potential basis of self-perception in infancy.' *Developmental Psychology 21,* 963–973.

Baron-Cohen, S., Jolliffe, T., Mortimore, C. and Robertson, M. (1997) 'Another advanced test of theory of mind: Evidence from very high functioning adults with autisms or Asperger Syndrome.' *Journal of Child Psychology and Psychiatry 38,* 813–822.

Baron-Cohen, S. and Swettenham, J. (1996) 'The relationship between SAM and ToMM: Two hypotheses.' In P. Carruthers and P.K. Smith (eds) *Theories of Theories of Mind.* Cambridge: Cambridge University Press.

Baron-Cohen, S., Tager-Flusberg, H. and Cohen, D.J. (1993) *Understanding Other Minds: Perspectives from Autism.* Oxford: Oxford University Press.

Baron-Cohen, S., Tager-Flusberg, H. and Cohen, D.J. (eds) (2000) *Understanding Other Minds: Perspectives from Autism and Developmental Cognitive Neuroscience.* Oxford: Oxford University Press.

Baron-Cohen, S., Wheelwright, S., Hill, J., Raste, Y. and Plumb, I. (2001) 'The "Reading the Mind in the Eyes" Test revised version: A study with normal adults, and adults with Asperger syndrome or high-functioning autism.' *Journal of Child Psychology and Psychiatry 42,* (2), 241–251.

Beebe, B., Jaffe, J., Feldstein, S., Mays, K. and Alson, D. (1985) 'Interpersonal timing: The application of an adult dialogue model to mother–infant vocal and kinesic interactions.' In T.M. Field and N.A. Fox (eds) *Social Perception in Infants.* Norwood, NJ: Ablex.

Bion, W.R. (1962) *Learning from Experience.* London: Heinemann.

Bjerregaard, B. and Lizotte, A.J. (1995) 'Gun ownership and gang membership.' *The Journal of Criminal Law and Criminology 86,* 37–58.

Blair, R.J.R. (1995) 'A cognitive developmental approach to morality: Investigating the psychopath.' *Cognition 57*, 1–29.

Blair, R.J.R., Jones, L., Clark, F. and Smith, M. (1997) 'The psychopathic individual: A lack of responsiveness to distress cues?' *Psychophysiology 34*, (2), 192–198.

Blair, R.J.R., Morris, J.S., Frith, C.D., Perrett, D.I. and Dolan, R.J. (1999) 'Dissociable neural responses to facial expression of sadness and anger.' *Brain 122*, (5), 883–893.

Bleiberg, E. (2001) *Treating Personality Disorders in Children and Adolescents: A Relational Approach.* New York: Guilford Press.

Bogdan, R.J. (1997) *Interpreting Minds.* Cambridge, MA: MIT Press.

Bolton, D. and Hill, J. (1996) *Mind, Meaning and Mental Disorder.* Oxford: Oxford University Press.

Bowlby, J. (1969) *Attachment and Loss, Vol. 1: Attachment.* London: Hogarth Press and the Institute of Psycho-Analysis.

Brazelton, T., Kowslowski, B. and Main, M. (1974) 'The origins of reciprocity: The early mother–infant interaction.' In M. Lewis and L. Rosenblum (eds) *The Effect of the Infant on Its Caregivers.* New York: John Wiley.

Brazelton, T.B. and Tronick, E. (1980) 'Preverbal communication between mothers and infants.' In D.R. Olson (ed) *The Social Foundations of Language and Thought.* New York: Norton.

Bushman, B.J. and Baumeister, R.F. (1999) 'Threatened egotism, narcissism, self-esteem, and direct and displaced aggression: Does self-love lead to violence?' *Journal of Personality and Social Psychology 75*, 219–229.

Cassam, Q. (ed) (1994) *Self-knowledge.* Oxford: Oxford University Press.

Coid, J.D. and Dodge, K.A. (1998) 'Aggression and antisocial behaviour.' In W. Damon (ed) *Handbook of Child Psychology (5th ed.) Vol. 3: Social, Emotional, and Personality Development.* New York: Wiley.

Corkum, V. and Moore, C. (1995) 'Development of joint visual attention in infants.' In C. Moore and P. Dunham (eds) *Joint Attention: Its Origins and Role in Development.* New York: Erlbaum.

Cox, M. (1982) 'The psychotherapist as assessor of dangerousness.' In J.R. Hamilton and H. Freeman (eds) *Dangerousness: Psychiatric Assessment and Management.* London: Alden Press.

Crick, N.R. and Dodge, K.A. (1994) 'A review and reformulation of social information-processing mechanisms in children's social adjustment.' *Psychological Bulletin 115*, 74–101.

Csibra, G. and Gergely, G. (1998) 'The teleological origins of mentalistic action explanations: A developmental hypothesis.' *Developmental Science 1*, (2), 255–259.

Csibra, G., Gergely, G., Brockbank, M., Biro, S. and Koós, O. (1999) 'Twelve-month-olds can infer a goal for an incomplete action.' Paper presented at the 11th Biennial Conference on Infant Studies (ICIS), Atlanta, Georgia.

DeCasper, A.J. and Fifer, W.P. (1980) 'Of human bonding: Newborns prefer their mothers' voices.' *Science 208*, 1174–1176.

Denham, S.A., Zoller, D. and Couchoud, E.A. (1994) 'Socialization of preschoolers' emotion understanding.' *Developmental Psychology 30*, 928–936.

Dennett, D. (1987) *The Intentional Stance.* Cambridge, MA: MIT Press.

Dodge, K.A., Pettit, G. and Bates, J.E. (1994) 'Socialization mediators of the relation between socioeconomic status and child conduct problems.' *Child Development 65*, 649–665.

Dunn, J. (1996) 'The Emanuel Miller Memorial Lecture 1995. Children's relationships: Bridging the divide between cognitive and social development.' *Journal of Child Psychology and Psychiatry 37*, 507–518.

Dunn, J., Brown, J. and Beardsall, L. (1991) 'Family talk about feeling states and children's later understanding of others' emotions.' *Developmental Psychology 27*, 448–455.

Dunn, J., Brown, J., Somkowski, C., Telsa, C. and Youngblade, L. (1991) 'Young children's understanding of other people's feelings and beliefs: Individual differences and their antecedents.' *Child Development 62*, 1352–1366.

Dywan, J. and Bowers, K.S. (1983) 'The use of hypnosis to enhance recall.' *Science 222*, 184–185.

Elliott, D., Hamburg, B. and Williams, K. (1998) *Violence in American Schools.* Cambridge: Cambridge University Press.

Fantz, R. (1963) 'Pattern vision in newborn infants.' *Science 140*, 296–297.

Farrington, D.P. (1989) 'Early predictors of adolescent aggression and adult violence.' *Violence and Victims 4*, 79–100.

Field, T. (1979) 'Differential behavioral and cardiac responses of three-month-old infants to a mirror and peer.' *Infant Behaviour and Development 2*, 179–184.

Fodor, J. (1987) *Psychosemantics.* Cambridge, MA: MIT Press.

Fodor, J.A. (1992) 'A theory of the child's theory of mind.' *Cognition 44*, 283–296.

Fonagy, P. (1991) 'Thinking about thinking: Some clinical and theoretical considerations in the treatment of a borderline patient.' *International Journal of Psycho-Analysis 72*, 1–18.

Fonagy, P. (1995) 'Playing with reality: The development of psychic reality and its malfunction in borderline patients.' *International Journal of Psycho-Analysis 76*, 39–44.

Fonagy, P. (1997a) 'Attachment and theory of mind: Overlapping constructs?' *Association for Child Psychology and Psychiatry Occasional Papers 14*, 31–40.

Fonagy, P. (1997b) 'Multiple voices versus meta-cognition: An attachment theory perspective.' *Journal of Psychotherapy Integration 7*, 181–194.

Fonagy, P. (1999) 'The transgenerational transmission of holocaust trauma. Lessons learned from the analysis of an adolescent with obsessive-compulsive disorder.' *Attachment and Human Development 1*, 92–114.

Fonagy, P. (2000) 'Attachment and borderline personality disorder.' *Journal of the American Psychoanalytic Association 48*, (4), 1129–1146.

Fonagy, P., Gergely, G., Jurist, E. and Target, M. (2002) *Affect Regulation, Mentalization and the Development of the Self.* New York: Other Press.

Fonagy, P., Steele, H., Moran, G., Steele, M. and Higgitt, A. (1991) 'The capacity for understanding mental states: The reflective self in parent and child and its significance for security of attachment.' *Infant Mental Health Journal 13*, 200–217.

Fonagy, P., Steele, M., Moran, G.S., Steele, H. and Higgitt, A. (1993) 'Measuring the ghost in the nursery: An empirical study of the relation between parents' mental representations of childhood experiences and their infants' security of attachment.' *Journal of the American Psychoanalytic Association 41*, 957–989.

Fonagy, P., Steele, M., Steele, H., Higgitt, A. and Target, M. (1994) 'Theory and practice of resilience.' *Journal of Child Psychology and Psychiatry 35*, 231–257.

Fonagy, P., Steele, M., Steele, H., Leigh, T., Kennedy, R., Mattoon, G. and Target, M. (1995) 'The predictive validity of Mary Main's Adult Attachment Interview: A psychoanalytic and developmental perspective on the transgenerational transmission of attachment and borderline states.' In S. Goldberg, R. Muir and J. Kerr (eds) *Attachment Theory: Social, Developmental and Clinical Perspectives.* Hillsdale, NJ: The Analytic Press.

Fonagy, P. and Target, M. (1996) 'Playing with reality I: Theory of mind and the normal development of psychic reality.' *International Journal of Psycho-Analysis 77*, 217–233.

Fonagy, P. and Target, M. (1997) 'Attachment and reflective function: Their role in self-organization.' *Development and Psychopathology 9*, 679–700.

Fonagy, P. and Target, M. (2000) 'Playing with reality III: The persistence of dual psychic reality in borderline patients.' *International Journal of Psychoanalysis 81*, (5), 853–874.

Fonagy, P., Target, M. and Gergely, G. (2000) 'Attachment and borderline personality disorder: A theory and some evidence.' *Psychiatric Clinics of North America 23*, 103–122.

Fonagy, P., Target, M., Steele, M. and Steele, H. (1997a) 'The development of violence and crime as it relates to security of attachment.' In J.D. Osofsky (ed) *Children in a Violent Society.* New York: Guilford Press.

Fonagy, P., Target, M., Steele, H. and Steele, M. (1998) *Reflective-Functioning Manual, Version 5.0, for Application to Adult Attachment Interviews.* London: University College London.

Fonagy, P., Target, M., Steele, M., Steele, H., Leigh, T., Levinson, A. and Kennedy, R. (1997b) 'Morality, disruptive behavior, borderline personality disorder, crime, and their relationships to security of attachment.' In L. Atkinson and K.J. Zucker (eds) *Attachment and Psychopathology.* New York: Guilford Press.

Freud, S. (1914) 'On narcissism: An introduction.' In J. Strachey (ed) *The Standard Edition of the Complete Psychological Works of Sigmund Freud, Vol. 14.* London: Hogarth Press.

Gazzaniga, M.S. (1985) *The Social Brain: Discovering the Networks of the Mind.* New York: Basic Books.

Gergely, G. (2001) 'The development of understanding of self and agency.' In U. Goshwami (ed) *Handbook of Childhood Cognitive Development.* Oxford: Blackwell.

Gergely, G. and Csibra, G. (1996) 'Understanding rational actions in infancy: Teleological interpretations without mental attribution. Symposium on "Early Perception of Social Contingencies".' Paper presented at the 10th Biennial International Conference on Infant Studies, Providence, RI, USA.

Gergely, G. and Csibra, G. (1997) 'Teleological reasoning in infancy: The infant's naive theory of rational action. A reply to Premack and Premack.' *Cognition 63*, 227–233.

Gergely, G. and Csibra, G. (1998) 'La interpretacion teleologica de la conducta: La teoria infantil de la accion racional [The teleological interpretation of behaviour: The infant's theory of rational action].' *Infancia y Aprendizaje 84*, 45–65.

Gergely, G. and Csibra, G. (2000) 'The teleological origins of naive theory of mind in infancy.' Paper presented at the Symposium on 'Origins of Theory of Mind: Studies with Human Infants and Primates'. Presented at the 12th Biennial International Conference on Infant Studies (ICIS), Brighton, England.

Gergely, G., Koós, O. and Watson, J.S. (in press) 'Contingency perception and the role of contingent parental reactivity in early socio-emotional development: Some implications for developmental psychopathology.' In J. Nadel and J. Decety (eds) *Imitation, Action et Intentionalité*. Paris: Presses Universitaires de France.

Gergely, G. and Watson, J. (1996) 'The social biofeedback model of parental affect-mirroring.' *International Journal of Psycho-Analysis 77*, 1181–1212.

Gergely, G. and Watson, J. (1999) 'Early social-emotional development: Contingency perception and the social biofeedback model.' In P. Rochat (ed) *Early Social Cognition: Understanding Others in the First Months of Life*. Hillsdale, NJ: Erlbaum.

Gilligan, J. (1997) *Violence: Our Deadliest Epidemic and its Causes*. New York: Grosset/Putnam.

Harpold, J.A. and Band, S.R. (1998) *Lessons Learned: An FBI Perspective: School Violence Summit*. Little Rock, AR: Behavioral Science Unit, FBI Academy.

Harter, S. (1999) *The Construction of the Self: A Developmental Perspective*. New York: Guilford Press.

Hirschfeld, L. and Gelman, S. (1994) *Mapping the Mind: Domain Specificity in Cognition and Culture*. New York: Cambridge University Press.

Hobson, R.P. (1993) *Autism and the Development of Mind*. London: Lawrence Erlbaum.

Hughes, C., Dunn, J. and White, A. (1998) 'Trick or treat? Uneven understanding of mind and emotion and executive dysfunction in "hard-to-manage" preschoolers.' *Journal of Child Psychology and Psychiatry 39*, 981–994.

Jaffe, J., Beebe, B., Feldstein, S., Crown, C.L. and Jasnow, M.D. (2001) 'Rhythms of Dialogue in Infancy.' *Monographs of the Society for Research in Child Development 66*, (2).

James, W. (1890) *Principles of Psychology*. New York: Henry Holt and Co.

Jenkins, J. and Astington, J.W. (1996) 'Cognitive factors and family structure associated with theory of mind development in young children.' *Developmental Psychology 32*, 70–78.

Johnson, J.G., Cohen, P., Brown, J., Smailes, E.M. and Bernstein, D.P. (1999) 'Childhood maltreatment increases risk for personality disorders during early adulthood.' *Archives of General Psychiatry 56*, 600–605.

Johnson-Reid, M. and Barth, R.P. (2000) 'From maltreatment report to juvenile incarceration: The role of child welfare.' *Child Abuse and Neglect 24*, (4), 505–520.

Kernberg, O.F. (1976) *Object Relations Theory and Clinical Psychoanalysis.* New York: Aronson.

Kernberg, O.F. (1982) 'Self, ego, affects and drives.' *Journal of the American Psychoanalytic Association 30*, 893–917.

Kernberg, O.F. (1983) 'Object relations theory and character analysis.' *Journal of the American Psychoanalytic Association 31*, 247–271.

Kernberg, O.F. (1984) *Reflections in the Mirror: Mother–child Interactions, Self-awareness, and Self-recognition.* New York: Basic Books, Inc.

Kihlstrom, J.F. (1994) 'Hypnosis, delayed recall and the principles of memory.' *International Journal of Clinical and Experimental Hypnosis 42*, 337–345.

Klein, M. (1946) 'Notes on some schizoid mechanisms.' In M. Klein, P. Heimann, S. Isaacs and J. Riviere (eds) *Developments in Psychoanalysis.* London: Hogarth Press.

Kohut, H. (1971) *The Analysis of the Self.* New York: International Universities Press.

Kohut, H. (1977) *The Restoration of the Self.* New York: International Universities Press.

Laub, J.H. (1998) 'The interdependence of school violence with neighbourhood and family conditions.' In D.S. Elliot, B. Hamburg and K.R. Williams (eds) *Violence in American Schools: A New Perspective.* New York: Cambridge University Press.

Lecours, S. and Bouchard, M.-A. (1997) 'Dimensions of mentalisation: Outlining levels of psychic transformation.' *International Journal of Psycho-Analysis 78*, 855–875.

Legerstee, M. and Varghese, J. (2001) 'The role of maternal affect mirroring on social expectancies in two- to three-month-old infants.' *Child Development 72*, 1301–1313.

Leslie, A.M. (1994) 'TOMM, ToBy and agency: Core architecture and domain specificity.' In L. Hirschfeld and S. Gelman (eds) *Mapping the Mind: Domain Specificity in Cognition and Culture.* New York: Cambridge University Press.

Levinson, A. and Fonagy, P. (submitted) 'Attachment classification in prisoners and psychiatric patients.'

Lewis, M., Allessandri, S.M. and Sullivan, M.W. (1990) 'Violation of expectancy, loss of control and anger expressions in young infants.' *Developmental Psychology 26*, (5), 745–751.

Lewis, M. and Brooks-Gunn, J. (1979) *Social Cognition and the Acquisition of Self.* New York: Plenum Press.

Loeber, R. and Stouthamer-Loeber, M. (1998) 'Development of juvenile aggression and violence: Some common misconceptions and controversies.' *American Psychologist 53*, 242–259.

Lyons-Ruth, K. (1996) 'Attachment relationships among children with aggressive behavior problems: The role of disorganized early attachment patterns.' *Journal of Consulting and Clinical Psychology 64*, 64–73.

Lyons-Ruth, K., Bronfman, E. and Atwood, G. (1999) 'A relational diathesis model of hostile-helpless states of mind: Expressions in mother–infant interaction.' In J. Solomon and C. George (eds) *Attachment Disorganization.* New York: Guilford Press.

Lyons-Ruth, K. and Jacobovitz, D. (1999) 'Attachment disorganization: Unresolved loss, relational violence and lapses in behavioral and attentional strategies.' In J. Cassidy and P.R. Shaver (eds) *Handbook of Attachment Theory and Research.* New York: Guilford.

McDougall, J. (1989) *Theaters of the Body: A Psychoanalytic Approach to Psychosomatic Illness.* New York: W.W. Norton and Co.

Main, M. and Goldwyn, R. (1994) *Adult Attachment Rating and Classification System, Manual in Draft, Version 6.0.* Unpublished manuscript: University of California at Berkeley.

Main, M. and Hesse, E. (1990) 'Parents' unresolved traumatic experiences are related to infant disorganized attachment status: Is frightened and/or frightening parental behavior the linking mechanism?' In M. Greenberg, D. Cicchetti and E.M. Cummings (eds) *Attachment in the Preschool Years: Theory, Research and Intervention.* Chicago: University of Chicago Press.

Main, M. and Hesse, E. (1992) 'Disorganized/disoriented infant behaviour in the Strange Situation, lapses in the monitoring of reasoning and discourse during the parent's Adult Attachment Interview, and dissociative states.' In

M. Ammaniti and D. Stern (eds) *Attachment and Psychoanalysis.* Rome: Gius, Latereza and Figli.

Main, M. and Solomon, J. (1986) 'Discovery of an insecure-disorganized/ disoriented attachment pattern.' In T.B. Brazelton and M.W. Yogman (eds) *Affective Development in Infancy.* Norwood, NJ: Ablex.

Malatesta, C.Z., Culver, C., Tesman, J.R. and Shepard, B. (1989) 'The development of emotion expression during the first two years of life.' *Monographs of the Society for Research in Child Development 54*, 1–104.

Malatesta, C.Z. and Izard, C.E. (1984) 'The ontogenesis of human social signals: From biological imperative to symbol utilization.' In N.A. Fox and R.J. Davison (eds) *The Psychobiology of Affective Development.* Hillsdale, NJ: Erlbaum.

Matthys, W., Cuperus, J.M. and van Engeland, H. (1999) 'Deficient social problem-solving in boys with ODD/CD, with ADHD, and with both disorders.' *Journal of the American Academy of Child and Adolescent Psychiatry 38*, 311–321.

Meins, E., Ferryhough, C., Fradley, E. and Tuckey, M. (2001) 'Rethinking maternal sensitivity: Mothers' comments on infants' mental processes predict security of attachment at 12 months.' *Journal of Child Psychology and Psychiatry 42*, 637–648.

Meltzoff, A.N. (1990) 'Foundations for developing a concept of self: The role of imitation in relating self to other and the value of social mirroring, social modeling and self practice in infancy.' In D. Cicchetti and M. Beeghly (eds) *The Self in Transition: Infancy to Childhood.* Chicago: University of Chicago Press.

Meltzoff, A.N. and Moore, M.K. (1977) 'Imitation of facial and manual gestures by human neonates.' *Science 198*, 75–78.

Meltzoff, A.N. and Moore, M.K. (1989) 'Imitation in newborn infants: Exploring the range of gestures imitated and the underlying mechanisms.' *Developmental Psychology 25*, 954–962.

Mitchell, R.W. (1993) 'Mental models of mirror self-recognition: Two theories.' *New Ideas in Psychology 11*, 295–325.

Morton, J. and Johnson, M.H. (1991) 'CONSPEC and CONLEARN: A two-process theory of infant face recognition.' *Psychological Review 98*, 164–181.

Neisser, U. (1988) 'Five kinds of self-knowledge.' *Philosophical Psychology 1*, 35–59.

NICHD Early Child Care Research Network (1996) 'Characteristics of infant child care: Factors contributing to positive caregiving.' *Early Childhood Research Quarterly 11*, 269–306.

Papousek, H. and Papousek, M. (1974) 'Mirror-image and self recognition in young human infants: A new method of experimental analysis.' *Developmental Psychobiology 7*, 149–157.

Papousek, H. and Papousek, M. (1987) 'Intuitive parenting: A dialectic counterpart to the infant's integrative competence.' In J.D. Osofsky (ed) *Handbook of Infant Development.* New York: Wiley.

Patterson, G.R., Reid, J.B. and Dishion, T.J. (1992) *Antisocial Boys.* Eugene, OR: Castalia.

Perner, J. (1991) *Understanding the Representational Mind.* Cambridge, MA: MIT Press.

Perner, J., Ruffman, T. and Leekman, S.R. (1994) 'Theory of mind is contagious: You catch it from your sibs.' *Child Development 65*, 1228–1238.

Piaget, J. (1936) *The Origins of Intelligence in Children.* New York: International Universities Press, 1952.

Pines, M. (1982) 'Reflections on mirroring.' *Group Analysis 15* (supplement).

Pope, A.W. and Bierman, K.L. (1999) 'Predicting adolescent peer problems and antisocial activities: The relative roles of aggression and dysregulation.' *Developmental Psychology 35*, 335–346.

Povinelli, D.J. and Eddy, T.J. (1995) 'The unduplicated self.' In P. Rochat (ed) *The Self in Infancy: Theory and Research.* Amsterdam: Elsevier.

Repacholi, B.M. and Gopnik, A. (1997) 'Early reasoning about desires: Evidence from 14- and 18-month-olds.' *Developmental Psychology 33*, 12–21.

Rochat, P. and Morgan, R. (1995) 'Spatial determinants in the perception of self-produced leg movements in three- to five-month-old infants.' *Developmental Psychology 31*, 626–636.

Ruffman, T., Perner, J., Naito, M., Parkin, L. and Clements, W. (1998) 'Older (but not younger) siblings facilitate false belief understanding.' *Developmental Psychology 34*, (1), 161–174.

Sander, L.W. (1970) 'Regulation and organization of behavior in the early infant–caretaker system.' In R. Robinson (ed) *Brain and Early Behavior.* London: Academic Press.

Sandler, J. (1987) *Projection, Identification, Projective Identification.* London: Karnac Books.

Schmuckler, M.A. (1996) 'Visual-proprioceptive intermodal perception in infancy.' *Infant Behavior and Development 19*, 221–232.

Schneider-Rosen, K. and Cicchetti, D. (1991) 'Early self-knowledge and emotional development: Visual self-recognition and affective reactions to mirror self-image in maltreated and non-maltreated toddlers.' *Developmental Psychology 27*, 481–488.

Schuengel, C., Bakermans-Kranenburg, M.J., van IJzendoorn, M.H. and Blom, M. (1999) 'Unresolved loss and infant disorganisation: Links to frightening maternal behavior.' In J. Solomon and C. George (eds) *Attachment Disorganization*. New York: Guilford.

Segal, H. (1964) *Introduction to the Work of Melanie Klein*. New York: Basic Books.

Slade, A., Belsky, J., Aber, L. and Phelps, J.L. (1999) 'Mothers' representations of their relationships with their toddlers: Links to adult attachment and observed mothering.' *Developmental Psychology 35*, (3), 611–619.

Smith, C. and Thornberry, T.P. (1995) 'The relationship between child maltreatment and adolescent involvement in delinquency.' *Criminology 33*, 451–477.

Solomon, J. and George, C. (1999) *Attachment Disorganization*. New York: Guilford.

Spiegel, D. and Scheflin, A.W. (1994) 'Dissociated or fabricated? Psychiatric aspects of repressed memory in criminal and civil cases.' *International Journal of Clinical and Experimental Hypnosis. Special Issue: Hypnosis and Delayed Recall – I, 42*, 411–432.

Stern, D.N. (1977) *The First Relationship: Mother and Infant*. Cambridge, MA: Harvard University Press.

Stern, D.N. (1985) *The Interpersonal World of the Infant: A View from Psychoanalysis and Developmental Psychology*. New York: Basic Books.

Tomasello, M. (1999) *The Cultural Origins of Human Cognition*. Cambridge, MA: Harvard University Press.

Trevarthen, C. (1979) 'Communication and cooperation in early infancy: A description of primary intersubjectivity.' In M.M. Bullowa (ed) *Before Speech: The Beginning of Interpersonal Communication*. New York: Cambridge University Press.

Tronick, E.Z. (1989) 'Emotions and emotional communication in infants.' *American Psychologist 44*, 112–119.

Tronick, E.Z. and Gianino, A.F. (1986) 'The transmission of maternal disturbance to the infant.' In E.Z. Tronick and T. Field (eds) *Maternal Depression and Infant Disturbance.* San Francisco: Jossey Bass.

Tyson, P. and Tyson, R.L. (1990) *Psychoanalytic Theories of Development: An Integration.* New Haven and London: Yale University Press.

Valois, R. and McKewon, R. (1998) 'Frequency and correlates of fighting and carrying weapons among public school adolescents.' *American Journal of Health Behavior 22*, 8–17.

van IJzendoorn, M.H., Moran, G., Belsky, J., Pederson, D., Bakermans-Kranenburg, M.J. and Kneppers, K. (2000) 'The similarity of siblings' attachments to their mothers.' *Child Development 71*, 1086–1098.

Verlinden, S., Hersen, M. and Thomas, J. (2000) 'Risk factors in school shootings.' *Clinical Psychology Review 20*, 3–56.

Walker, H., Irvin, L.K. and Sprague, J.R. (1997) *Violence Prevention and School Safety: Issues, Problems, Approaches, and Recommended Solutions.* Eugene, OR: Institute on Violence and Destructive Behavior, University of Oregon.

Watson, J.S. (1972) 'Smiling, cooing, and "the game".' *Merrill-Palmer Quarterly 18*, 323–339.

Watson, J.S. (1979) 'Perception of contingency as a determinant of social responsiveness.' In E.B. Thoman (ed) *The Origins of Social Responsiveness.* New York: Lawrence Erlbaum.

Watson, J.S. (1985) 'Contingency perception in early social development.' In T.M. Field and N.A. Fox (eds) *Social Perception in Infants.* Norwood, NJ: Ablex.

Watson, J.S. (1994) 'Detection of self: The perfect algorithm.' In S. Parker, R. Mitchell and M. Boccia (eds) *Self-Awareness in Animals and Humans: Developmental Perspectives.* Cambridge: Cambridge University Press.

Watson, J.S. (1995) 'Self-orientation in early infancy: The general role of contingency and the specific case of reaching to the mouth.' In P. Rochat (ed) *The Self in Infancy: Theory and Research.* Amsterdam: Elsevier.

Wellman, H. (1990) *The Child's Theory of Mind.* Cambridge, MA: Bradford Books/MIT Press.

Wellman, H.M. and Phillips, A.T. (2000) 'Developing intentional understandings.' In L. Moses, B. Male and D. Baldwin (eds) *Intentionality: A Key to Human Understanding.* Cambridge, MA: MIT Press.

Wells, L.E. and Rankin, J.H. (1988) 'Direct parent controls and delinquency.' *Criminology 26*, 263–285.

Whiten, A. (1991) *Natural Theories of Mind.* Oxford: Basil Blackwell.

Wimmer, H. and Perner, J. (1983) 'Beliefs about beliefs: Representation and constraining function of wrong beliefs in young children's understanding of deception.' *Cognition 13*, 103–128.

Winnicott, D.W. (1956) 'Mirror role of mother and family in child development.' In D.W. Winnicott (ed) *Playing and Reality*. London: Tavistock.

Winnicott, D.W. (1971) 'Transitional objects and transitional phenomena.' In D.W. Winnicott (ed) *Playing and Reality*. London: Tavistock.

CHAPTER 2

Attachment Representation, Attachment Style or Attachment Pattern?

Usage of Terminology in Attachment Theory

Thomas Ross

SUMMARY

In recent years attachment research has experienced much attention within the field of psychotherapy research. During the 'attachment boom' there has been an explosion of terms relating to different theoretical constructs of attachment. A review of the recently published attachment literature abstracts from January 2000 until May 2002 revealed a multitude of terms used in a rather confusing way. In this chapter the usage of terms is discussed with respect to their core meaning, and the adequacy of their application is evaluated. In order to provide a basis for empirical comparisons, social science requires a clear and specific conceptualisation of terminology. The terms 'attachment style', '– representation', '– pattern', '– quality', '– status', '– organisation', '– class/classification', and '– type/prototype' are discussed in some detail and suggestions for further usage are made.

INTRODUCTION

In his writings about attachment John Bowlby integrated elements of psychoanalysis, ethology, and control- and learning theory into a theory which
has greatly influenced theoretical concepts of developmental psychology,
clinical psychology, psychoanalysis, and psychiatry. In his works on 1. 'attachment', 2. 'separation', 3. 'loss, sadness and depression' he focused on
the central role of interpersonal relationships for social development and
psychological functioning throughout life (Bowlby 1969, 1973, 1980).
His theoretical considerations of attachment relationships were led by one
central observation: in case of perceived physiological or psychological
threat or danger, children tend to preserve their psychological integrity by
seeking protection with primary caregivers. He developed two major
hypotheses regarding the origin of inter-individual differences of attachment:

1.   Through a history of responsive care, children will evolve
       expectations (inner working models) of their caregivers' likely
       responses to signs of distress or other signals of the desire for
       contact. The specific prediction, then, is that caregiver
       responsiveness early in infancy is related to individual
       differences in attachment security later in infancy. In the most
       simple terms, Bowlby postulated that what infants expect is
       what has happened before.

2.   The second hypothesis concerned the likely consequences of
       individual differences in attachment security for the child's
       development, particularly personality development (Bowlby
       1973). Bowlby argued that because attachment relationships
       are internalised or represented, these early experiences and
       subsequent expectations get taken forward to serve later
       behavioural and emotional adaptation, even in totally new
       contexts and with different people.

In particular, inner working models are a foundation not only for expectations concerning the self, but also for later relationships with caregivers and
non-caregivers alike. Parental responsivity is an important basis for the
evolving child–parent relationship. The experience of a predictable world
of interpersonal relationships leads to the development of a stable self or
self-perception via invariant and stable perception of effective communica-

tion of behavioural signals. Thus there are implications for later efficacy, self-esteem, and involved social relationships (Marvin and Britner 1999).

The first to provide a formal description of individual differences in infants' attachment security was Mary Ainsworth (Ainsworth 1967). Inspired by Bowlby's theory and her own observations of caregiving practices and infant behaviour in Uganda, she developed the 'strange situation' test (Ainsworth *et al.* 1978), which is a method for assessing individual differences in attachment behaviour of infants. More attachment measures were devised, and in 1985 the Adult Attachment Interview (AAI, George, Kaplan and Main 1985), the first method to assess and evaluate attachment representations in adolescents and adults, was published.

Many measures have been published and applied since then. Simultaneously, there has been a considerable increase of terminology, the usage of terms depending on the type of measure. While the constructs of the inner working model, maternal sensitivity and sensitive responsiveness are clearly conceptualised, the same cannot be said for the terms used to describe different psychobiological adaptation strategies and the classification of individual differences. The most important are (in alphabetical order):

- attachment classification
- attachment pattern
- attachment organisation
- attachment quality
- attachment representation
- attachment status
- attachment style
- attachment type or prototype.

These terms appear in virtually all recent books, book chapters, monographs, and papers on attachment theory in a similar context (see Bartholomew and Perlman 1994; Cassidy and Shaver 1999; Crittenden and Claussen 2000; Murray Parkes, Stevenson-Hinde and Marris 1991; Simpson and Rholes 1998).

In May 2002 I conducted a literature review using the databases Psychlit, Psychinfo, Medline and the German databases Psyndex and

Dimdi. The search focused on the most recent publications, from January 2000 until spring 2002. The search was based on abstracts, not on the corresponding original publications. Applying the search terms 'attachment style', 'attachment representation', 'attachment status', 'attachment quality' and 'attachment organisation', and their German equivalents, produced a total of 377 entries. The following table shows all terms with a minimum of five entries.

Table 2.1 Number of attachment terms in a sample of 377 literature entries (January 2000–May 2002)	
Term	*Number of entries*
attachment style	252
attachment representation	66
attachment pattern	41
attachment quality	28
attachment status	22
attachment organisation	16
attachment classification	9
attachment type/prototype	8
attachment category	7
attachment model*	5

* *This term appeared only in German references, as 'Bindungsmodell'.*

In addition, the following terms were occasionally found in direct connection with attachment constructs:

- 'attachment orientation' was mentioned four times
- 'attachment relationship'
- 'dimension' and '– group' were each mentioned twice

- 'attachment configuration', '– rating', '– feature', '– tendency', '– strategy', '– history', '– orientation', '– response' and '– profile' were each mentioned once.

In many cases different attachment terms were found within a single abstract. The term 'attachment disorganisation' was found twice, the terms 'attachment disorder', 'attachment difficulty' and 'attachment pathology' were also found once each. The usage of 'attachment disorganisation' and 'attachment disorder' was directly related to the assignment of subjects to attachment categories, which is theoretically unsound. There was no such association for the terms 'attachment difficulty' and 'attachment pathology'. But these terms still imply a strong normative judgement, which is empirically not justified. Some abstracts contained four different terms for the description of the same fact.

The categorisation of adaptive strategies was found to vary considerably with respect to both the theoretical models on which they are based, and the methodological access different authors choose in accordance with their theoretical focus (see Table 2.2).

The theoretical development of attachment constructs and the choice of a categorical concept cannot be understood without recognising the pioneering work of Ainsworth *et al.* (1978) and subsequent attempts to operationalise attachment in adults (Adult Attachment Interview, George, Kaplan and Main 1985; Current Relationship Interview, Crowell and Owens 1998; Attachment Style Questionnaire, Hazan and Shaver 1987, 1990). Methodology plays an important role in this context. Attachment style categories, as derived from attachment questionnaires, largely result from factor analytical techniques. The resulting dimensions are then labelled with a plausible terminology. This handling is of course not unusual; but depending on the normative sample and the items used, it also provides different factor solutions.

Table 2.2 Terminology used by different authors in order to describe different strategies of sociobiological adaptation in situations eliciting attachment behaviour (selection)

Ainsworth et al. (1978) (Strange Situation)	George, Kaplan and Main (1985)	Hazan and Shaver (1987)	Bartholomew (1990)	Pilkonis (1988, 1995)
secure	secure	secure	secure	secure features
anxious-avoidant	dismissing		dismissing	• obsessive-compulsive features • defensive separation • lack of interpersonal sensitivity
anxious-resistant	enmeshed, preoccupied	anxious-ambivalent	preoccupied	• excessive dependency • borderline features • excessive care
disorganised	disorganised			mixed insecure
		anxious-avoidant	fearful-avoidant	
	cannot classify			

From a singular point of view, this is not problematic. But there has been no formal examination of the terminology used in relation to attachment measures, or of the methodological implications this has for comparing the results and conclusions of different studies. As a result, discrepancies in methodology are often not identified and taken into account. However, when attachment is measured, the term 'attachment style' is frequently used, but this is also true for semi-structured interview techniques (Interpersonal Relations Assessment (IRA), Pilkonis 1988; Pilkonis et al. 1995) and it remains unclear whether attachment styles that are being measured by different methods actually relate to a single theoretical construct. The core questions are: Does attachment style A measured by method A correspond to attachment style B measured by method B? And why do very structurally different measures such as semi-structured interviews (IRA) and attachment questionnaires (Adult Attachment Questionnaire, Feeney and Noller 1992) both indicate 'attachment style' classifications when it is likely that these measures touch very different aspects of attachment? Furthermore, there has been a recent trend to expand the original three- or four-category model and to name the new categories according to clinical observation. Although this research strategy might be pragmatic and is corroborated by empirical results (Pilkonis 1988; Pilkonis *et al.* 1995), a large-scale comparison of methods in attachment research is only possible if the numerous existing categories are cut down to three or four. This is necessary because, in order to yield good results, the categories need to match up conceptually as well as in the terminology used. This is often not the case.

The following discussion focuses on the usage of terms with respect to their core meaning, and evaluates the adequacy of their application. Suggestions are made on how to use terms consistently in order to conceptualise individual differences in attachment.

DEFINITIONS

Style and attachment style

The term 'style' (Old English 'stile'; French 'style'; Old French also 'stile'; Latin 'stilus') originally meant 'spike, pointed instrument used for writing'. By way of metonymic transformation the meaning changed from a description of the writing instrument to the mode of writing and talking. In today's usage the term 'style' has a wide range of meanings. It refers to:

> the way in which something is said, done, expressed, or performed: (a style of speech and writing); the combination of distinctive features of literary or artistic expression, execution, or performance characterising a particular person, group, school, or era; sort; type: (a style of furniture); quality of imagination and individuality expressed in one's actions and tastes: (does things with style); a comfortable and elegant mode of existence: (living in style); a mode of living: (the style of the

very rich); the fashion of the moment, especially of dress; vogue; a particular fashion: (the style of the 1920s); a customary manner of presenting printed material, including usage, punctuation, spelling, typogra-
phy, and arrangement. The style term is also used in the natural
sciences, particularly in botany, zoology, and medicine. (*The American
Heritage Dictionary of the English Language* 2000)

While 'style' was long used to describe an individualistic mode of doing
something, in the nineteenth century the meaning of the word was
broadened. Further, 'style' is used, for example, to refer to rhetorical orna-
mentation and personality characteristics.

Nowadays 'style' is used to refer to a living style; this includes not only
aesthetic elements, but also a general way of looking at things. 'Style' is
understood as a symbol, or a set of symbols, standing for general feeling and
wellness.

In *developmental and social psychology* the term 'cognitive style' is well
known and refers to more or less constant personal features of information
processing (Higgins 1996).

Attachment theorists use the term 'style' in describing manifest aspects of
attachment behaviour, for example, in the above-mentioned Interpersonal
Relations Assessment (IRA, Pilkonis 1988; Pilkonis *et al.* 1995), and also in
questionnaires designed to assess a self-report of a subject's own psychological experience and behaviour. As one's own perspective is always
modulated by internal states (i.e. the self-concept of a person) and evaluates
life events in fundamentally different ways, compared to an external person,
self-report cannot be taken as an objective illustration of external behaviour.
Questionnaires always produce selective self-descriptions or indirect
images of the self-concept. The answers are the results of the perceptive
processes of the subjects, who process mental information selectively and in
a subjectively organised manner, and cannot, therefore, be objectively quan-
tified (Höger 2002). These perceptions are influenced, in addition, by
memory processes. Furthermore, memory recall depends on individual
dynamics which are, according to attachment theory, also marked by early
life experiences; and so the existing attachment pattern (the element that the
questionnaires are meant to reflect) influences the answering process (the
imaging process) and can no longer be viewed as a direct description of
experiences in connection with the attachment system (Höger 2002). In
other words: the inner working model constituting the attachment style

interferes with subjective information processes in relation to manifest behaviour. Self-report measures do not reflect direct manifestations of attachment behaviour. Also, it is important to understand that theoretical constructs change over time and lose their original connotations. Following these lines of thought it is important to distinguish strictly between the terms describing specific constructs ('attachment representation', 'inner working model', 'attachment style') and the regular use of a given term (see Dozier and Tyrell 1998).

The term 'attachment style' should therefore be understood as follows: an attachment style denotes manifestly observable aspects of attachment behaviour; assessing the visible results of an internal psychological process dealing with attachment stimuli must be the core research issue. An attachment style is then seen as a result of one or more subjective processing strategies of internal and external perceptions which are shaped by inter-personal life experiences.

Representation and attachment representation

The term 'representation' is derived from the Latin verb 'repraesentare' and has in modern languages (English 'representation', French 'representation', Spanish 'representación') the meaning of 'symbol, image, depiction, illus-tration, or sign'.

Representation refers to the 'act of representing, in any sense of the verb; the act of representing or the state of being represented' (*Webster's Revised Unabridged Dictionary* 1996). A representation is also:

> something that represents, as an image or likeness of something; an account or statement, as of facts, allegations, or arguments; an expostu-lation; a protest; a presentation or production, as of a play. The state or condition of serving as an official delegate, agent, or spokesperson. The right or privilege of being represented by delegates having a voice in a legislative body. A body of legislators that serve on behalf of a con-stituency. (*The American Heritage Dictionary of the English Language* 2000)

In law, representation refers to 'a statement of fact made by one party in order to induce another party to enter into a contract'. In mathematics, it is 'a homomorphism from an algebraic system to a similar system of matrices'. A representation can also be 'a new presentation; as in re-presentation of facts previously stated' (*The American Heritage Dictionary of the English Language* 2000).

In philosophy 'representation' is a classic term of epistemology, but it has also entered into the fields of psychology and cognitive science. In politics and law, representation relates to doing something on behalf of others. In the philosophical and psychological tradition representation has four major meanings (Scheerer 1992, p.790):

- image in a broad sense, i.e. a mental state with cognitive content

- image in a narrow sense, i.e. a mental state reproducing an earlier mental state

- depiction, meaning a structural illustration through pictures, symbols and signs of all kinds

- representing another person.

First of all, a representation requires a 'presentation' that it relates to. The usage of both terms was discussed mainly in the nineteenth and early twentieth centuries, but is inconsistent today. 'Presentation' tends to be used when the (direct) presence of an idea in the consciousness is focused. On the other hand, 'representation' denotes a process that continues as a conscious idea is reproduced, adapted, handled, or arranged. This is, for example, the case with recalled memories, which often take the form of images (Scholz 1992, p.827).

In the second half of the twentieth century 'mental representation' became a key term for theoretical accounts in psychology and philosophy. This was especially the case in cognitive sciences and the psychoanalytic philosophy of mind. In a broad sense all those theories of mind are representational which, intending to explain the behaviour and mental processes of man, use the term 'mental representation' to mean *intrapsychic entities* that entail syntactic and semantic attributes and belong to a *representational system* (Scheerer 1992, pp.837ff.). In the 1950s, however, representational theories of mind, especially in psychology, were overpowered and widely replaced by behaviourism (Skinner 1953, 1957, 1958). In the years since the cognitive turn, the term 'mental representation' has once again played a major role, especially when referring to knowledge representation[1] of perception and meaning (Anderson 2000). In artificial intelligence (AI) research the term 'representation' is used to illustrate a representation to the mind in the form of an idea or image. More common terms in relation to that meaning are 'mental representation' and 'internal representation', which are used as synonyms (WordNet 1997). Mental representations are most frequently referred to as processing internal symbols (the principle of structured representations). Representations in that sense are internal states that can be interpreted semantically, and display a transparent structure that allows them to transform by means of syntactic rules. By applying these syntactic rules, complex representations can be inferred from simple ones, using context-free semantics. The following dimensions and types of representation can be distinguished (Scheerer 1990):

- *Local representation*: every representation has its 'place'. In the case of distributed representation, a given place can be part of different representations, and sometimes a representation is distributed over all available positions of the representing element.

- *Symbolic representations* consist of symbols depicting discrete states that can be semantically interpreted and syntactically linked. According to symbol processing theory all representations must be symbolic.

- *Propositional representations* refer to propositions relating to those states that bear truth value and are part of an inferential network.

- *Intrinsic and extrinsic representations*: an intrinsic representation is a representation which contains the relations that are symbolised by the representation itself; they are self-referential. In extrinsic representations the relations are additionally named, as is the case in verbal descriptions of physical conditions.

- In artificial intelligence research, representations are referred to as *formal symbols or images*. What is represented is knowledge, memory, problem situations and so on – structures that have representational function. A formal illustration is chosen which describes a certain knowledge structure exactly and economically. A representation entails a representing system and a sytem represented; and the aspects or characteristics representing and to be represented in conjunction with the mathematical relation connecting the two systems.

Attachment representations are intrinsic, symbolic representations containing an experience-based image of the subjective interpersonal reality. They cannot be measured directly and may be concluded in retrospect as a latent dimension. The term 'attachment representation' is closely linked to the construct of 'inner working models' (Bowlby 1969). This refers to a system of conscious or unconscious rules for organising attachment-related information, as well as to more or less limited access to this information (Main *et al.* 1985). Thus, the inner working model of a person can be understood as a consequence of an intrapsychic image of interpersonal relationship regulation.

Attachment theory applies to the term 'attachment representation' in those cases when reflection or anchoring of actually experienced interpersonal relationship sequences within the psychic apparatus are meant. The reflection of reality is not isomorphic, but it always reflects an adaptive intrapsychic coping strategy of relationship experience in conjunction with specific memory systems (semantic versus episodic, procedural memory; Tulving 1972, 1983, 1986). The behavioural aspect (attachment style) may correspond with the intrapsychic domain (attachment representation), but there is no necessity for this; therefore the two concepts have to be distinguished conceptually and verbally (Bartholomew and Shaver 1998; Crowell *et al.* 1999).

Pattern and attachment pattern

The word 'pattern' stems from Middle English 'patron' and Old French 'patron', and is defined as 'anything proposed for imitation; an archetype; an exemplar; that which is to be, or is worthy to be, copied or imitated; as, a pattern of a machine' (*The American Heritage Dictionary of the English Language* 2000).

In *Webster's Revised Unabridged Dictionary* (1996) the term 'pattern' is defined as 'a model or original used as an archetype, a model considered worthy of imitation'. It also denotes 'a representative sample, a specimen of something'. Third, it is used as 'a consistent, characteristic form, style, or method, such as a composite of traits or features characteristic of an individual or a group: one's pattern of behaviour'. Furthermore it represents 'a plan, diagram, or model to be followed in making things; as something intended as a guide for making something else: a dress pattern'. The pattern term is also used in combination with aviation or football: 'a flight pattern or pass pattern'. As a technical term (founding) a pattern is 'a full-sized model around which a mould of sand is made, to receive the melted metal'.

In everyday life one implication of the term 'pattern' is that of colourfulness. Another implication is the difference of basic elements constituting a higher order entity. When a living or dead object is looked at, an evaluation or assessment of the object takes place. Parts of the whole are integrated using different weights. In another context the term 'pattern' is used to describe an instruction or 'construction plan' (e.g. for sewing clothes).

The psychology of perception is mainly concerned with the psycho-physiological preconditions or processes of pattern perception and interpretation. Some elements of a perception stimulus are put together in order to form a unified perception, and these perceptions are then compared with previously stored information in the memory system (Posner 1976, 1991; Anderson 1988).

Attachment theorists use the pattern term inconsistently. It is often applied when there can be no clear and unequivocal classification and when the main categories 'secure', 'insecure-avoidant', 'insecure-ambivalent', 'insecure-disorganised' and 'cannot classify' are weighed up (Ainsworth *et al.* 1978, 1985; George, Kaplan and Main 1985). By including elements of different classes into the classification process, there is an implicit transition from a categorical to a dimensional assessment with the poles secure–insecure; at least, there is a weakening of categorical boundaries. Consequently, the categorical system is replaced by a dimensional one. A good example is the recent measure by Brennan and Shaver (Brennan and Shaver 1995; Brennan *et al.* 1998) which is based on seven scales derived by factor analysis (frustration with partners, proximity-seeking, self-reliance, ambivalence, trust/confidence in others, jealousy/fear of abandonment, and anxious clinging to partner) and two underlying dimensions (anxiety and avoidance).

Problems arise with respect to the identification of attachment patterns, because they cannot be identified as dimensions (Höger 2002). A *dimension* denotes the order of objects under the same aspect following the principle of quantitative grading. However, attachment patterns are adaptive strategies of the attachment behaviour system, which is triggered by insecurity or anxiety. As these adaptive strategies are qualitatively different, they cannot be meaningfully described by a quantitative dimension (i.e in terms of more or less security). A good counter-example, however, is the handling of the Interpersonal Relations Assessment (IRA), which allows us to identify attachment patterns – in this case used as a synonym for 'attachment styles'.

The IRA is a clinical interview to assess the biography, focusing on interpersonal relations.

The so-called prototype rating splits the 'classic' categories of the Adult Attachment Interview (AAI) into seven prototypes which are assigned to a secure, insecure-avoidant, insecure-ambivalent, or insecure-mixed category. The prototypes are:

- secure features
- excessive dependency
- borderline features
- excessive care
- obsessive-compulsive features
- defensive separation
- lack of interpersonal sensitivity.

The prototypes are then ranked with respect to their importance or their relative weight. The most dominant prototype is ranked 1 and the least important 7. The first two ranks determine the assignment of a person to one of four main categories, which correspond partly, although not to a very high degree, to categories used in the AAI (secure, insecure-avoidant, insecure-ambivalent, mixed-insecure).[2] In this case it seems sensible to speak of attachment patterns, because the ranking method renders possible a true pattern of attachment styles, belonging to different attachment categories. Consequently, there has been a tendency in recent years to include elements of non-dominant attachment categories in the classification of attachment representations. In this respect evaluation by means of the AAI is a matter of determining an attachment pattern rather than a singular categorisation. When psychobiologically adaptive strategies of attachment are assigned to only one category, as is the case with non-dimensional questionnaires, the term 'attachment pattern' should not be applied.

Quality and attachment quality

The 'quality' term is very old but it was only when Aristotle theorised about it in his 'Categories' that it became widely acknowledged. Aristotle understood 'quality' as an abstract characteristic owned by one or more concrete entities. He distinguished the members of this category from those of other categories, most notably 'substance', 'quantity', and 'relations'. Four types of quality are defined by Aristotle (Rath 1998):

- state and attitude; attitudes are of longer duration and of lower variability than states

- disposition; the natural ability or disability to do something

- affective qualities; they are referred to as qualities of the senses (sweetness or warmth), bringing about affections in the senses, but also as enduring or congenital dispositions of mind (rage or madness)

- figure and shape of things – relating to characteristics of geometrical lines and areas, or to the form of physical items.

Historically important is the distinction between *primary* and *secondary* qualities. 'Primary qualities' refers to those characteristics of things which can be mapped as mathematical or quantitative counterparts of the secondary qualities, which for their part are defined by the physical senses. Primary qualities are *processes of matter*, for example, changes of physiological states in nerve cells after activation. By contrast, secondary qualities are the impressions and sensations caused by physiological changes (Pieper 1997; Rath 1998). In order to understand the usage of the 'quality' term in attachment literature, it is important to acknowledge the significance of 'quality of judgement'. The quality of judgement first appears in Aristotle's writings (Drieschner and Harjes 1989, pp.1780ff.).

Equally important for understanding the modern use of 'quality' is Kant's distinction of judgements. In his work *Kritik der reinen Vernuft* (*Critique of Pure Reason*, Heidemann (ed.) 1985) he distinguished between judgements and categories, both of which relate to the generic schemata 'quantity', 'quality', 'relation' and modality'. In Kant's terms, 'quality' comprises *affirmative* (S is P: reality) *negative,* (S is not P: negation) and *infinite* (S is Not-P: limitation) judgements. To determine a quality, a judgement (evaluation of the subject in question) is always needed.

According to the above, 'attachment quality' must be understood as a secondary (sensory) quality which requires as a precondition a characteristic psychophysiological reaction resulting from early attachment experiences. The attachment system of an insecure-avoidant person, for instance, will produce unpleasant feelings (affections in Aristotle's sense) in attachment-eliciting situations (close, emotionally significant contacts between two people). Consequently, the person will then tend to avoid this type of close interpersonal relations.

Because 'quality' is in modern understanding not free of judgement (viz. the relative 'goodness' of one object as compared to a similar one) it seems better not to use this term but to apply other, more neutral alternatives ('attachment representation', 'attachment style', 'attachment pattern').

Status and attachment status

The 'status' of a person is referred to as 'the relative position or standing of things or especially persons in a society; standing' (for example: the status of a person is that of a guest). Second, it describes 'high standing or prestige: a position of status in the community'. In law, status relates to the 'legal character or condition of a person or thing: the status of a minor'. A fourth major meaning of the term is 'state of affairs; situation'. (*The American Heritage Dictionary of the English Language* 2000). 'Status' is also referred to as:

> the relative rank that an individual holds, with attendant rights, duties, and lifestyle, in a social hierarchy based upon honour or prestige. Status may be ascribed – that is, assigned to individuals at birth without reference to any innate abilities – or achieved, requiring special qualities and filled through competition and individual effort. Status is often ascribed on the basis of sex, age, family relationships, and birth, placing one into a particular social group. Achieved statuses may be based on education, occupation, marital status, and other factors. A person may be said to occupy a high position when he is able to control, by order or by influence, other people's conduct; when he derives prestige from holding important office; or when his conduct has earned the esteem of his fellows. Relative status is a major factor determining the behaviour of people toward one another; and competition for status seems to be a prime pursuit. Status is closely correlated with etiquette and morality and in many societies rises with the liberal use of wealth (gift exchange; potlatch). In most Western urban-industrial societies, such attributes as a respected occupation, the possession and consumption of material goods, physical appearance and dress, and etiquette and manners have become more important than lineage in determining one's social status. Status groups are aggregates of persons arranged in a hierarchical social system. Such groups differ from social classes in being based on consid-

erations of honour and prestige, rather than on purely economic status.
(*Encyclopedia Britannica* 2001)

The 'status' of a person viewed from a social psychology perspective is connected with social identity and implies social attribution processes (Brown 1990; Tajfel 1978; Tajfel and Turner 1986). The attribution process does not arise only from a group but from the person herself, and there is a complex interaction of attribution and rejection of 'status types', expectancies, control and strategies. An interesting feature to note in this context is the 'halo effect' – which characterises the well-known finding that a certain personal characteristic (status symbol) is implicitly generalised to other personality features (Cook and Campbell 1979).

The term 'attachment status' implies the expectation of typical attachment behaviour on the one hand, and a hierarchical structure of attachment on the other. This implication is problematic, because a completely unbiased assessment of 'status' does not exist. There is, in the common usage of the term, an inherent tone of prejudice, indicating a dimension of pathology in the sense of 'good' (secure attachment) and 'bad' (insecure attachment).

Even if a biased understanding is not intended by theorists using this term, its usage might be misleading. Although it is true that individuals with insecure attachment (especially those with 'disorganised' or 'cannot classify' attachment classification) display a high vulnerability for a multitude of pathological features (Dozier *et al.* 1999; Greenberg 1999), it is also true that the relative risk must be interpreted against the background of a diathesis-stress model. The majority of insecurely attached individuals do not show signs of psychopathology, independent of their attachment classification (see the meta-analyses of van IJzendoorn and Bakermans-Kranenburg 1996, and Mickelson, Kessler and Shaver 1997). Being closely linked to the concept of 'sociological status', one might assume that the 'status' term bears not only a judgement, but also a notion of social superiority (in terms of a higher adaptive and functional capability) of securely attached individuals as compared with insecurely attached people. There would be no empirical justification for such an assumption. Additionally, there is no unequivocal knowledge on how the construct of life satisfaction, which is difficult to operationalise, relates to basic constructs of attachment theory. It therefore makes sense to refrain from using the term 'attachment status'.

Organisation and attachment organisation

An organization refers to the 'persons (or committees or departments, etc.) who make up a governing body and who administer something (an administrative and functional structure)' (*Merriam Webster Dictionary* 1994). The term also denotes 'a group of people who work together; an organized structure for arranging or classifying; an ordered manner; orderliness by virtue of being methodical and well organized; the act of organizing a business or business-related activity' (*WordNet* 1997) and 'the activity or result of distributing or disposing persons or things properly or methodically (organization arrangement); the act of or process of organizing or of being organized' (*Merriam Webster Dictionary* 1994).

The term 'organisation' applies both to the process of organising and to social institutions or systems such as administrative facilities, industry, schools or hospitals; to momentary, stable or variable behavioural processes or activities; and to the working structures underlying social systems.

More recently, theories originating in natural sciences have been applied to describe self-determined, dynamic and chaotic processes of self-organisation in administrations and industrial organisations (Dorsch, Häcker and Stapf 1994, p.532).

In attachment theory the term 'attachment organisation' is mostly used in connection with the intrapsychic representation structure of attachment experiences. Applying the AAI terminology (George, Kaplan and Main 1985), attachment representations can be structured in organised or disorganised ways. The usage of the term 'attachment organisation' is therefore adequate only when assumptions about the intrapsychic structure of attachment experiences can be empirically tested. This is mainly the case with measures using discourse analytic techniques for the analysis of narratives (for instance the AAI). In relation to attachment questionnaires, 'organisation' should not be used.

Class/classification and attachment class/classification

The term class first came into wide use in the early 19th century, replacing such terms as rank and order as descriptions of the major hierarchical groupings in society. Besides being important in social theory, the concept of class as a collection of individuals sharing similar economic circumstances has been widely used in censuses and in studies of social mobility. Social classes must be distinguished from status groups; the former are based primarily upon economic interests, while the latter are constituted by evaluations of the honour or prestige of an occupation, cultural position, or family descent. A class is defined as a group sharing the same socio-economic status; as the social rank, especially high social rank; high quality; a group, set, or kind sharing common attributes; a major category in biological taxonomy ranking above the order and below the phylum or division; a collection of adjacent and discrete or continuous values of a random variable; set, a division or rating based on grade or quality; best of its kind. Class is also a mathematical term. And it is referred to as a body of students meeting regularly to study the same subject and the period during which such a body meets. (*Merriam Webster Dictionary* 1994)

The term 'classification' denotes the 'act, process, or result of classifying. It is often used as a synonym for category or class' (*The American Heritage Dictionary of the English Language* 2000). 'Classification' is also referred to as 'a group of people or things arranged by class or categories; a restriction imposed by the government on documents or weapons that are available only to certain authorized people' (*WordNet* 1997). In biology, classification refers to the 'establishment of a hierarchical system of categories on the basis of presumed natural relationships among organisms. The science of biological classification is commonly called taxonomy' (*The American Heritage Dictionary of the English Language* 2000).

In psychology or medicine the term 'classification' refers to diagnostic processes. Subjects are assigned one or more previously defined categories or classes. Classification is primarily an action or a number of actions with the aim of organising objects or facts with respect to features they have in common. Classification also involves neglecting details; a classified object or fact is imprecise with respect to certain characteristics regarded as unimportant. In addition to the process of classifying, the 'classification' term also refers to the membership of subjects to a class of characteristics; it denotes process and result of actions simultaneously.

In social and mass psychology a class denotes a significant multitude of people who are equally ranked in the societal hierarchy.

In social psychology the 'class' term encompasses a certain judgement; it highlights differences among people with respect (for example) to the financial ability to acquire goods; or to the relative rank of people in the production process.

The natural sciences treat the 'class' term differently. The *formation* of classes is accomplished by the use of order criteria, and the *process of making* classes is referred to as classification (systematic order of empirically observable natural objects).

Attachment classifications are a mixture of natural and artificial classifications: natural, because behavioural characteristics are directly observable (strange situation test) or identifiable by means of discourse analysis of interview transcripts; artificial, because the principles of classification are applied to the objects depending on theoretical foci (for example, the classification of attachment behaviour in three or four categories using mathematical methods). In order to clearly distinguish process and result of an action, it is advisable to use 'classification' only for the process of classifying objects or subjects and to name the result of such a process 'attachment representation' or 'attachment style'.

Type/prototype and attachment type/prototype

'Type' is derived from late Latin 'typus' meaning image, and from Greek 'typos', meaning impression. A type refers to:

> a number of people or things having in common traits or characteristics that distinguish them as a group or class; the general character or structure held in common by a number of people or things considered as a group or class; a person or thing having the features of a group or class; an example or a model having the ideal features of a group or class; a person regarded as exemplifying a particular profession, rank, or social group: a group of executive types; a restaurant frequented by tourist types; a figure, representation, or symbol of something to come, such as an event in the Old Testament that foreshadows another in the New Testament; a taxonomic group, especially a genus or species, chosen as the representative example in characterising the larger taxonomic group to which it belongs; printing: a small block of metal or wood bearing a raised letter or character on the upper end that leaves a printed impression when inked and pressed on paper; such pieces considered as a group; printed or typewritten characters; a size or style of printed or typewritten characters; a typeface: a sans-serif type; a

pattern, a design, or an image impressed or stamped onto the face of a coin.

As verb – to type – it is used as a synonym to writing (to write something with a typewriter). (*The American Heritage Dictionary of the English Language* 2000)

In *Webster's Revised Unabridged Dictionary* (1996) 'type' is referred to as 'a combining form signifying impressed form; stamp; print; type; typical form; representative; as in stereotype phototype, ferrotype, monotype'. In programming theory a type or data type is 'a set of values from which a variable, constant, or other expression may take its value' (*Free On-line Dictionary of Computing* 1993).

In the twentieth century, psychology and psychiatry became a fruitful application field for typological thought and the 'type' term. There is a multitude of different type terms and typologies, such as the basic types of the human physiognomy and character, or the different phenomena of psychological life.

Differential psychology introduced the term 'psychological type' – typos – at the beginning of the twentieth century. A psychological type is a disposition of a neutral psychological or psychophysiological manner which applies to a group of people in a comparable way; and this group is not necessarily closed (Gachowetz 1994, pp.820ff.).

A great number of typologies of personality have been devised, and some are known to have existed for more than 2000 years. Especially the more recent ones are empirically tested; some of these are still influential for research in psychology and psychiatry.[3]

In the social sciences, 'type' is used to refer to phenomena which return with a certain accuracy and likelihood. Typically, reoccurring relations (laws) between phenomena can be found. In this context Menger (1883) introduced the term 'real type'. Real types are referred to as basic forms of real manifestations leaving space and time for further development and characteristics of the phenomena.

The term 'ideal type' has been extraordinarily important for the development of theories in social sciences. An ideal type, in the social sciences, is a mental construct derived from observable reality, although not conforming to it in detail because of deliberate simplification and exaggeration (Weber 1904). 'It is not ideal in the sense that it is excellent, nor is it an average; it is, rather, a logical ideal used to order reality by selecting and accentuating certain elements' (*Encyclopedia Britannica* 2001).

Prototype

The term 'prototype' is derived from Latin *prototypus* and means 'original, primitive'. A prototype is 'an original type, form, or instance serving as a basis or standard for later stages; an original full-scale and usually working model of a new product or new version of an existing product; an early, typical example'. In biology, it is 'a form or species that serves as an original type or example' (*The American Heritage Dictionary of the English Language* 2000).

With regard to attachment research it was Pilkonis (1988; Pilkonis *et al.* 1991) who introduced 'prototype' (IRA) into the field. In Germany the IRA was adapted by Strauß and Lobo (1997, 1999). As a term drawing on a long history in social science, and describing clinical manifestations of attachment behaviour which partly overlap and cannot strictly be assigned to categories, it seems adequate to use the type/prototype term. In this context it denotes categorisation attempts as descriptive heuristics which still need to be empirically validated and do not (yet) qualify as categories.

CONCLUSION

The usage of terms applied in order to denote attachment constructs is heterogeneous. The terms 'attachment representation', 'attachment style', and 'attachment prototype' are used adequately and they are terms relating to the corresponding construct. They are applied with respect to the intrapsychic mode of handling interpersonal relationship experiences ('attachment representation') or relate to manifest behavioural correlates of attachment ('attachment style'). When the research focus lies on testing clinical hypotheses and differentiation of manifest attachment behaviour ('attachment style'), the usage of 'attachment type/prototype' seems appropriate. 'Attachment pattern' and 'attachment organisation' are applied in inconsistent ways. For further usage it is important to clearly distinguish these terms from 'attachment representation', 'attachment style' and 'type/prototype'. 'Attachment status', '– quality' and '– classification' (as a result of a classification process) are useless because they hold no additional information beyond what is denoted by the above-mentioned terms. Furthermore, they contain social connotations which might lead to misunderstandings when discussing human attachment. The same applies to the occasionally appearing terms 'attachment pathology', '– disorder', '– disorganisation' and '– difficulty'. Even more than the previously criticised terms 'attachment status', '– quality', and '– classification', they imply social judgements which are not empirically justified.

NOTES

1. While in the 1980s representations were considered to be identical with data (Roitblat 1982), this is no more the case in more recent accounts of the matter. While every representation must be implemented by some data structure, the representational property is in the correspondence to something in the world and in the constraint that correspondence imposes. Therefore, a knowledge representation (KR) is most fundamentally a surrogate, a substitute for the thing itself, used to enable an entity to determine consequences by thinking rather than acting, i.e. by reasoning about the world rather than taking action in it (Davies *et al.* 1993).

2. For example, a person is rated as follows: 1. secure (most dominant prototype), 2. borderline features, 3. obsessive compulsive features, 4. excessive dependency, 5. excessive care, 6. defensive separation, 7. lack of interpersonal sensitivity (least dominant prototype). Prototype 1 is thought to correspond with the secure/autonomous category of the Adult Attachment Interview (AAI); excessive care, borderline features, and excessive dependency are theoretically linked to ambivalence with respect to attachment (AAI: enmeshed/preoccupied); and obsessive compulsive features, defensive separation and lack of interpersonal sensitivity relate to avoidant attachment behaviour (AAI: dismissing attachment category). The person rated above thus displays a mixed pattern of attachment prototypes pertaining to security [secure (prototype 1)], ambivalence [borderline features (prototype 2)], avoidance [obsessive compulsive features (prototype 3)], ambivalence [excessive dependency (prototype 4)], ambivalence [excessive care (prototype 5)], avoidance [defensive separation (prototype 6)], avoidance [lack of interpersonal sensitivity (prototype 7)].

3. Perhaps the oldest personality theory known is contained in the cosmological writings of the Greek philosopher and physiologist Empedocles and in related speculations of the physician Hippocrates. Empedocles' cosmic elements – air (with its associated qualities, warm and moist), earth (cold and dry), fire (warm and dry), and water (cold and moist) – were related to health and corresponded (in the above order) to Hippocrates' physical humours,

which were associated with variations in temperament: blood (sanguine temperament), black bile (melancholic), yellow bile (choleric), and phlegm (phlegmatic). This theory, with its view that body chemistry determines temperament, has survived in some form for more than 2,500 years (*Encyclopedia Britannica* 2001).

Another most influential typology in the history of psychology was devised by Kretschmer: In his book *Körperbau und Charakter* (*Physique and Character*) (1977), he distinguished basic body constitutions (athletic, asthenic, leptosom, pycnic) and linked them with different forms of temperament (schizotymic and cyclothymic). Kretschmer drew back on the idea of an innate biological type; in this view, type is empirically measurable.

REFERENCES

Ainsworth, M.D. (1967) *Infancy in Uganda: Infant Care and Growth of Love.* Baltimore: The Johns Hopkins University Press.

Ainsworth, M.D. (1985) 'Patterns of attachment.' *Clinical Psychologist 38*, 27–29.

Ainsworth, M.D., Blehar, M., Waters, E., and Wall, S. (1978) *Patterns of Attachment: A Psychological Study of the Strange Situation.* Hillsdale, NJ: Erlbaum.

Anderson, J.R. (1988) *Kognitive Psychologie.* Heidelberg: Spektrum der Wissenschaft.

Bartholomew, K. (1990) 'Avoidance of intimacy: An attachment perspective.' *Journal of Social and Personal Relationships 7*, 147–178.

Bartholomew, K., and Perlman, D. (eds) (1994) *Attachment Processes in Adulthood. Advances in Personal Relationships, Vol. 5.* London: Jessica Kingsley Publishers.

Bartholomew, K., and Shaver, P.R. (1998) 'Methods of assessing adult attachment: Do they converge?' In J.A. Simpson and W.S. Rholes (eds), *Attachment Theory and Close Relationships.* New York: Guilford Press.

Bowlby, J. (1969) *Attachment and Loss. Attachment.* New York: Basic Books.

Bowlby, J. (1973) *Attachment and Loss. Separation.* New York: Basic Books.

Bowlby, J. (1980) *Attachment and Loss. Loss, Sadness and Depression.* New York: Basic Books.

Brennan, K.A., Clark, C.L. and Shaver, P.R. (1998) 'Self-report measurement of adult attachment: An integrative overview.' In J.A. Simpson and W.S. Rholes (eds) *Attachment Theory in Close Relationships.* New York: Guilford Press.

Brennan, K.A. and Shaver, P.R. (1995) 'Dimensions of adult attachment, affect regulation, and romantic relationship functioning.' *Personality and Social Psychology Bulletin 21*, (3), 267–283.

Brown, R. (1990) 'Beziehungen zwischen Gruppen.' In W. Stroebe, M. Hewstone, J-P. Codol and G.M. Stephenson (eds) *Sozialpsychologie*. Berlin: Springer.

Cassidy, J., and Shaver, P.R. (eds) (1999) *Handbook of Attachment. Theory, Research, and Clinical Implications*. New York: Guilford Press.

Cook, T.D. and Campbell, D.T. (1979) *Quasi-experimentation*. Chicago: Rand McNally.

Crittenden, P.M. and Claussen, A.H. (eds) (2000) *The Organization of Attachment Relationships: Maturation, Culture, and Context*. New York: Cambridge University Press.

Crowell, J.A. and Owens, G. (1998) *Current Relationship Interview and Scoring System. CRI manual 4.0*. State University of New York at Stony Brook.

Crowell, J.A., Fraley, C., and Shaver, P.R. (1999) 'Measurement of individual differences in adolescent and adult attachment.' In J. Cassidy and P.R. Shaver (eds) *Handbook of Attachment. Theory, Research, and Clinical Implications*. New York: Guilford Press.

Davies, R., Shrobe, H. and Szolovits, P. (1993) 'What is a knowledge representation?' *AI Magazin 14*, (1), 17–33.

Dorsch, F., Häcker, H. and Stapf, K.H. (eds) (1994) *Dorsch Psychologisches Wörterbuch*. 12. Ed. Bern: Huber.

Dozier, M. and Tyrrell, C. (1998) 'The role of attachment in therapeutic relationships.' In J.A. Simpson and W.S. Rholes (eds) *Attachment Theory and Close Relationships*. New York: Guilford.

Dozier, M., Chase Stovall, K. and Albus, K.E. (1999) In J. Cassidy and P.R. Shaver (eds) *Handbook of Attachment. Theory, Research, and Clinical Implications*. New York: Guilford Press.

Drieschner, M. and Harjes, H.P. (1989) 'Qualität des Urteils.' In J. Ritter and K. Gr ünder (eds)*Historisches Wörterbuch der Philosophie, Vol. 7*. Basel: Schwabe and Co.

Encyclopedia Britannica (2001) Deluxe Edition CD-Rom: Britannica.com.

Feeney, J.A. and Noller, P. (1992) 'Attachment style and romantic love: Relationship dissolution.' *Australian Journal of Psychology 44*, (2), 69–74.

Free On-line Dictionary of Computing (1993) http://foldoc.doc.ic.ac.uk/foldoc/index.html

Gachowetz, H. (1994) 'Typologie.' In F. Dorsch, H. Häcker and K.H. Stapf (eds) *Dorsch Psychologisches Wörterbuch*. 12. Ed. Bern: Huber.

George, C., Kaplan, N. and Main, M. (1985) 'The Adult Attachment Interview.' Unpublished manual. University of California, Berkeley.

Greenberg, M.T. (1999) 'Attachment and psychopathology in childhood.' In J. Cassidy and P.R. Shaver (eds) *Handbook of Attachment. Theory, Research, and Clinical Implications*. New York: Guilford Press.

Hazan, C. and Shaver, P. (1987) 'Romantic love conceptualized as an attachment process.' *Journal of Personality and Social Psychology 52*, (3), 511–524.

Hazan, C. and Shaver, P. (1990) 'Love and work: An attachment theoretical perspective.' *Journal of Personality and Social Psychology 59*, 270–280.

Heidemann, I. (1985) (ed) Kant, I. *Kritik der reinen Vernunft* (1. Ed. 1790) Nachdruck. Stuttgart: Reclam.

Higgins, E.T. (Ed) (1996) *Social Psychology. Handbook of Basic Principles*. New York: Guilford.

Höger, D. (2002) 'Fragebögen zur Erfassung von Bindungsstilen.' In B. Srauß, A. Buchheim and H. Kächele (eds) *Klinische Bindungsforschung: Theorien, Methoden, Ergebnisse*. Stuttgart: Schattauer.

Kretschmer, E. (1977) *Körperbau und Charakter. Untersuchungen zum Konstitutionsproblem und zur Lehre von den Temperamenten* (26. Ed.) Berlin: Springer.

Main, M., Kaplan, N. and Cassidy, J. (1985) 'Security in infancy, childhood, and adulthood: A move to the level of representation.' In I. Bretherton and E. Waters (eds) *Growing Points of Attachment Theory and Research. Monographs of the Society for Research in Child Development 50*, 66–106.

Marvin, R.S. and Britner, P.A. (1999) 'Normative development. The ontogeny of attachment.' In J. Cassidy and P.R. Shaver (eds) *Handbook of Attachment. Theory, Research, and Clinical Implications*. New York: Guilford Press.

Menger, C. (1883) *Untersuchungen öüber die Methode der Socialwissenschaften und der politischen Ökonomie*. Leipzig: Duncker and Humblot.

Merriam Webster Dictionary (1994) 10th edition. In *Encyclopedia Britannica* (2001) Deluxe Edition CD-Rom: Britannica.com.

Mickelson, K.D., Kessler, R.C. and Shaver, P.R. (1997) 'Adult attachment in a nationally representative sample.' *Journal of Personality and Social Psychology 73*, 1092–1106.

Murray Parkes, C., Stevenson-Hinde, J. and Marris, P. (1991) (eds) *Attachment Across the Life Cycle*. London: Tavistock.

Pieper, A. (1997) (ed) *Aristoteles.* M ünchen: Deutscher Taschenbuchverlag.

Pilkonis, P.A. (1988) 'Personality prototypes among depressives: Themes of dependency and autonomy.' *Journal of Personality Disorders 2,* 144–152.

Pilkonis, P., Heape, C., Proietti, J., Clark, S., McDavid, J. and Pitts, T. (1995) 'The reliability and validity of two structured diagnostic interviews for personality disorders.' *Archives of General Psychiatry 52,* 1025–1033.

Pilkonis, P.A., Heape, C.L., Ruddy, J. and Serrao, P. (1991) 'Validity in the diagnosis of personality disorders: The use of the LEAD standard.' *Journal of Consulting and Clinical Psychology 3,* 46–54.

Posner, M.I. (1976) *Kognitive Psychologie.* M ünchen: Juventa.

Posner, M.I. (ed) (1991) *Contemporary Approaches to Cognitive Psychology.* Varanasi: Rishi Publications.

Rath, I.W. (1998) *Aristoteles. Die Kategorien.* Stuttgart: Reclam.

Roitblat, H.L. (1982) 'The meaning of representation in animal memory.' *Behavioral Brain Science 5,* 353–406.

Scheerer, E. (1990) *Berichte aus dem Zentrum föür interdisziplinäre Forschung der Universität Bielefeld: Projekt Mind and Brain Nr. 72.*

Scheerer, E. (1992) 'Repräsentation.' In J. Ritter and K. Gr nder (eds)*Historisches Wörterbuch der Philosophie ,Vol. 8.* Basel: Schwabe and Co.

Scholz, O.R. (1992) 'Repräsentation.' In J. Ritter and K. Gr ünder (eds) *Historisches Wörterbuch der Philosophie, Vol. 8.* Basel: Schwabe and Co.

Simpson, J.A. and Rholes, S.W. (1998) *Attachment Theory and Close Relationships.* New York: Guilford.

Skinner, B.F. (1953) *Science and Human Behaviour.* New York: Macmillan.

Skinner, B.F. (1957) *Verbal Behaviour.* New York: Appleton-Century-Crofts.

Skinner, B.F. (1958) 'Teaching machines.' *Science 128,* 969–977.

Strauß, B. and Lobo, A. (1997) 'Das Beziehungsprototypenverfahren zur Erfassung von Bindungsqualitäten im Erwachsenenalter nach Pilkonis.' Unpublished manual. University of Jena, Germany.

Strauß, B. and Lobo-Drost, A. (1999) 'Das Erwachsenen-Bindungsprototypen-Rating (EBPR) Version 1.0.' Unpublished manual.

Tajfel, H. (1978) *Differentiation Between Social Groups. Studies in the Social Psychology of Intergroup Relations.* London: Academic Press.

Tajfel, H. and Turner, J. (1986) 'The social identity theory of intergroup behaviour.' In G. Austin and S. Worchel (eds) *The Social Psychology of Intergroup Relations.* Chicago: Nelson-Hall.

The American Heritage Dictionary of the English Language. Fourth edition (2000). Boston: Houghton Mifflin.

Tulving, E. (1972) 'Episodic and semantic memory.' In E. Tulving and W. Donaldson (eds) *Organization of Memory.* New York: Academic Press.

Tulving, E. (1983) *Elements of Episodic Memory.* London: Clarendon Press.

Tulving, E. (1986) 'What kind of hypothesis is the distinction between episodic and semantic memory?' *Journal of Experimental Psychology 12,* 307–311.

van IJzendoorn, M.H. and Bakermans-Kranenburg, M.J. (1996) 'Attachment representations in mothers, fathers, adolescents, and clinical groups: A meta-analytic search for normative data.' *Journal of Consulting and Clinical Psychology 64,* 8–21.

Weber, M. (1904) *Die Objektivität sozialwissenschaftlicher und sozialpolitischer Erkenntnis.* T übingen: Mohr.

Webster's Revised Unabridged Dictionary. 1913 Edition (1996) http://humanities.uchicago.edu/forms_unrest/webster.form.html

WordNet® 1.6 (1997) Princeton University. http://www.cogsci.princeton.edu /cgi-bin/webwn

CHAPTER 3

Fragmented Attachment Representations

Franziska Lamott, Elisabeth Fremmer-Bombik and Friedemann Pfäfflin

This chapter takes as examples the attachment representations of violent and severely traumatised women, and with the help of selected case vignettes discusses particularly incoherent narratives which up until now have usually been characterised as 'cannot classify' (Hesse 1996). Apart from the three traditional classifications 'secure' (F), 'insecure-distanced' (Ds) and 'insecure-enmeshed' (E), it is established practice to classify two additional modes, namely 'unresolved-traumatised' (U), which can combine with each of the three classifications mentioned above and which is distinguished by a partial disorganisation, and the 'cannot classify' (CC) category, which hitherto has mainly been understood as a kind of remainder category. We suggest taking its specific characteristics, i.e. the total incoherence of the narrative, into account, and understanding it as a sign of fragmentation. Using case vignettes, we want to demonstrate its specific quality and suggest interpreting it as a category of its own, which we call 'fragmented' (FRAG).

SAMPLE

The study draws on attachment representations of 33 severely traumatised women who committed crimes of murder or manslaughter and were either convicted and received a prison sentence (Sample 1 [prison sample]; n = 19), or were sentenced to confinement in a secure forensic psychiatric clinic (Sample 2 [forensic psychiatric sample]; n = 14) (Lamott *et al.* 1998; Lamott 2000; Lamott and Pfäfflin 2001). While the women in Sample 1 had mostly suffered physical and sexual abuse during their childhood, the women in Sample 2 were for the most part traumatised by the death of significant others or by a depressive and suicidal mother. The women in both samples had experienced their criminal acts as additional traumas.

METHOD AND RESULTS

Adult Attachment Interviews (AAI) were performed. In Sample 1, attachment representations were classified as *insecure* in 74 per cent (n = 14) and as *secure* in 26 per cent (n=5). In Sample 2 the percentage of the *insecure* classification was even higher and amounted to 93 per cent (n = 13), whereas only one woman (7%) was classified as *secure*. The majority of the women had not come to terms with their trauma and qualified for the additional category U/CC. (U = *unresolved trauma*; Gloger-Tippelt and Hoffmann 1997. CC = *cannot classify*; Hesse 1996). The classification U/CC was found in 58 per cent of Sample 1 and in 50 per cent of Sample 2. Finally, some narratives were particularly incoherent and could only be classified as CC. Drawing upon selected case vignettes, the authors will focus on these incoherent narratives, which were found in 16 per cent of Sample 1, and 36 per cent of Sample 2. The authors suggest classifying them as fragmented (FRAG).

CATEGORIES OF ATTACHMENT REPRESENTATIONS IN THE NARRATIVE CONTEXT

At the beginning stage of attachment research, the attachment relationship and the exploratory behaviour of children were central. During the 1980s a 'move to the level of representation' (Main, Kaplan and Cassidy 1985; Dornes 1998) and an interest in the symbolisation of attachment developed, with the focus on mental representation in adults. The constructs 'attachment representation' and 'internal working model' (Bowlby 1969; Main *et al.* 1985) characterise in different theoretical backgrounds the intra-psychic processing of attachment and relationship experiences (Fremmer-Bombik 1995). The differing conceptual representations indicate two theoretical strands converging in attachment theory: that of psychoanalysis and that of behavioural and systems theory. While psychoanalysis, in the sense of 'attachment representation', brings into focus on the one hand the intra-psychic representations of (partial) object relationships, and on the other the internalised 'interaction forms' (Lorenzer 1970), the 'internal working model' borrowed from behavioural and systems theory emphasises more strongly the constructive aspect of attachment-relevant experiences for behavioural control. Attachment representations and internal working models unconsciously regulate, to a great extent, the direction and organisation of attention and memory, as well as access to knowledge of oneself and access to others. According to Bowlby (1969), both constructs, which are to be understood as synonyms, take on the task of simulating (that is, anticipating) events in the real world, in order to put an individual in the position of being able to plan his or her actions. In this way attachment representations are decisive for the perception, treatment, and ultimately also the concrete overcoming of conflict-laden relationships (Fremmer-Bombik and Grossmann 1993; Grossmann 2000).

For the empirical comprehension of attachment representations, attachment theory provides a semi-structured, qualitative interview, the Adult Attachment Interview (AAI) developed by George, Kaplan and Main (1985). With 18 central questions which refer to early childhood memories, to indifferent or supportive parents, and to separation due to death or desertion, the relevance for the reported experience of the interviewee is given pride of place. The transcript of this interview is the basis for text analysis which focuses upon the attachment representations preserved in the narrative structures. By means of discourse analytical methods, the coherence and incoherence of the text are primarily examined; in other words, it is not the content of the related story that is of primary importance for the evaluation, but rather the way in which life events such as separation and loss are reported. The AAI comes close to the unconscious processes via the mistakes, Freudian slips, and breaks in the text. In the evaluation it focuses upon the 'organisation of attachment-relevant information in the sense of a defence concept' (Buchheim, Brisch and Kächele 1998, p.134). Such a method, which concentrates more on the form than the content, is useful, particularly when viewed against the background of knowledge of the processes of de-symbolisation of traumatic experience. Traumata are frequently not symbolised verbally, so that the blocked-off material tends rather to find expression in incoherence, pseudo-poetic phrases and illogical material (Kü chenhoff 1998; Fischer and Riedesser 1998).

The Adult Attachment Interview classifies three central attachment representations (Main *et al.* 1985; Main 1991):

1.   *Secure* (free to evaluate, secure-autonomous = F). With securely attached persons, the coherent form of the text, the way in which they talk about early experiences, is decisive. Semantic and episodic memories correspond to each other, evaluations are substantiated by concrete memories. Even negative childhood experiences, if reflected upon, can lead to a secure, autonomous attachment. Securely attached persons have access to a 'broad emotional range of coherent representations of good and bad attachment experiences' (Köhler 1998, p.373). In this context, Fonagy (1998) emphasises that free, undistorted cognitive and emotional processes are the result of a successful containment and an indication of secure attachment. In this way, a number of securely attached interviewees of the study stand out through a reflexive attachment behaviour during the interview, that is, through their meta-cognitive abilities and reflective function (Fonagy 1998). They appear open, well balanced and reflective, and frequently also exhibit an understanding for the behaviour of their parents. The negative experiences of early childhood are integrated and accordingly are experienced as part of a coherent self.

2.   *Insecure-distanced* (dismissing = Ds). Distanced or defensive behaviour is typical of the dismissing attachment representation. What is particularly noticeable is the considerable degree of repression and splitting. The relationship to the parents is either idealised (in the case of missing episodic memories), or described in negative and dismissive terms. The interviewees seem to be cut off from their attachment

experiences. Most of their statements are incomplete and their memories fragmentary. The significance of the relationships is either idealised or devalued; the interviewees want to appear independent. Their language is abstract, the frequent use of nouns instead of verbs is striking, as is the use of absolutes and disassociation ('you' instead of 'I') (Gloger-Tippelt and Hoffmann 1997, p.170). The interview situation itself is also characterised by a distanced, evasive attitude on the part of the interviewees. Their answers are short or lengthy, or noncommittal.

3.   *Insecure-enmeshed* (enmeshed-preoccupied = E). Persons who conspicuously struggle with their past in interviews exhibit particularly clearly the enmeshed relationship mode. Their memories are mostly pervaded by rancour and anger, or by a resigned, almost depressive passivity. Participants who exhibit these representations are bound up in their conflicts and maintain their internalised conflicts. The cognitive and affective aspects of mental representations of the self or others indicate insecurity and unsuccessful containment (K üchenhoff 1998). In addition, the involvement allows neither autonomy nor intimacy. These persons' accounts are inconsistent, with endless incomplete sentences about their childhood experiences. Frequently past conflicts seem still to be present, which is an indication of a lack of understanding of experienced psychical dependency.

Besides these three main classifications, *additional and independent modes* characterising the text were identified which denote:

4.   *Unresolved-traumatised* (unresolved trauma = U) attachment status (Gloger-Tippelt and Hoffmann 1997, p.166). This classification precedes the three main classifications and is regarded as an extension of the main classifications. The classification 'unresolved' can combine with each of the three attachment representations mentioned above and is not simply a fourth model. Texts which are characterised by the U category are distinguished by a partial disorganisation. Partial, in this context, means that the text becomes broken and incoherent at those points in the interview when a concrete trauma such as

separation, maltreatment or abuse is talked about. Here spatial and temporal disorientation often occur. The topic is usually unresolved sorrow to do with the loss of an object in childhood. As well as the partial collapse of the discourse strategies, the dominant attachment representations (F, E, and Ds) can, as a rule, be recognised. Text qualities which indicate unprocessed traumatic experiences in life history correspond to the disorganised and disoriented attachment models of childhood. They were identified with more than random frequency in borderline patients (Fonagy *et al.* 1995, Stalker *et al.* 1995), in persons with post-traumatic distress reactions (e.g. after sexual abuse; Fonagy *et al.* 1995, Stalker and Davies 1995) or in persons exhibiting severe suicidal symptomatology (Adam *et al.* 1994).

5.   As a further mode, Hesse (1996) described an organisational form of the text that he termed *cannot classify* (= CC), as it could not be classified in any one particular direction. He found these totally incoherent texts frequently in connection with severe psychiatric disturbances. Whilst the U category characterises a collapse in limited sections of the text centred around a trauma, but at the same time attachment-relevant, the CC category evinced a global collapse of all discourse strategies throughout the whole text.

In our view, this text quality, which Hesse (1996) collected under the category 'cannot classify', should not be understood as just a remainder category but rather as having its own characteristics, which takes into account the special character of the inner condition represented in the text. Other than in the case of untreated traumatised persons, no dominant attachment representation (F, Ds, E) can be found. We would therefore suggest the term *fragmented attachment representation* (= FRAG) for the CC-category, as texts broken up in such a way are extremely contradictory, illogical to incomprehensible, and not infrequently seem 'mad'. The inter- viewees alternate desultorily between suggestions of strategies and are extremely trying as social interlocutors.

CLINICAL EXAMPLES FOR FRAG

With the help of some transcripts of interviews, the special features of this classification will now be elucidated. First, the biographical background is outlined, before the 'fragmentation' of the attachment representations is extricated from the text. As the interview characteristically contains only fragments of biography, the life history was (re-)constructed from the case records. In this way a coherent history evolves, produced by the authors 'at one remove', and forms the background for the fragmented attachment representations of the subjects. This trick is not only necessary for didactic reasons in the presentation of this text, but is also fundamental in both the everyday and scientific processes of recognition for understanding a life history which in itself is presented as fragmented.

Case vignette A

In the prison Ms A, a thin, sad and discouraged young woman of 26, turns up for the interview (interviewer: F. Lamott). She appears both shy and insecure. It is difficult to judge her age; she looks like a small, prematurely aged girl who always reverts to inappropriate giggles under stress.

Her natural father deserted the family when she was two years old. Her parents divorced and a short time later her mother married an American who was with the military police in military barracks in Germany. Ms A attended an American pre-school and learned English. When she was six years old her half-sister was born. She describes her mother as cold and unloving. She was often beaten and had to sit still for hours, tied to a chair, or was locked in the toilet. She remembers that in these situations she took refuge in the world of her imagination and played 'mother and child' with toilet rolls, either 'cuddling' or beating them.

> F.L.: So when, when you were sad and distressed, what did you do?
>
> Ms A: I took refuge in my imaginary world (mhm – *Ms A laughs*) and imagined things (mhm) that could be good and that (mhm) or could look like that (*Ms A laughs* – mhm).
>
> F.L.: And what was it that could be good?

Ms A: I don't really know any more (mhm) I mean – (mhm) how should I explain it (mhm) yes changing things somehow.

F.L.: So better than the situation in which one is?

Ms A: Yes, yes.

F.L.: So playing mother and child and (yes) good mother?

Ms A: Yes, good mother.

F.L.: And the child feels happy and, and...

Ms A: Yes, but not always.

F.L.: But not always (*F.L. and Ms A laugh*).

Ms A: Well yes...

F.L.: The child might also be naughty.

Ms A: Yes.

F.L.: And then you were angry (yes) with the child? (Mhm).

Ms A: Yes, but not always (mhm) so there was also (um ah) another role (mhm) I mean the other way around.

F.L.: You mean that you played the mother?

Ms A: Yes, and the mother wasn't so nice (mhm) she then (*Ms A laughs*) the child and the child died and (# # = *incomprehensible speech*) (mhm mhm) and sometimes some sort of illness (mhm) (*Ms A laughs, embarrassed*) and – the mother was helpless (mhm) I mean she wasn't always nasty it was only that she was helpless (mhm mhm – *Ms A laughs*), I (*clears her throat* – mhm) – about the whole thing (*Ms A laughs, embarrassed* – mhm).

Ms A is ignored, left alone, and badly nourished. In spite of this she continues to love her mother. Her stepfather beats her, too, especially when he is drunk. One year after the birth of her half-sister, Ms A is sent to her grandmother, her natural father's mother, whom she describes as understanding and tolerant. She attends a special school.

During this period (she says in the interview) her father's brother makes sexual advances towards her, exposing himself to her. While she is relating this episode she giggles and says that she brought him to his senses by saying you didn't do that kind of thing within the family. Later, when she was 17 (she continues) her natural father also wanted to have sexual relations with her, which she refused – again she refers, giggling, to the family situation. A short time later she entered an intimate relationship with her father's other brother, which lasted a year.

At the age of 20, following an apprenticeship as a domestic helper, she marries the man who is to be the father of her child, a musician. Shortly after the birth of her first child she falls pregnant again. Her second daughter dies at the age of six months.

Ms A talks of an 'accident', but she brought about her baby's death herself. It is June. Ms A goes to the fair in the late morning with her husband and her two daughters. The baby cries continuously, Ms A cannot quieten the child and becomes increasingly on edge and angry, as she has no idea why the child is crying. She was probably hungry, according to the judgement, but this does not occur to Ms A. She leaves her husband at the fair and rushes home with the baby, which refuses to be pacified. The child's constant crying brings her increasingly into a state of desperation and anger. She tries to stop the baby's crying by shaking her and shouting at her, hitting the child, throttling her, before eventually banging her head against a table top. The baby is silent. Finally she washes her and puts her to bed. At this point the child is still alive. But as a result of internal injuries and head and brain injuries, she dies during the night. When Ms A's husband returns home he finds the dead child and forces his wife to inform the police. She admits what she has done in front of the examining magistrate. In the trial she retracts her confession and changes her story a number of times: she banged into the doorframe with the child by accident, it fell on the floor by accident, etc. Ms A, who during the trial is judged to be intellectually limited and to have diminished responsibility (German Penal Code § 21), is sentenced to a term of imprisonment for manslaughter (German Penal Code § 212), which she serves in a penal institution.

Ms A – according to the judgement – did not want to kill her child. But bringing up her child had proved too much for the young mother who had herself suffered terrible deprivation. It seems as though she treated children like dolls, and was not able to form an attachment with them, just as she herself had never experienced a stable attachment with her own parents. Every time she lost her temper she came into conflict with herself – on the one hand she wanted to spare her child what she had experienced, but on the other hand she was not able to control her compulsive outbursts. The result was that when she lost her temper, she always hit herself first in the face with her fists before she began to beat the children ever more wildly. Ms A suffers from the 'accident', as she herself frequently calls her action. When her defence lawyer confronted her with pictures of the dead baby girl, she broke down and wanted to take her own life.

The evaluation of the interview does not exhibit a dominant attachment representation. The inadequate giggling, the fragile relationship to the interviewer (poised between closeness and distance), the incoherent character of the narrative, and the increasingly broken nature evident in the text are, however, irritating. Only partly comprehensible fragments can be found, but these are scattered throughout the text and bear no relationship to the narrative as a whole.

The fragmented attachment representations have structural similarities with the interactive experiences typical for borderline patients, which are reflected in a disintegrated and inconsistent self-esteem and an unstable relationship to others. The object relationships are on the one hand characterised by a lack of distance to the object, and on the other hand by the functionalisation of the other to narcissistic self-regulation (Kernberg 1993, 2000).

The following passage on the report of serial abuse within the family illustrates the fragile nature and the violation of the rules of dialogue. The text has a tendency towards 'madness'.

> F.L.: And how old were you when you were – when it happened?
>
> Ms A: (mhm) The first time the brother the butcher the job as butcher is (mhm mhm – *Ms A laughs*) yes uh... (*pause, 3 seconds*) it was the time when when my grandpa was still alive.
>
> F.L.: Mhm, you were still very small.
>
> Ms A: Yes.
>
> F.L.: Mhm.

Ms A: And a lot later my dad wanted to try it too I could tell (mhm) a lot later 17 or so (mhm) and then I said no – so Dad I've got to go now (mhm) it's getting too weird now (mhm) the thing with my dad (#) (*Ms A laughs*) (mhm) (# #) that was something sacred for me (mhm) – loving and honouring his father and his mother (mhm) (mhm) and that uh – they treated me so badly (mhm) I still honoured them (mhm) yes, yes.

F.L.:   And the other uncle who wasn't a butcher?

Ms A: Uh, he sells sells houses and with him I had um – had (mhm) a love affair (mhm).

F.L.:   At 17?

Ms A: Yes yes (mhm) – uh.

F.L.:   Because you said (#).

Ms A: Eh?

F.L.:   You had a love affair with him now.

Ms A: No.

F.L.:   Ah (no) that's what I heard or did I misunderstand you?

Ms A: (*pause, 2 seconds*) I've forgotten now too (*F.L. and Ms A laugh*) don't know either (mhm).

F.L.:   But now that's, uh, the relationship doesn't exist, it's – over now?

Ms A: Yes, it's over, I made it clear that (*pause, 2 seconds*) for me (mhm) now personally and I did it – me was for me well then – what – thing is (mhm) that that for me is my my is sacred for me (mhm – *Ms A laughs* – mhm) my family is sacred for me (mhm – *Ms A laughs*) I stand by that – and that's what I then – uh explained to my uncles too (mhm) even earlier too (mhm) I told him, hey you listen that's not on okay (mhm mhm mhm) and we have to stop that (mhm mhm) otherwise – uh (mhm – *Ms A laughs*) I can't see any chance for me to stay here any longer (mhm) or something like that yes.

F.L.:   And how did you feel then, was it difficult for you?

Ms A: Yes it was pretty difficult (mhm) when that with my uncle the one who's a butcher (mhm) that was pretty difficult (mhm) really (*Ms A laughs* – mhm) and what happened with my second uncle – it just – something just got into me something.

F.L.:   You were a little older then (*Ms A laughs*) weren't you?

Ms A: Yes (mhm) and then I just – just told him plainly (mhm) and then said well… (*pause, 2 seconds*) it's my family see and the other thing – we'll keep for us (mhm) that's got nothing to do with anybody (mhm) we have to keep that to ourselves first (mhm) and then we can let it run (mhm – *Ms A laughs* – mhm mhm) yes and then they accepted it – (*Ms A laughs* – mhm mhm) yes but it was pretty bad – um the thing with my uncle 'cos – (#) the one who was a butcher (mhm – # # # – *Ms A laughs*) um I told my grandmother (mhm) my grandmother told my granny – the mother of my three fathers [*sic*] (mhm) but she didn't believe it (mhm) yes and yes I thought okay – then not in my way (mhm mhm mhm – *Ms A laughs*).

This section of the interview demonstrates that the main function of the internal working model, focusing in anticipation on the reactions of the interlocutor, is not successful (Fremmer-Bombik 1995). The life experiences are so inconsistent that integration within a unified working model of relationships fails; only fragments of attachment representations occur, and the surrounding world remains unpredictable. In the combination CC/U/E3[1] (Main and Goldwyn 1994), the evaluation of the interview presents fragments of unprocessed trauma and of apprehensive involvement. Unstable attachments themselves impede the development of integrated working models. If this difficult process is also hindered by ill-treatment resulting in anxiety and a fear of being deserted, then these disconnected fragments of emotional and cognitive representations dominate and deposit themselves as risk factors.

Case vignette B

Ms B is in prison for the second time for attempted murder. Both times her victims survived. In both cases the victims were intimate and close friends of the perpetrator. There is something irritating about Ms B, an average sized, stocky woman in jeans and a long pullover. For the interview (F. Lamott) she is wearing a pair of tinted glasses and has put her shoulder-length hair up under a crocheted hat. You can't see her eyes. Her conduct is conspicuous: exaggeratedly 'unfeminine' manner, somewhat unwieldy in her physical movements, the way she holds her cigarette, how she draws on it, the gestures and facial expressions, how she establishes contact with the interviewer – challenging, always slightly ironic and yet somehow matey.

Ms B has thirteen siblings: five half-brothers and -sisters her father brought with him into her parents' marriage, seven real brothers and sisters (of whom she is the second youngest), and after her mother married again, one more half-brother.

When she is two years old her father dies. He leaves behind him a farm. Ms B cannot remember her father; nevertheless she speaks of her great love for him and believes herself to be very like him.

F.L.:   Let's talk briefly about your father now. He died when you were two.

Ms B: Exactly.

F.L.:   I don't suppose you remember him at all?

Ms B: No only a picture, see? But I really love him more than anything really I can, I mean okay I can't talk much about it but a picture like that I look just like him and also what my mother told me about what it was like back then so (mhm).

F.L.:   …whom did you feel closer to, your father or your mother?

Ms B: I feel closer to my father although although I never knew him (mhm, mhm) – but I always wanted to be like him although I didn't know what he was like see? (mhm) Only what I heard about him.

After the father's death the children were put into a number of homes. Not long after, the mother married again but Ms B's hope that she would now be taken home was not realised: '…our mother would only fetch us (mhm) when she remembered that she had children, you see (mhm) and when she was fed up with us again we were taken away again (mhm)' Her childhood consisted of continuous change between stays in different places. 'I didn't know where I belonged', and 'If you don't get any love, then (you) are alone outside yourself [sic]'. Indeed she frequently acted during the interview as though she were standing 'outside herself', as if one part of her would speak and the other look at her. Standing outside oneself is a metaphor for being split, disassociated, not in contact with oneself and the situation one is in, having to separate from unbearable feelings as not one's own.

In one of the homes she developed a close relationship to a nun, whom she called her 'favourite nun', and made her an 'ersatz mother':

F.L.:   How would you describe your relationship to her?

Ms B: Well it was love I suppose but there was always a kind of weight there see? (mhm) You could never give them a hug, well yes but never really tender 'cos, you know 'cos they're nuns (mhm) that's nothing different 'cos they do their work (mhm) are there for everyone (mhm) but so that you could say hey come on I'm really going to (mhm) depend on you (mhm) or you need it sometimes (mhm) see? And that wasn't really there (mhm) this absolute physical contact see? (mhm). Only her apron belonged to me see? I suppose you could say I was in love with her apron, see? (mhm) That I could behind (##).

F.L.:   Connection to her?

Ms B: Yes that's it.

F.L.:   In tow?

Ms B: Yes (mhm, mhm).

When she was five or six the nun died and the burial was a terrible experience for the little girl. She was forced to look at the dead woman laid out in her coffin. A short time later her mother came and took her and her older sister home with her. But she never really felt safe there. There were a lot of arguments and her mother drank and beat her children.

F.L.:   Did you sometimes feel threatened by your mother as a
             child?

Ms B: Oh you know – let's say I overlooked a lot because I loved
             her (mhm) – and I also forgave beating me almost beat me
             to death because I sometimes didn't know uh why (mhm)
             see? Because – sometimes I knew because – this man my
             stepfather he raped me and my sister see? So – as a child I
             sometimes thought about that – that she might have hated
             us because we took her husband away from her I don't
             know what goes on in a woman's head (mhm) than I some-
             times thought that 'cos she she got divorced then – and
             that was actually okay see? She actually calmed down a bit
             then.

This text passage shows a curious generation role reversal. It seems as
though the daughter were the mother and the mother the daughter: she
'overlooked a lot' of what her mother did, and her mother hated her (instead
of protecting her from her stepfather) because she had taken her husband
away from her; that was the reason for the beatings. Seen psychodynamically, Ms B takes on the guilty role and the responsibility for her
mother's aggressive actions. In order to protect the object she loves, she
identifies herself with the aggressor (Fischer and Riedesser 1998; Herman
1998; Hirsch 1987) – a method of shaping a relationship which can frequently be found in her life. The whole text is characterised by diffuse generation and gender relationships.

During the interview, when Ms B talks about her mother's lack of love,
she relates a brief episode which happened between her and her mother
when she was 15 years old. The scene of this attack appears familiar but
under different conditions (see Lamott 2000).

Ms B: Well that's actually what I'm missing today actually you
             know for sheer she's endless barriers or she can't show
             people love or approach you of her own accord (mhm)
             except for when she was drunk see? (mhm) – And I
             couldn't either 'cos I've got my walls too somehow got
             (mhm) she was always offish see? (mhm) Unless I got her
             drunk sometimes on purpose we drank and then she
             always danced with me like that then somehow she just

> wanted to dance was more fun and warmer and I used that yes then I hugged her 'cos I never felt that otherwise never had you know (mhm) so my whole (mhm) my whole life I was never really allowed to hug her this see I don't know why? – Uh and then when she was drunk then I hugged her see? (mhm) And that was okay for me (mhm) yes but and then that was enough too (mhm).

It is as if the pubescent Ms B were now achieving, cunningly in male identification, what had been denied her all her life. What is remarkable is that Ms B also shows exaggerated familiarity with the interviewer when describing this attack.

After leaving secondary school she decides she wants to become a mechanic. But nobody is willing to train her as an apprentice; she becomes a salesgirl. At the age of 18 she marries; one year later the marriage has already ended in divorce. She does not feel comfortable beside her husband and after the divorce moves in with a girlfriend, with whom she has a love affair. After they have lived together for some time, the conflicts become more frequent and they decide on a trial separation. During this period her girlfriend takes her own life. Ms B feels responsible for the suicide. She moves into the red-light district and lives with a woman there who 'turns tricks' for her. When the woman also decides to move out, Ms B tries to stop her with all means at her disposal. The conflict escalates: in a bar Ms B points a gun at her girlfriend with the intention of shooting her. One of the guests places himself between them and is fatally hit. Ms B is sentenced to years of imprisonment for manslaughter.

In prison she meets a woman with whom she moves in after her release. But her happiness is again short-lived and after a year her girlfriend decides to leave her. Ms B pleads with her and tries to persuade her to stay with her. But her girlfriend's decision is final and she moves out of their shared flat. She lies in wait for her ex-girlfriend, intending to try and change her mind. The woman, accompanied by two men, refuses again, upon which Ms B stabs her with a knife. It is only the presence of the two men that saves her life. Ms B was sentenced to ten years' imprisonment for attempted murder. In the psychiatric report submitted to the court, antisocial behavioural tendencies were described, but Ms B was declared fully responsible.

At the end of the interview, when asked to evaluate her life history experiences, Ms B's inner turmoil and fragile identity are particularly obvious in the incoherence of the text.

> *F.L.:* Is there anything in particular that you would regard as having learnt from your childhood experiences? You said before that uh you drew strength uhm from the fact that you were forced to fight?

> *Ms B:* Yes I learnt how I didn't want to be (mhm) see? I learnt how to hate how to kill how everything see? (mhm) And I'm still working hard at that (mhm) – very 'cos I know I know myself (mhm) 'cos nobody knows themselves properly see? (mhm) Every day you're new yes (mhm) but I know what I'm capable of (mhm) you know what I mean (mhm) what some people don't know yet (mhm) 'cos I've experienced almost everything and know what I don't want to be (mhm). Yes now I'm now I'm actually what I am at heart I'd say (mhm) yes (mhm) what I couldn't be 'cos it was always suppressed yes (mhm) – and now I'd just like to show feelings I want to live I want (mhm) to give love (mhm) really (mhm). I want to be my other half now (mhm) see? That's a bit schizophrenic but aren't we all? Yes yes our other half's waving to us (mhm) – yes? (*pause, 8 seconds*) I always say (##) you need schizophrenia to exist in this world ha ha ha.

The evaluation of the interviews with Ms B reveals clearly fragmented attachment representations (FRAG): CC/U/Ds3/F1/E3. As well as a number of unresolved traumas, fragments of attachment representations can be found which can be ordered as follows: first, there are insecure-distanced or dismissing representations, with a clear lack of emotional involvement; second, secure ones that show a burdened, but worked-through childhood; and third, there are insecure-enmeshed representations filled with anxiety. What is fundamental, however, shows itself less in partial aspects, but rather in the whole text itself, which is incoherent and fragmented.

CONCLUSIONS

As the discourse analytical evaluation of the narrative taken from the Adult Attachment Interview begins primarily with the way in which life history events are discussed, it also provides statements about the quality of incoherent texts, making this method especially suitable for analysing the narrative structure of severely traumatised and disturbed persons. That may at first sound paradoxical, as not only the narrated history but also the interaction between interviewer and interviewees is directly affected by the insecure and fragmented attachment. As these people are mostly no longer in a position to create coherent life histories, the interviewers, analysts or researchers – as in the examples given here – find themselves in the position of relief designers who use additional information from files, judgements or psychiatric reports to construct a biographical foil which makes it possible to illustrate more clearly the brittleness of fragmented attachment representations (FRAG).

Meanwhile, a number of investigations on the relationship between psychic disorders and attachment representations are available, which Dozier, Chase Stovall and Albus (1999), in Cassidy and Shaver's *Handbook of Attachment,* have collected in the form of a meta-analysis. However, since in all studies the data collected by means of the AAI was evaluated according to either the classification with three (F, E, Ds) or the classification with four alternatives (F, E, Ds, U), by focusing on the CC-category this chapter presents a differentiation that until now has been given almost no consideration in meta-analysis. Hesse, in his discussion of the subject, emphasises the CC-category, stating that this is 'by no means a simple "waste bin" for random cases' (Hesse 1996, p.9). So, in order to be more precise in classification, we have introduced the term 'fragmented attachment representations (FRAG)', since in the analysis of the narrative the focus is on the fragmentation of the text. The individual fragments reflect inconsistent experiences and don't allow one to identify specific attachment representations, yet are characterised by specific forms of defence. Thus the whole text gives the impression of being incoherent, chaotic, and for the most part incomprehensible. This particular text quality 'has recently been found related to histories of psychiatric disorder, to marital and criminal violence, and to experiences of sexual abuse' (Hesse 1996, p.9). In a Dutch study on violent offenders in prison, van IJzendoorn *et al.* (1996) – like Stalker and Davies (1995) with sexually abused women – found an over-representation of CC, which, in the terminology suggested by us, would correspond to fragmented attachment representations.

Future research should concentrate on these fragmented attachment representations which, so it seems, can be found above all in the forensic field. Not only might this lead one to expect more exact recognition of the attachment representations of severely traumatised and disturbed persons; it may also point the way forward for therapeutic approaches and prognoses on release.

NOTE

1.   The number (i.e. the 3) denotes a subclassification of enmeshed-preoccupied attachment representation (for example: E2 stands for a preoccupied representation dominated by anger and E3 denotes a preoccupied attachment representation characterized by anxiety). See Main and Goldwyn (1994).

REFERENCES

Adam, K., Keller, A., West, M., Larose, S. and Goszer, L. (1994) 'Parental representation in suicidal adolescents: A controlled study.' *Australian and New Zealand Journal of Psychiatry 28*, 418–425.

Bowlby, J. (1969) *Attachment and Loss. Vol. 1: Attachment.* New York: Basic Books.

Buchheim, A., Brisch, K.H. and Kächele, H. (1998) 'Einfü hrung in die Bindungstheorie und ihre Bedeutung f ür die Psychotherapie.' *Psychotherapie, Psychosomatik, medizinische Psychologie 48*, 128–138.

Cassidy, J. and Shaver, P. (eds) (1999) *Handbook of Attachment.* New York and London: Guilford Press.

Dornes, M. (1998) 'Bindungstheorie und Psychoanalyse.' *Psyche 52*, 299–348.

Dozier, M., Chase Stovall, K. and Albus, K.E. (1999) 'Attachment and psychopathology in adulthood.' In Cassidy, J. and Shaver, P. (eds) *Handbook of Attachment.* New York and London: Guilford Press.

Dulz, B. and Jensen, M. (1997) 'Vom Trauma zur Aggression – von der Aggression zur Delinquenz. Einige überlegungen zu Borderline-Störungen.' *Persönlichkeitsstörungen, Theorie und Therapie 1*, 109–117.

Fischer, G. and Riedesser, P. (1998) *Lehrbuch der Psychotraumatologie.* Mü nchen: Reinhardt.

Fonagy, P. (1998) 'Metakognition und Bindungsfähigkeit des Kindes.' *Psyche*
52, 349–368.

Fonagy, P., Steele, H., Steele, M., Mattoon, G. and Target, M. (1995)
'Attachment, the reflective self, and borderline states. The predictive
specificity of the Adult Attachment Interview and pathological emotional
development.' In Goldberg, S., Muir, R. and Kerr, J. (eds) *Attachment
Theory: Social Developmental and Clinical Perspectives.* New York: The Analytic
Press.

Fremmer-Bombik, E. (1995) 'Innere Arbeitsmodelle von Bindung.' In Spangler,
G. and Zimmermann, P. (eds) *Die Bindungstheorie. Grundlagen, Forschung und
Anwendung.* Stuttgart: Klett-Cotta.

Fremmer-Bombik, E. and Grossmann, K.E. (1993) 'Über die lebenslange
Bedeutung frü her Bindungserfahrungen.' In Petzold, H.G. (ed) *Früöhe
Schädigungen – späte Folgen? Psychotherapie und Babyforschung Vol. 1.*
Paderborn: Junfermann Verlag.

George, C., Kaplan, N. and Main, M. (1985) 'The Adult Attachment Interview.'
Unpublished manuscript. Berkeley: University of California.

Gloger-Tippelt, G. and Hofmann, V. (1997) 'Das Adult Attachment Interview:
Konzeption, Methode und Erfahrungen im Deutschen Sprachraum.'
Kindheit und Entwicklung 6, 161–172.

Grossmann, K.E. (2000) 'Die Entwicklung von Bindungsqualität und
Bindungsrepräsentation: Auf der Suche nach der Überwindung psychischer
Unsicherheit.' In Endres, M. and Hauser, S. (eds) *Bindungstheorie in der
psychotherapeutischen Praxis.* Mü nchen: Ernst Reinhardt.

Herman, J. (1998) *Die Narben der Gewalt. Traumatische Erfahrungen verstehen und
öüberwinden.* M ünchen: Kindler.

Hesse, E. (1996) 'Discourse, memory, and the adult attachment interview: A
note with emphasis on the emerging "cannot classify" category.' *Infant
Mental Health Journal 17*, 4–11.

Hirsch, M. (1987) *Realer Inzest. Psychodynamik des Missbrauchs in der Familie.*
Berlin, Heidelberg and New York: Springer.

Kernberg, O. (1993) *Psychodynamische Therapie bei Borderline-Patienten.* Bern:
Hans Huber.

Kernberg, O. (2000) 'Borderline-Persönlichkeitsorganisation und
Klassifikation der Persönlichkeitsstörungen.' In Kernberg, O., Dulz, B. and
Sachsse, U. (eds) *Handbuch der Borderlinestörungen.* Stuttgart, New York:
Schattauer.

Köhler, L. (1998) 'Zur Anwendung der Bindungstheorie in der psychoanalytischen Praxis.' *Psyche 52*, 369–398.

K üchenhoff, J. (1998)'Trauma, Konflikt, Repräsentation.' In Schlösser, A.M. and Höhfeld, K. (eds) *Trauma und Konflikt.* Giessen: Psychosozial.

Lamott, F. (2000) 'Traumatische Reinszenierungen – ü ber den Zusammenhang von Gewalterfahrung und Gewalttätigkeit von Frauen.' *Recht und Psychiatrie 18*, 56–62.

Lamott, F. and Pfäfflin, F. (2001) 'Ergebnisse der Untersuchung Trauma, Beziehung und Tat – Bindungsrepräsentationen von Frauen, die getötet haben.' *Monatsschrift föür Kriminologie und Strafrechtsreform 84*, 10–24.

Lorenzer, A. (1970) *Sprachzerstörung and Rekonstruktion.* Frankfurt a.M.: Suhrkamp.

Main, M. (1991) 'Metacognitive knowledge, metacognitive monitoring, and singular (coherent) vs. multiple (incoherent) model of attachment: Findings and directions for future research.' In Parkes, C.M., Stevenson-Hinde, J. and Marris, P. (eds) *Attachment Across the Life Cycle.* London: Routledge.

Main, M. and Goldwyn, R. (1994) 'Adult Attachment Scoring and Classification System.' Unpublished manuscript. University of Berkeley, CA.

Main, M., Kaplan, N. and Cassidy, J. (1985) 'Security in infancy, childhood and adulthood: A move to the level of representation.' In Bretherton, I. and Waters, E. (eds) *Growing Points of Attachment Theory and Research.* Monographs of the Society for Research in Child Development, Vol. 50, pp.66–106.

Spangler, G. and Zimmermann, P. (1995) *Die Bindungstheorie. Grundlagen, Forschung und Anwendung.* Stuttgart: Klett-Cotta.

Stalker, C. and Davies, F. (1995) 'Attachment organization and adaption in sexually-abused women.' *Canadian Journal of Psychiatry 20*, 234–240.

van IJzendoorn, M.H., Feldbrugge, J.T.M., Derks, F.C.H., de Ruiter, C., Verhagen, M.F.M., Philipse, M.W.G., van der Staak, C.P.F. and Riksen-Walraven, J.M.A. (1996) 'Attachment representations of personality disordered criminal offenders.' Unpublished manuscript.

Part II

Clinical Issues

CHAPTER 4

The Link Between Childhood Trauma and Later Violent Offending[1]

The Application of Attachment Theory in a Probation Setting

Paul Renn

INTRODUCTION

Research findings relating to young offenders show a history of maltreatment and loss in up to 90 per cent of the sample population (Boswell 1996; Fonagy *et al.* 1997). These findings accord with my clinical experience as a probation officer working with adult offenders in the community. In particular, I find that those who commit violent offences have themselves been victims of childhood abuse and/or suffered neglect or loss experienced as catastrophic. Indeed, the acting out of unresolved childhood trauma in a criminal way is a consistent feature in the behaviour of those with whom I work and, moreover, strongly associated with substance misuse.

The case study that follows illustrates the clinical application of attachment theory in a probation setting. It is presented as an example of my work with violent offenders and with the intention of emphasizing the connection between childhood trauma and subsequent violent offending. It elucidates the way in which attachment theory may be used to explicate offending behaviour and to assess risk in a forensic setting. In line with Boswell's (1998) advocacy of research-minded practice, the study seeks to demonstrate the importance of asking offenders about their traumatic backgrounds at the point of assessment. The therapeutic model shows that the application of attachment theory in brief, time-limited work may enhance the offender's capacity for narrative intelligibility, leading to an integration of dissociated thoughts and emotional affect, and to a concomitant cessation of violent behaviour.

THEORETICAL PARADIGM

Attachment theory played a central part in my assessment of the offender and I anticipated that this approach would underpin my intervention with him. As indicated above, I have found attachment theory a powerful tool in explicating offending behaviour and assessing risk and, furthermore, eminently adaptable to working effectively with offenders in a probation setting. From this developmental perspective the person's inner world of subjective experience is structured, shaped and organized by patterns of attachment and interpersonal interactions into representational models (Bowlby 1969, 1980).

With regard to traumatic childhood experiences involving separation and loss, Bowlby (1969) found that when a young child is unwillingly separated from the attachment figure, he or she shows distress. In the event of the separation being prolonged, necessitating the child being placed in unfamiliar surroundings, such distress is likely to become intense. Typically, the child's distress follows a sequence of protest, despair, and emotional detachment. Bowlby (1969) suggests that these phases may be linked to three types of responses, viz., separation anxiety, grief and mourning, and defence. Further, he argues that these responses are phases of a single process – that of mourning separation and loss. The traumatic quality of the child's grief reaction is encapsulated in Bowlby's poignant observation that 'Loss of a loved person is one of the most intensely painful experiences any human being can suffer' (Bowlby 1980, p.7).

Bowlby (1979, 1980) emphasizes that generally the crucial process of mourning takes place in the context of the family's characteristic attachment behaviour towards the child. He contends that the family may either facilitate the expression of grief by responding sympathetically to the child's distress, or adopt an inhibiting attitude that causes the child to suppress or avoid typical feelings of fear of abandonment, yearning and anger. Bowlby (1979, 1980) stresses that a supportive and sympathetic attitude within the family may lead to a process of healthy mourning in children as young as two years. The process consists of normal behavioural responses of anxiety and protest, despair and disorganization, and detachment and reorganization. By means of this process, the loss is gradually accepted by the child, whose capacity to form new attachment bonds is restored following a period of disorganization.

By contrast, in pathological mourning the child's unexpressed, ambivalent feelings of yearning for, and anger with, the attachment figure become split off into segregated or dissociated systems of the personality, and the loss may be disavowed. As a consequence, and in the absence of a trusted substitute attachment figure, the child has little alternative but to move precipitously to a defensive condition of emotional detachment, thereby internalizing a mental model of attachment that is dismissing or avoidant of affective states associated with separation and loss. In instances such as these, the child's attachment behaviour system remains deactivated because attachment-related information is being defensively and selectively excluded from consciousness (Bowlby 1980, 1988).

In describing childhood pathological mourning, Bowlby (1979) makes the important point that his hypothesis is not confined to the actual death of, or separation from, the attachment figure. Indeed, he stresses that the child may experience separation and loss in numerous, less overt ways – for example, in the form of threats of abandonment, parental rejection, depression, neglect and/or abuse, as well as loss of love (Bowlby 1979, 1988). Bowlby (1979) emphasizes that the common factor in these various situations is the child's loss of a parent to love and to attach to.

In developing Bowlby's theoretical concepts, Main, Kaplan and Cassidy (1985) suggest that patterns of secure and insecure attachment organization, internalized in the form of working models, are representational of states of mind in relation to patterns of attachment. Further, Main et al.'s (1985) research indicates that, once established, patterns of attachment tend to persist over time and become actively self-perpetuating because information experienced as potentially disruptive is countered by perceptual and behavioural control mechanisms. Internal working models are, therefore, thought to mediate experience of actual relationships and events, and to guide and direct feelings, behaviour, attention, memory and cognition. The authors' findings support Bowlby's (1979) contention that mental models shaped by childhood experiences of pathological mourning may be activated under conditions of separation and loss in adulthood, together with the expression of dysfunctional anger, hatred and aggression.

In the course of their research, Main and her colleagues (1985) employed the Adult Attachment Interview (George, Kaplan and Main 1984) in order to classify parental states of mind with respect to attachment. Using this research tool and Ainsworth et al.'s (1978) Strange Situation procedure, which observes and classifies the attachment status of children, Main et al. (1985) established a link between four distinct narrative styles and four corresponding patterns of attachment behaviour. These findings were confirmed by Main in a follow-up study (1991) and, together, demonstrate that each pattern of attachment organization has as its precursor a specific pattern of mother–infant interaction and its own behavioural sequelae. Again, this research suggests that malignant childhood events relevant to attachment, such as separation and loss, may cause difficulty in integrating and organizing information, and that such difficulty may play a determining role in the creation of security in adulthood. As noted above, Main et al. (1985) conclude that internal working models derived from insecure patterns of attachment organization are resistant to change because error-correcting information is being defensively and selectively excluded from consciousness, resulting in perceptual distortion of relationships and events. The authors' findings of research undertaken in Baltimore have been replicated in studies carried out in Germany by Grossman and Grossman (1991).

Along similar lines, Peterfreund (1983) suggests that different internal working models are in operation during different activities and in different situations, making predictive calculation and adaptive behaviour possible. In advocating a 'heuristic', as opposed to a 'stereotypical', approach to the process of psychoanalytic therapy, he too stresses the significance of information processing and error-correcting feedback in this process, arguing that these are the means by which perceptually distorted internal working models are modified, updated and fine-tuned. Peterfreund's synthesizing approach reflects both Bowlby's emphasis on empirical observation of human relationships and the fact that many of the concepts underpinning attachment theory are derived from cognitive psychology and developmental psychology. Attachment theory, therefore, may be seen as a bridge between cognitive science and psychoanalysis (Holmes 1993).

In line with this thinking, my work with offenders is informed by findings from developmental studies, adult attachment research, and trauma research. In combination with interactional and developmental perspectives in psychoanalysis, such findings provide a particular way both of listening to the offender's narrative and of understanding the clinical process (Slade 1999). In accordance with this view, Stern (1998) argues that 'search strategies' which explore the client's past are an integral aspect of the therapeutic process, contending that 'In good part, the treatment is the search' (p.203). As with attachment theory, Stern's (1985, 1998) perspective views psychopathology as arising out of an accumulation of maladaptive interactive patterns that result in character and personality types and disorders in adulthood.

THE OFFENDER – JOHN: PERSONAL HISTORY

John, the subject of this case study, has given his permission for this chapter to be published. Names have been changed, however, and personal circumstances disguised in order to protect identities. John is 48 years old and grew up in a large family, being one of eight children. He is the youngest of four brothers, one of whom died several years ago, and has two older and two younger sisters. He spoke of his father as being 'distant and always at work', and his mother as 'over-protective', recalling that she had played out an elaborate pretence in respect of his father's occupation by telling neighbours he worked in a bank, whereas, in fact, he was a barman. John completed his secondary education at the age of 15, leaving school with no exam qualifications. By this time, he was misusing illicit drugs and alcohol. He went on to develop a dependency on the latter. As a consequence of this problem, John's employment record is inconsistent and, in the main, consisted of manual and semi-skilled work.

John has had a series of unstable relationships with women, characterized by drink-related violence, controlling behaviour, possessiveness and sexual jealousy on his part. Because of his problematic behaviour towards women, John consulted his GP when aged 18. He was referred for psychiatric assessment but not offered ongoing treatment. John married when aged 28, but insisted 'There never was a true love', adding 'I haven't wanted to commit myself'. He avoided doing so in part by 'always having relationships with two women at the same time'. This situation obtained during the course of his 13-year-long marriage, which John described as an 'on-off affair'. He related how he would often pick fights with his wife so as to give himself an excuse to leave home and go on a drinking binge. The marriage was childless, but John has three children from a subsequent relationship which, typically, was brief, intermittent and volatile. He has had no contact with his children for several years and was unaware of their current whereabouts. At the time we met, John was largely estranged from his own family and not in an intimate relationship.

Forensic history

John has been involved with the criminal justice system for over 30 years, appearing before the courts for the first time as a juvenile. Though he has convictions for motoring offences and, when younger, burglary, drink-related violence is the most prominent and consistent feature of his offending behaviour. This commenced in adolescence and, as mentioned above, was the reason why John was eventually referred for psychiatric assessment. He has convictions for grievous bodily harm, assault with intent, assault on the police, possession of a firearm, and criminal damage, on one occasion going to his ex-partner's home armed with an axe, which he used to break in. John has been subject to a range of sentences including discharges, fines, probation, community service, and imprisonment. He has had numerous sojourns in rehabilitation units for his alcohol problem but always returned to misusing drink. One of his brothers also has an alcohol problem but John is the only member of the family to become embroiled with the law.

The index offence

The index offence was committed five years ago and consisted of a serious assault on John's partner, Sylvia. The couple had been in a relationship for two years, but lived separately. John came to suspect Sylvia of being sexually involved with someone else. He went to her home in a drunken state one evening and accused her of having sex with another man, calling her a 'slag and a whore'. When Sylvia denied John's accusation he attacked her with his fists and feet in a blind, uncontrollable rage, causing serious injury to her head and body and desisting only when finally she told him 'what he wanted to hear'. At court, the photographic evidence of Sylvia's injuries was said to be 'horrific'. John denied the offence when arrested, maintaining that Sylvia's injuries were self-inflicted. He was convicted following a jury trial and sentenced to two-and-a-half years' imprisonment.

First contact

John's case was allocated to me when I transferred to the probation office in his home area. His reputation at the office was that of a perpetual client with whom everything had been tried. I wrote to John in prison to introduce myself as his new throughcare officer. In his reply, he alluded to the attack on Sylvia, saying, 'It wasn't anger, it was alcohol talking, I'm not angry by nature'. Though clearly John was distancing himself from his anger and violence in this statement, there was at least an implicit admission of his assault on Sylvia.

The initial assessment

I met John for the first time during his temporary release from prison on home leave. He had managed to retain his local authority tenancy by subletting to a male alcoholic friend, but previously had lived alone. John was due to be released on parole licence a month later and his period of supervision would run for eight months. At this first meeting, I asked John specific questions about childhood experiences in respect of separation, loss and abuse. He was clearly surprised and puzzled by the tenor of my questions as he had not been asked about such issues before. After some initial hesitation, John spoke of having had frequent separations from his family from about the age of five years. These were the result of a series of operations for ENT problems necessitating his hospitalization. He recalled struggling with the nursing staff on one occasion as he fought to retain consciousness while being held down and given 'gas'.

Despite these traumatic experiences, John's narrative style when discussing them was dismissive, in that he did not believe they had had an adverse effect on him. The dismissive quality of his narrative, together with his propensity for violence in intimate relationships, indicated that he might have developed an insecure-avoidant pattern of attachment organization (Main 1991; Main *et al.* 1985; Main and Weston 1982). Given these clinical features, I held in mind the possibility that John might have responded to the enforced separation from his family by precipitously entering a state of emotional detachment (Bowlby 1973, 1979). In reviewing studies linking insecurely attached children and subsequent criminal behaviour, Fonagy and his colleagues (1997) suggest that insecure attachment constitutes a distinct risk factor. Further, Fonagy *et al.* (1997) argue that patterns of attachment operate as mechanisms of defence to help the child cope with idiosyncrasies of parental caregiving, and that criminality involves disturbance of attachment processes. These findings accord with de Zulueta's (1993) proposal that 'violence is attachment gone wrong'.

It soon became clear that John's ideal view of himself was that of a passive, non-violent man who, in his own words, 'wouldn't hurt a fly'. My tentative hypothesis at this point was that John was carrying powerful unprocessed emotional pain; that he was disowning feelings of anger and hatred, and that, since he lacked the capacity to contain and transform such emotions, these built up in response to stressor events, generating intense internal conflict which eventually became overwhelming. At such times, John resorted to binge drinking. Under the disinhibiting effect of alcohol his split-off emotional turmoil was unleashed and acted out in the form of a violent rage. This clinical picture indicated that John might be prone to experiencing a traumatic stress reaction when embroiled in an intense, emotionally-charged situation (de Zulueta 1993; Herman 1992). From this perspective, traumatic affect is seen as having a disorganizing effect on mental functioning, and to be a significant motivating factor in the manifestation of violent behaviour (Tyson and Tyson 1990).

I harboured reservations about John's ability to engage in a therapeutic process. These misgivings centred on the fact that he was denying the index offence and that his record of attending appointments when supervised in the past had not exactly been exemplary. Further, as noted above, John was resistant to the idea that past experience may have a maladaptive effect on behaviour in the present, specifically in relation to his alcohol misuse, as he had been told at a rehabilitation unit that 'alcoholism is a disease'. He therefore expressed a good deal of scepticism about the prospect of change, having passively accepted this fatalistic diagnosis. Nevertheless, I explained what our work together would involve, should he decide on this option, emphasizing the collaborative nature of the process. John responded by saying that he would 'give it a go' as nothing else he had tried had been successful. He signed a standard medical consent form giving me permission to contact his GP in order to discuss any relevant issues.

Time framework

Given the setting within which I work, my intervention with John would be brief and time-limited, hence speed in assessing the clinical issues was a major consideration. In fact, I had a total of 13 sessions with John, each session lasting an hour. A follow-up meeting was held six months after his supervisory period had ended. I incorporate such meetings into my practice, seeing these as serving a dual purpose of evaluating the effectiveness of my work and providing the offender with a sense of continuity and connection to a secure base (Bowlby 1988), or at least to one experienced as secure enough. In my experience, the availability of an ongoing link at this critical time helps preclude the often-noted (though anecdotal) phenomenon whereby the offender re-offends towards the end of the supervisory period, seemingly as a reaction to the loss of a relationship that has become significant.

Therapeutic intervention

The first meeting following John's release from prison focused on helping him to recognize and own his disturbing thoughts and feelings. An example of this difficulty arose when John spoke in mild terms about the friend whom he had allowed to stay at his home while he was in prison. John returned to find the place a complete tip and rent arrears of over £1000 owing to the Housing Department. At first John spoke of feeling 'a bit let down' and, later, when I questioned his passive response, of being 'angry and annoyed', vacillating between these two attitudes. It seemed to me that John was quite confused as to how he actually felt about his friend and in two minds about how to respond, speaking in the same breath of going to reason with this person and of beating hell out of him!

This narrative appeared to provide a glimpse of the conflict characterizing John's representational world of object relations or confused, unstable, internal working models of attachment. He seemed on the one hand to be

identifying with the hurt, angry, disappointed child who had been let down
and whose trust had been betrayed; on the other, to be identifying with a
dismissing parent who deflected and perhaps even forbade the expression
of difficult thoughts and painful feelings. This situation seemed to be
re-created in the session, in that John anxiously deflected any attempt on my
part to connect with him on an emotional level. Indeed, I felt under
immense pressure not to talk about meaningful issues and events and I
experienced a sense of futility and despair.

It would have been all too easy to succumb to the sense of hopelessness
that I was experiencing, and so given up the attempt to engage John.
Instead, I sought to understand his emotional state and subjective experience. In ways not too dissimilar from the stress-inducing aspects of the
Strange Situation procedure (Ainsworth *et al.* 1978) and the Adult Attachment Interview (George *et al.* 1984), I viewed the emotionally heightened
exchange with John as having elicited archaic interactive patterns of attachment. These mental models took the form of nonverbal, non-reflective procedural memories, and were expressed in his behavioural performance, the
observation of which provided a basis for me to experience, share and match
his affective state (Beebe, Jaffe and Lachmann 1992; Beebe and Lachmann
1992; Stern 1985, 1998).

Despite the intensity of the interaction, my reading of John's overt
behaviour influenced me to stay in the affective moment, which I viewed as
an unconscious communication of unmanageable feelings. I decided to
share aspects of my countertransferential experience of being with him,
wondering whether the powerful thoughts and feelings stimulated in me
mirrored something of his own experience (Casement 1990; Maroda
1991). John confirmed that he had felt a mounting sense of anxiety, verging
on panic, adding that he usually avoids talking about his feelings. Avoidance
of this sort, particularly in men, may reflect the way in which gender, culture
and inner prohibition coalesce, resulting in a defensive splitting of thought
from feeling. From a developmental perspective, such behaviour may also
indicate a failure of affective development and a concomitant incapacity to
regulate emotional states when under stress (Schore 1994). Research
suggests that in such instances, the lack of a contingent parental response to
the child's attachment signals may, if characteristic of the relationship, come
to be associated with negative affect and escalating arousal, leading to
prolonged and severe states of withdrawal. The internalization of such

interactive patterns may interfere with the subject's optimal regulation of arousal and thus compromise his or her capacity to stay attentive and process information (Beebe, Jaffe and Lachmann 1992).

Disclosure of childhood trauma

Somewhat paradoxically, John appeared relieved by the dawning realization that inner emotions may be recognized, shared and understood (Benjamin 1995). Seemingly in consequence of this intersubjective experience, a more reflective mood and positive affective state prevailed. This exchange, in turn, appeared to evoke in John memories of a traumatic event that had taken place when he was aged eight. Tentatively, John related how he and his then best friend, Ricky, had been playing near a fast-flowing river. John's memories of the event were somewhat vague and hazy, but he recalled that Ricky had slipped from the moss-covered embankment into the river and drowned. John came to believe that people suspected him of having pushed his friend into the river. Indeed, I found myself silently questioning whether John might have had a hand in Ricky's death. Again, I observed the nuances of his facial expressions, direction of gaze, vocal inflections, bodily orientation and gesture when discussing this traumatic event, as well as monitoring my own affective responses, but I detected nothing in John's overt behaviour at that time, nor subsequently, to indicate that his narrative was anything other than authentic in regard to this matter. I therefore concluded that Ricky's death had, indeed, been a tragic accident.

In addition to feeling blamed and accused, John came to view himself as a 'bad' person because his attempts to save Ricky had failed. John went on to speak of having confused and intangible memories of being in court in the aftermath of Ricky's death and of growing up feeling burdened by 'guilt'. The court in John's memory was probably that of the coroner who carried out the inquiry into the circumstances of Ricky's death. It seemed likely that, in a similar way to those who live through a major disaster, John experienced a deep sense of guilt at having survived when Ricky had died (de Zulueta 1993; Herman 1992) and that this whole situation was exacerbated by his having to appear at the coroner's court.

I wondered whether the trauma of Ricky's drowning had activated John's earlier trauma, that of being separated from his family and held down and 'gassed' in hospital – drowning in gas, as it were. This observation seemed to resonate with John's subjective experience. He became deeply

thoughtful and reflective, sitting in silence for a considerable time. He
looked sad and forlorn and his eyes brimmed with tears. When he surfaced
from this pensive mood he appeared to recognize aspects of himself as if for
the first time. He spoke about persistent feelings of sadness, anxiety and
watchfulness, and he questioned whether these could be linked to his disturbing childhood experiences. It seemed that the recollection of these
state-dependent memories had started the process of unlocking the affective
components of John's unresolved trauma (Stern 1985). Despite the similarity in our ages, my primary countertransference at this point was that of a
benign, concerned parent seeking to understand and ameliorate a child's
confused state and emotional distress. Although the session had been challenging and intense, John seemed buoyed up and expressed the hope that
ghosts could finally be laid to rest. His positive affective response and dis-
closure of unresolved childhood trauma suggested that a secure-enough
therapeutic alliance had been speedily established.

Repetition of the trauma

During subsequent sessions, John and I tried to give meaning to what, in
symbolic terms, he was acting out unconsciously by means of his offending
behaviour. It seemed to me, at least in part, that he was re-enacting a destructive and self-destructive pattern of behaviour in identification with the
'bad', traumatized eight-year-old child who had been unable to mourn
Ricky's death and was left carrying a tremendous burden of guilt. My
hypothesis was that an aspect of this re-enactment involved John being
drawn compulsively and repetitively to stand accused in the dock of a court,
thereby reliving the trauma and, at the same time, confirming his negative
core assumption or fantasy of himself as a bad, guilty person. Moreover, I
wondered whether the experience of being adjudged guilty and sentenced
to a period of incarceration had the temporary effect of assuaging John's
deep and pervasive sense of badness. This hypothesis rang true for John and
became a key therapeutic metaphor in our work (Stern 1985). Further, the
co-construction of significant events in John's childhood seemed to go
some way towards filling gaps in his personal history by beginning to
provide his fragmented experience with coherent narrative meaning
(Holmes 1996; Main 1991; Main et al. 1985). John elaborated on these
thoughts, saying that he feels safe and secure in prison, whereas on the
outside he is continually assailed by feelings of panic, anxiety and an

impending sense of danger, as if something dreadful were about to happen. In phenomenological terms, it would seem that John's unresolved trauma was experienced as 'a fear of a breakdown that had already happened' but had not been 'remembered', and thus was prone to being repeated at an unconscious level of functioning (Winnicott 1974, p.104).

Continuous assessment and ongoing intervention

At this point in my work with John my assessment had crystallized. Keeping relevant research findings in mind, I based my assessment of John on the theoretical premise that cognitive-affective states associated with his traumatic experiences had been subject to perceptual distortion, defensive exclusion and selective inattention (Bowlby 1980; Main *et al.* 1985). In line with Herman (1992), I surmised that the lack of an appropriate response to John's trauma had left him with a pervasive sense of alienation and disconnection in his relationships. I concluded, therefore, that the main therapeutic task was to facilitate a process of mourning by assisting him to make connections between detached, split-off thoughts and emotional affect associated with the traumatic events he had described (Bowlby 1973, 1979, 1988; Spezzano 1993). This work had, of course, already commenced to some extent during the assessment process, reflecting Stern's (1998) contention, noted above, that the search process is, in itself, therapeutic.

By this stage, John seemed committed to working on these unresolved issues and he stuck doggedly to the task, appearing to have an active need to tell his story and create a narrative. He admitted to being desperate for a drink after the previous session, but told me that instead he had made a conscious effort to think about what we had discussed. In line with Main's (1991) research into metacognitive monitoring, I had enjoined John in quite a directive way to develop a dialogue with himself. This involved using thought and his mind in a new and novel way so as to contain and assimilate raw psychic pain, and stepping outside of himself in order to observe his thoughts, feelings and behaviour. Following Fonagy *et al.'s* (1997) development of Main's (1991) research, these strategies were designed to enhance John's reflective function, thereby increasing his capacity to contemplate and understand both his own and others' mental states in a coherent way. The overall therapeutic aim was to assist John better to regulate his emotional and mental anguish without becoming overwhelmed to the extent that he acted out by misusing alcohol and behaving violently. As we have seen, the process involved the evocation of key traumatic experiences preserved in his childhood memories, making these available for dyadic regulation and ideational elaboration (Schore 1994; Spezzano 1993; Stern 1985).

As the weeks went by, John reported that he was keeping his drinking within sensible limits. He looked healthier, with clear eyes and a better colour to his complexion, and he seemed more at ease with himself. The impression of John being less anxious and conflicted was quite pronounced, and he related how, prior to this improvement, the mere act of leaving home to catch a bus to the town centre would engender anxiety, panic and a sense of danger which he would quell with drink. John also reported noting changes in the way he was responding to others, and they to him, acknowledging that in the past he would often deal with his aggressive impulses by provoking aggression in others, thereby giving himself a ready excuse to be violent and resort to alcohol misuse. He spoke of decorating his flat, and we came to see this as an external manifestation of the tidying up his inner life was undergoing. He went on to recall feeling acutely persecuted and paranoid as a child following Ricky's death, saying that he lived in a state of fear and anxiety about the prospect of being attacked by Ricky's family because 'they thought I'd killed Ricky'. Such fears may well have been realistic but, in my opinion, were also likely to have been fuelled by fantasies of retaliation which flourished in the absence of an affectively attuned, containing parental response. It seemed to me that John's later violent behaviour reflected Greenberg, Speltz and DeKlyen's (1993) proposal that children who are insecurely attached develop an internal working model of relationships characterized by anger, mistrust and hostility. As noted above, Main *et al.*'s (1985) longitudinal research supports the proposition that internal working models developed in childhood tend to persist over time.

Certainly, lack of trust became a major issue for John as he developed into adolescence and adulthood, together with clinical issues of control, autonomy, dependence, separation and loss. He spoke of his surprise at being able to talk to me about personal and painful matters, and he went on to risk rejection by asking if he could contact me after his parole licence had ended, should a crisis arise. I agreed to this request, viewing it in terms of an adult relational need rather than an infantile desire, and, as mentioned previously, said that I would like to have a follow-up meeting in any event. This exchange seemed to indicate that John was internalizing his relationship with me in the form of a secure-enough base, but that he still needed to feel there would be the opportunity for direct proximity-seeking should something untoward occur (Bowlby 1980, 1988). I was encouraged by the fact that John was beginning to make links between his traumatic childhood experiences and the anxiety, panic and aggression manifested in later years. He seemed increasingly able to appraise the significance and meaning of these distressing affects (Schore 1994), and to use the working alliance, or developing attachment relationship, to negotiate and reorganize unresolved clinical issues (Stern 1985).

Childhood amnesia/dissociation

Some confirmation of this progress occurred towards the end of the session. John related that when he was aged 28 and on the point of marrying, 'My mother told me I'd changed when I was eight'. Apparently, she had offered no explanation as to why this should have happened. Significantly, John went on to say that, to this day, no one in his family has ever alluded to Ricky's death, adding that he had suffered 'amnesia' between the ages of eight and eleven. It seemed to me that, lacking the emotional and cognitive capacities to assimilate the traumatic event unaided, John's only option was to resort to a form of dissociation; that is, an altered, detached state of consciousness (de Zulueta 1993; Herman 1992). For whatever reason, it would appear that John's parents were insensitive to his needs and unable to help him deal with the aftermath of the tragedy, perhaps misguidedly believing that ignoring the event was for the best. Indeed, there was nothing to suggest they were intentionally cruel or malign but rather that for reasons stemming from their own attachment histories, they were defensively excluding from consciousness John's attachment behaviour cues (Main *et al.* 1985).

The information provided by John, when I listened to it with relevant research findings in mind, led me to surmise that his parents had been unable to comfort and soothe his distress because of the fear this evoked in themselves (Lyons-Ruth and Jacobovitz 1999; Schore 1994). In this case, it is likely that John came to perceive his parents' dismissing, non-reflective response to his fear as both frightening and frightened, and so to experience his own state of arousal as a danger signal for abandonment (Main and Hesse 1990). In consequence of the family's disorganized caregiving–

attachment system, and the insecurity to which this relational matrix gave rise, it would seem that John's attentional strategies were compromised and that he developed an exquisite vulnerability to trauma (Lyons-Ruth and Jacobovitz 1999). His subsequent behaviour suggests that he adapted to this unhappy situation by inhibiting his mentalizing capacity, becoming increasingly detached from his parents and from aspects of his subjective experience, particularly affective states of anxiety, fear and rage (Fonagy 1999). Although John's mother was physically present, she appears to have been inaccessible psychologically and emotionally, and therefore unavailable to help John develop the capacity for self-regulation of powerful negative affect. His subsequent misuse of addictive substances may be seen as having its aetiology in this very incapacity, with first drugs and then alcohol being used to suppress dreaded psychobiological states and hence restore a semblance of affect regulation (Schore 1994). In this context, it would seem reasonable to hypothesize that John's childhood attachment to his mother was characterized by what Settlage *et al.* (1990) and Schore (1994) term 'proximal separations'.

Discussion

John's material brought to mind research that addresses the aetiology of cognitive-affective disturbance in children. For example, Liotti (1992), following Main (1991), posits a connection between disorganized/disoriented attachment and dissociative disorders. According to Liotti's hypothesis, the child's disorganized/disoriented attachment behaviour corresponds to the construction of an internal working model of self and attachment figure that is multiple and incoherent, as opposed to singular and coherent. Liotti (1992) suggests that a multiple internal working model of this kind may predispose the child to enter a state of dissociation in the face of further traumatic experiences. Similarly, Davies and Frawley (1994), in their work with adult survivors of childhood sexual abuse, view dissociation as existing on a continuum, with multiple personality disorder or dissociative identity disorder (MPD/DID) representing the most extreme form of mental defence against severe, protracted trauma. This opinion is shared by Mollon (1996) who questions whether MPD/DID should be conceptualized as part of a broad grouping of trauma-based psychiatric disorders or as a unique form of personality organization deriving from dissociative and post-traumatic factors.

From a social constructivist perspective, Stern (1997) views cognition as an amalgam of thought and feeling and an integral aspect of a continuous phenomenological process operating within the interpersonal field. Under optimal conditions, this process functions to organize, structure and unify subjective experience, thereby providing the individual with a sense of coherence and meaning. However, Stern argues that experience may be split for defensive reasons in reaction to trauma and result in the isolation of emotion from mentation. Van der Kolk and Fisler (1995) found that, in effect, the traumatized subject is left in a state of 'speechless terror'. Lacking the words to describe the traumatic event or construct a coherent personal narrative, the individual experiences great difficulty in regulating internal states. Moreover, the authors' findings show that subjects traumatized in childhood experience more pervasive biological dysregulation than those first traumatized in adulthood. In both instances, however, the traumatic incident is initially 'remembered' in the form of fragmented somatosensory experiences (van der Kolk 1994). Similarly, McDougall (1985, 1989) argues that cumulative trauma consequent on a mother's insensitive way of handling and interacting with her infant may, during the course of development, lead to a split between word-presentations and affect-laden experiences. McDougall adopts Nemiah's (1978) and Sifneos's (1973) concept of alexithymia – that is, the inability to recognize and describe discrete emotional states. She postulates that affective reactions associated with the traumatizing caregiving process are either avoided or rapidly ejected from consciousness. As a result of this developmental failure, the individual may be susceptible to psychosomatic illness in later life.

Fonagy *et al.* (1997), in building on Main's (1991) research into metacognition, posit that the child's capacity to explore the mind of the other and develop as a thinking and feeling being arises within the matrix of a secure attachment relationship. Insecurity of attachment, on the other hand, undermines the child's capacity to reflect on and integrate mental experience. Such individuals, it is argued, lack insight into the representational basis of human interaction and intentionality. This being so, they resort to concrete solutions to intrapsychic and interpersonal problems, attempting to control their subjective states and self-cohesion through physical experience such as substance misuse, physical violence and crime.

Van der Kolk (1989), in reviewing studies pointing to the underlying physiology of attachment, posits that endorphin releasers are laid down in the early months of life within the context of attachment to caregivers with different styles of caregiving. He concludes that affectively intense experiences are accompanied by the release of these neurochemicals, and that this psychobiological process comes to be associated to states both of security and of trauma. With these findings in mind, Mitchell (2000) comments on the seemingly addictive propensity for repeatedly forging intimate adult relationships redolent of ties to early objects, even when these are traumatic. He suggests that such behaviour may reflect neurochemical, as well as psychological, derivatives.

Much of the aforementioned theory and research is derived from Bowlby (1988), who presented a paper in 1979 entitled 'On knowing what you are not supposed to know, and feeling what you are not supposed to feel'. Here, Bowlby cites findings by Cain and Fast (1972) to show how distorted communications between parent and child, which disconfirm the child's thoughts and feelings of real events, may engender intense guilt. Cognitive dissonance of this kind may lead the child to develop a chronic distrust of other people and of his or her own senses, together with a tendency to find everything unreal.

The response of John's parents (though he spoke only of his mother in this context) would seem to suggest that emotional states were characteristically dismissed and deflected. Moreover, as we have learned from John, his mother appears to have entered prolonged periods of denial during his childhood, seemingly prompted by feelings of shame and embarrassment, as evinced by her refusal to acknowledge the reality of her husband's actual employment status. As noted above, research has demonstrated a significant link between such parental characteristics in terms of a dismissing narrative style on the one hand and insecure-avoidant attachment behaviour in children on the other (Main 1991; Main et al. 1985; Main and Weston 1982). Further, as previously pointed out, children with an insecure-avoidant pattern of attachment have been found to show a marked lack of empathy towards peers in distress. Indeed, Main and Weston (1982) observed a distinct tendency in such insecurely attached children to behave in an aggressive and hostile way, as did Grossman and Grossman (1991). In John's case – as with so many men who suffer unresolved childhood trauma – substance misuse and violent behaviour followed. The links between these factors were, again, highly reminiscent of the work on trauma by de Zulueta (1993) and Herman (1992). They also accord with findings cited by West and George (1999). These show that male perpetrators of adult relational violence report a high incidence of childhood histories of severe abuse and trauma (Downey, Khoun and Feldman 1997; Herman and van der Kolk 1987; Kalmuss 1984).

Session eight: gender identity

During the eighth meeting with John issues surrounding sexuality and gender were discussed. Given the avoidant pattern of attachment behaviour characterizing John's adult intimate relationships, I silently questioned the security of his masculine identity. Despite being a stocky, powerfully built and somewhat gruff and macho man, John was sporting a long ponytail hairstyle. Moreover, as already noted, he generally adopted a passive, non-aggressive stance, seemingly disowning authentic thoughts and feelings in a way reminiscent of Winnicott's (1988) concept of the false self. John's style of relating at this point elicited feelings within me of inauthenticity and emotional disconnection. Thus prompted, I asked myself whether he might be employing a feminine identification in his interpersonal relationships as a defence against being overwhelmed by anger and rage deriving from archaic, ambivalent feelings of separation from and engulfment by the symbiotic mother (Stoller 1988).

On discussing the way in which men and women incorporate both masculine and feminine attributes, John's behavioural responses were initially aversive. His reaction put me in mind of the fact that heterosexual men not infrequently form temporary homosexual liaisons when imprisoned for any length of time. On discussing this delicate subject, I keenly observed John's behaviour for any indications of intrusiveness or persecution as I sought to establish a sense of emotional connection or intersubjective relatedness with him (Stern 1985, 1998). Again, I felt rather parental in the countertransference, as though fulfilling functions that were containing, emotionally, as well as informative on a cognitive level. The interactional aspect of the therapeutic process would seem to confirm the importance of applying a developmental model in clinical work with offenders, given the high incidence of unresolved childhood trauma in the offender population.

Following these exchanges John was able to elaborate on the experiences he had had while in prison. More generally, we explored how heterosexual men with an insecure sense of gender identity may manifest homosexual panic and deal with feelings of shame and anger by denying aspects of their sexuality that create anxiety, and instead projecting these onto others. A dialogue developed, exploring the way in which defensive behaviour of this kind, allied to a morbid fear of difference, may act as a touchstone for violence that targets minority groups, for example, 'gay bashing' and racist attacks. Although the latter appeared not to be features of John's pattern of offending behaviour, this discussion seemed further to enhance his reflective function or mentalizing capacity. He appeared gradually more able to perceive others as separate from himself and as having distinct feelings, intentions and desires (Fonagy *et al.* 1997).

Session nine: relapse and transference issues

Before the ninth session, John attended the funeral of a family friend. During this session, John volunteered the information that he had consumed about six pints of beer at the wake. We discussed this in the context of what the death of his friend had evoked in John. He said that his predominant feelings were of anxiety and guilt. John linked these feelings directly to a fearful anticipation that I would 'misjudge' him for drinking. I wondered whether this dynamic again constituted a transference re-enactment connected with John's childhood trauma, particularly the unmourned loss of Ricky. At that time, whether in reality or in fantasy, John did indeed feel misjudged and blamed for Ricky's death. Further, as we have seen, it would appear that his parents' response lacked empathy and was dismissive of his emotional pain and distress. On an unconscious level, therefore, John may well have been expecting a similar response from me, as it would seem that I was being attributed an archaic parental role in the transference (Sandler and Sandler 1998). His relapse provided the opportunity to resolve some of these issues, in that it enabled him to re-experience his traumatic attachment to a dismissing, emotionally unavailable parent in a way that was bearable (Holmes 1996). My task at such times was to survive John's omnipotent destructive fantasies without collapsing or retaliating (Winnicott 1988). This 'holding' response appeared to help John recognize my existence as a separate person, available to be used and related to intersubjectively (Benjamin 1995). Moreover, by relating to John in this unfamiliar way, I became a new developmental object, different from the original pathogenic object being sought in transferential re-enactments (Fonagy 1998; Hurry 1998; Schore 1994).

Session ten: the aetiology of John's violent behaviour

John opened the tenth session by saying he felt on an 'even keel', adding that he was continuing to spend a good deal of time thinking about past experiences, as well as monitoring his thoughts and feelings in the here-and-now, particularly when in an emotionally disturbed mood. At such times, in line with my suggestion, he would try to trace the immediate trigger of the affective distress and then make links between the past and the present. The therapeutic purpose of setting John this 'homework' was to encourage him to stay with the dreaded lived experience for long enough to reflect on and attempt to self-regulate primitive, unintegrated affective states. These problematic experiences would then be brought to sessions for collaborative exploration of their aetiology and meaning. My expectation was that this therapeutic intervention would gradually assist John to develop the capacity to elaborate and transform disturbing bodily experiences into a coherent narrative (Schore 1994; Spezzano 1993; Stern 1998). With regard to this process, Schore (1994) emphasizes that the therapist's own tolerance of affects will critically determine the range and types of emotion that may be explored or disavowed in the transference–countertransference relationship. It may be accepted that this consideration is of particular relevance in a forensic setting because the practitioner is often starkly confronted with the bleaker aspects of human experience and the darker side of human behaviour.

The session focused in a direct way on John's violence to women. This issue had been a delicate subject up until this point because his violent behaviour, especially in regard to women, jarred with his ideal self, leaving him feeling deeply shamed. At our first meeting John had displayed a pronounced tendency to minimize his culpability, and blame the victim. Indeed, we will recall that he had completely denied the offence initially and was convicted following a jury trial. John's capacity for denial brought to mind his mother who, as we have seen, deployed the self-same defence mechanism with equal conviction. In this context, I have learned from hard experience that working precipitously with denial is clinically sterile and counterproductive, generating intense feelings of frustration and rage in the participants as early parent–child roles and patterns of interaction get re-enacted in the transference–countertransference matrix. Fortunately, by this stage in my relationship with John a secure-enough working alliance had been forged, and so the time seemed ripe for us to work on this form of defensive behaviour. As we did so, John's split-off affect of shame and anger became increasingly available for interactive regulation. This process facilitated his gradual acceptance and active responsibility for his violent behaviour, and an enhancement of his ability to empathize with Sylvia.

My thinking in respect of John's violence was that he had split off states of anger, rage and yearning as a child, primarily in relation to his mother. This adaptive defence was needed because separations from her and the family had been managed insensitively, as had the later trauma in respect of Ricky, reflecting the family's disorganized caregiving–attachment system (Lyons-Ruth and Jacobovitz 1999). As noted above, the effects of these events and relational patterns had become frozen in time, being represented internally as perseverative, non-reflective, nonverbal procedural memories in the form of pre-symbolic interaction structures and internal working models. These mental models were, in turn, expressed in violent behavioural enactments in John's relationships, particularly at times of intense interpersonal stress (Beebe et al. 1992; Fonagy et al. 1997; Main et al. 1985; Schore 1994; Stern 1985, 1998; West and George 1999). This hypothesis received some confirmation when John went on to speak of becoming angry with a man who had recently beaten his wife. On discussing the incident, it became clear that much of the anger generated in John was not only because of the man's physical abuse of the woman. His feelings were also inflamed because this person had subsequently flatly denied that the assault had taken place, even though all his acquaintances knew full well that it had.

This scenario appeared to have powerful associations and resonances with John's childhood, in that, in a similar way, everyone had known that Ricky had drowned. As we have seen, despite the reality of this traumatic event, John's emotional and cognitive experience had been denied or, at best, unacknowledged, with Ricky's death becoming, in effect, a well kept family secret (Pincus and Dare 1990). In this way John's capacity for metacognitive monitoring was fatally compromised, since the information he was receiving about the traumatic event was contradictory and distorted. This, in turn, seems to have led to the development of a multiple, incoherent internal working model in respect of his attachment to his mother, and a concomitant state of dissociation (Liotti 1992; Main 1991). As Solomon and George (1996) found, disorganized attachment is characterized by controlling behaviour towards the attachment figure in the context of the child's feeling abandoned, helpless and vulnerable. This fraught situation is likely to have been exacerbated in John's case by the separations he had experienced at a younger age, when hospitalized and subjected to surgical intervention. The clinical evidence attested to these factors having contributed to the development of a predominantly insecure-avoidant pattern of attachment organization which, in line with Fonagy *et al.* (1997), I viewed as an adaptive defence mustered in the face of unattuned caregiving. Moreover, the overall clinical picture suggested that insecurity stemming from separation anxiety had interfered with John's capacity to differentiate himself psychologically from his attachment figure and thereby attain a state of 'mature dependence' (Fairbairn 1996). In this context, it is of interest to note that West and George (1999) suggest that psychological merging may explain the conflict between engulfment and abandonment that appears to be so characteristic of the physically abusive male.

As we have seen, Bowlby (1973) emphasizes that anger at an attachment figure who fails to provide the expected comfort at times of stress is a normal and integral aspect of the attachment system. It would appear that this safety valve was not available to John, as he lacked both external and internal permission to experience disturbing negative affect (Spezzano 1993). He had little option, therefore, but to develop a defensive organization against anger and rage, in part, identifying with the dismissing, non-reflective qualities and characteristics of his relationship with his mother as a way of defending against feelings of guilt and anxiety (Fonagy *et al.* 1997; A. Freud 1993). When these mental defences were overwhelmed, John's split-off, infantile, murderous rage was acted out with the violent, destructive force of an adult.

In the latest incident of this repetitive pattern, this internal dynamic was externalized, being displaced or redirected from John's original primary attachment figure (his mother) and projected onto Sylvia whom, at the point of the breakup of their relationship, he perceived as untrustworthy, rejecting and abandoning. Indeed, John's 'theory of mind' appears to have led him to expect betrayal and misattuned regulation at the hands of Sylvia (Fonagy *et al.* 1997; Schore 1994; West and George 1999), and so she became a vehicle for his intolerable and persecutory self states, that is, for the internalized aspects of his relationship with his mother that he experienced as frightening and unmanageable (Fonagy 1999). Further, aggression, rather than love, seems to have become an emotionally 'rewarding' way for John to express his ambivalent world of object relations (Dicks 1993).

Fear of abandonment, then, seems to have been the primary affect that led to the sudden activation of John's attachment behavioural system and identification with the disorganized internal working model of his relationship with his mother. As already noted, a salient feature of this mental model was John's expectation that his primary attachment figure would not be available or accessible at times of affective stress to provide comfort and protection (Schore 1994; West and George 1999). The clinical evidence, combined with John's forensic history, indicated that his mentalizing capacity was prone to becoming disorganized by intense separation anxiety and dysregulated fear, shame, hatred and rage when he felt threatened by the loss of a female partner with whom he had formed an intimate attachment.

The theoretical model of male violence proposed here converges with that delineated by West and George (1999). These authors contend that intimate adult relational violence is rooted in attachment disorganization, viewing this pattern as inextricably linked to unresolved trauma and to a segregated representational system characterized by dysregulated affect and pathological mourning. West and George (1999) suggest that the perpetrator's defensive and tightly controlled regulation of his attachment system breaks down at the moment of the assault as a consequence of his becoming flooded with negative affect and distorted perceptions deriving from his personal trauma. This formulation is consistent with my clinical experience and is detailed in diagrammatic form in Figure 4.1.

With regard to the index offence, the significance for John of Sylvia's perceived sexual infidelity lay in the fact that it represented her independence of mind and psychological separateness. In my opinion, any move by her towards a separate, independent existence would have conflicted with the explicit and implicit role expectations that John had brought to the relationship, being construed as a threat to his sense of security (Dicks 1993). Thus, John's violence was, in part, a frantic attempt to control Sylvia so as to ensure her continued availability, both to protect him against infantile loneliness and immature dependence (Dicks 1993; Fairbairn 1996) and to carry the alien, persecutory parts of himself (Fonagy 1999). The thought of being abandoned by Sylvia instilled terror in John because loss was experienced as a re-traumatization and, therefore, as a threat to the coherence and stability of his sense of self (de Zulueta 1993; Fonagy 1999; Herman 1992).

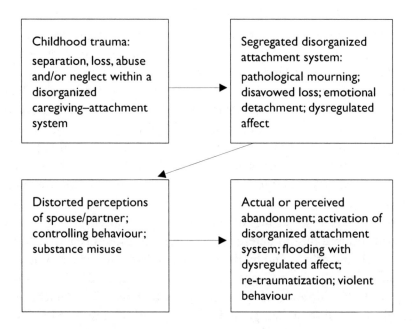

Figure 4.1 Relationship of childhood trauma to violent offending behaviour in adulthood

I was struck, moreover, by the fact that John's vicious assault on Sylvia had been triggered at the very point when she denied sexual infidelity, and that John continued to beat her mercilessly until she told him the 'truth'. Again, I silently wondered to what extent this ghastly episode was a re-creation in the present of unresolved aspects of John's childhood relationship with his mother, who throughout his life adamantly denied the reality of his traumatic experience (van der Kolk 1989, 1994). Thus, it would appear that John's violence had the effect not only of making him feel coherent and real, but also of eliciting from Sylvia the response he so desperately needed to hear – a voice that validated the 'truth' of his subjective experience (Fonagy 1999). Clearly, John's violent behaviour could easily have escalated out of control and led to a charge of murder or manslaughter, as in the case of other insecurely attached men who respond with extreme violence when abandoned by their female partners. Sharing these thoughts with John seemed to have a sobering effect on him and again engendered a state of deep, prolonged and silent reflection.

Session twelve: indications of change

At the twelfth session, John announced with great confidence that he no longer thought of himself as an alcoholic. I was surprised to see that he had had his hair cut short. I silently wondered whether this dramatic change in his personal appearance was emblematic of a firmer sense of masculine identity, together with a concomitant lessening of his need to defend against feelings of anger and aggression. In terms of Mahler, Pine and Bergman's (1985) process of separation-individuation, I asked myself whether John's apparent sense of a more secure male identity indicated the achievement of a higher level of psychological differentiation from the internalized symbiotic mother.

John again spoke of feeling more at peace with himself, seeing this as manifested in his ability to entertain more positive thoughts and feelings about himself and others, and by the fact that he had effected a reconciliation with his family and had got himself a job. He then drew a creative analogy with a childhood situation, telling me that he had underachieved educationally because he had gone deaf in one ear as a result of his ENT problems. Having been seated at the rear of the classroom, John had been unable to hear with clarity what the teacher was saying and his schoolwork suffered accordingly. Once this problem had been identified, John was brought forward to a front-row desk and subsequently came top of the class. With a twinkle in his eye, John said that now the problem of his unresolved trauma had been recognized he could move to the top of the class in terms of his emotional and psychological development!

Though clearly there were elements of affectionate teasing and idealization in this comment, it seemed to me that his narrative competence had markedly improved, in that he now appeared able to speak in a coherent, concise and plausible way about painful childhood events. This new-found autobiographical capacity seemed to indicate that John had begun to mourn and thereby integrate previously unassimilated traumatic experiences (Holmes 1996). Thus, from an attachment theory perspective, the positive therapeutic change reported by John and observed by me indicated that maladaptive internal working models of himself in relation to others, as well as to the traumatic event of Ricky's death, had begun to be modified and updated. In addition to the improvement in John's narrative intelligibility, change was manifested in his enhanced sense of security and reflective capacity.

The final session

At the final meeting, John reiterated his belief that a 'weight' had been lifted from him. Specifically, he spoke of no longer feeling persistently anxious, paranoid and persecuted, or of experiencing a deep and pervasive sense of sadness and depression. The abatement of these symptoms indicated that an enhancement had occurred in his capacity to use thought and language to transform dysregulated bodily experiences into subjective states of consciousness (Schore 1994). John was still in employment and managing his drinking. I confirmed that I would contact him in six months' time and that he could telephone me in between times, should the need arise. He expressed a sense of loss and frustration at not having had this kind of help years ago. He also questioned why, in over 30 years of being involved in the criminal justice system, no one had thought to talk with him about his early traumatic experiences, saying he felt that much of his life had been 'wasted' as a result. This situation emphasizes again the importance of obtaining relevant information about the offender's formative experiences and developmental history as part of a process of effective assessment, particularly in brief work. I thought that John's feelings of loss were being conflated with sadness at the ending of our relationship. I acknowledged the paradox he seemed to be highlighting – that even positive change involves loss in one form or another. On a positive note, I concluded that John's new-found ability to express attachment-related affective experiences was, in itself, evidence of the progress he had accomplished during the past eight months.

The therapeutic process

The progress made by John was dependent on his ability gradually to organize and integrate error-correcting information received as an ongoing aspect of the therapeutic process (Bowlby 1980, 1988; Main et al. 1985; Peterfreund 1983). Following Tronick et al. (1978), I viewed this process as consisting, in significant degree, of the moment-to-moment micro-repair of attunement or misaligned interaction – an intersubjective process operating at the level of procedural or implicit relational knowledge (Stern et al. 1998). This process was informed by the tracking and matching of subtle and dramatic shifts in John's mood-state as he narrated his story (Schore 1994). This interactive process led, in turn, to the recognition of a shared subjective reality (Fonagy 1998). By these means, my facilitating behaviours combined with John's capacity for attachment. Though operating largely out of conscious awareness, this reciprocal process permitted the development of a working alliance or attachment relationship (Schore 1994) that was secure enough to facilitate a collaborative exploration of painful, unresolved clinical issues linked to his misuse of alcohol and violent offending behaviour. As we have seen, key aspects of this intersubjective and reparative process were the dyadic regulation of dreaded states charged with intense negative affect (Schore 1994) and the co-construction of a coherent narrative (Holmes 1996). Thus, I became a new developmental object, the relationship with whom disconfirmed John's pathogenic transference expectations and enhanced his capacity for reflective thought (Fonagy 1998; Hurry 1998; Schore 1994). From a neurobiological perspective, Schore (1994) postulates that the process of affect regulation links nonverbal and verbal representational domains of the brain, thereby facilitating the transfer of implicit information in the right hemisphere to explicit or declarative systems in the left.

Follow-up contact

As agreed, I contacted John for a follow-up discussion six months later. His progress had been sustained, in that he was still in work, keeping his consumption of alcohol within sensible limits, and had not re-offended. Prior to the ending of John's supervisory period, I had liaised with his GP who, in consultation with John, agreed to refer him to the local mental health resource centre. John had attended an assessment session there with a clinical psychologist. It was mutually agreed that no further work was needed at that stage.

CONCLUSION

Given the wide incidence of intimate adult relational violence in Western society, understanding the clinical issues underlying such behaviour, and developing an effective therapeutic model to address the problem, are a pressing social concern. An important consideration in this context is the traumatic effect on children who repeatedly witness scenes of abusive male violence in the home (Cawson *et al.* 2000). I would argue that an attachment theory conceptualization, as outlined in this study and proposed by West and George (1999), has a significant contribution to make in this area of work. A diagram of the therapeutic model under discussion is set out in Figure 4.2.

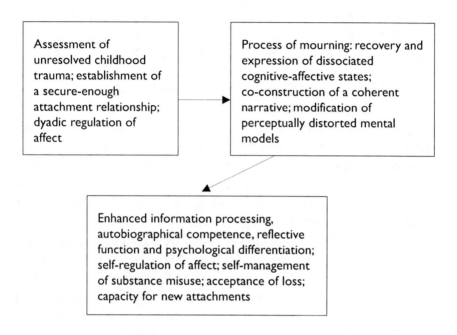

Figure 4.2 Conceptual structure of the proposed therapeutic model

Although Figure 4.2 indicates a linear therapeutic progression, in practice there is considerable interweaving of the clinical issues as these are worked on, in collaboration with the offender within an intersubjective process, as outlined above.

With regard to my brief intervention with John, it remains to be seen whether this will prove to be effective in the long term. I was keenly aware that far more could have been achieved therapeutically, not least in consolidating the progress he had made in regulating his affective states without resorting to alcohol misuse. This, however, was not a viable option, given the constraints of time and resources obtaining within the probation service and the limited period of his parole licence. Nevertheless, I consider that the work undertaken with John helped to resolve the childhood trauma underlying his adult violent offending behaviour. This, in turn, enhanced his sense of security and capacity for narrative competence and reflective function, thereby strengthening his ability to activate alternative models of interaction and take the other's perspective. These interlinking positive therapeutic changes should potentiate further personal growth and so provide John with a greater ability to empathize with others and make more moral, reasoned choices in the future (Fonagy and Target 1998; Holmes 1996).

More generally, I consider that this case study illustrates that it is not the traumatic childhood event in itself that is salient in personality development and adult psychopathology, but rather the characteristic caregiving–attachment system within which the child experiences the trauma. As noted above, research has demonstrated that the securely attached child develops the capacity to stay attentive and responsive to the environment, and to use error-correcting information to construct a coherent narrative when presented with scenarios involving separation and loss (Main 1991; Main and Hesse 1990; Main *et al.* 1985). It would seem reasonable to hypothesize, therefore, that the secure/autonomous adult has developed the mental capacity to process information more readily in the aftermath of a traumatic event than the insecure, disorganized subject whose ability to regulate states of arousal at moments of stress was compromised during early development. As Bowlby (1973, 1979) has observed, the quality of the emotional bond between the child and the caregiver will vitally influence whether mourning proceeds along a healthy path or takes a pathological course. From an attachment theory perspective, therefore, the overarching therapeutic task in my work with John was to help him to recover and express ambivalent thoughts and feelings linked to the trauma of unmourned childhood loss (Bowlby 1979).

Outcome

In a meta-analysis of outcome studies, Roth and Fonagy (1996) found that the extent to which ruptures of the working alliance were adequately addressed during the course of therapy was predictive of the efficacy of the intervention. The authors conclude that the relationship component is the common effective ingredient in positive outcomes. Their findings accord with my clinical experience in applying attachment theory in a probation setting, and would seem to confirm the respective findings of Schore (1994) and Stern *et al.* (1998), viz., that the interactive emotion-transacting aspect of the therapeutic encounter is the main mechanism of intrapsychic change.

Specific to a probation setting, it has been suggested that reconviction rates should be used to evaluate effectiveness and measure outcome (Chapman and Hough 1998). At the time of writing, John's name has not appeared on the local court list, nor have any requests for pre-sentence reports been received from non-local courts. It would seem reasonable to assume, therefore, that five years have elapsed since John last offended. Further, it may be accepted that identifying the links between John's insecure attachment, unresolved childhood trauma, emotional detachment, substance misuse and violent offending behaviour was vital in order to work with him both effectively and with expedition.

POSTSCRIPT

I met with John some six months after our follow-up contact to obtain his consent to publish an account of our work. He had remained largely free of symptoms of panic, persecution and depression, telling me, 'I feel a lot more confident than I used to,' and adding, 'I now think before I act.' John was still in work, even though this entails travelling some distance from his home. As we parted, he told me, 'I don't need the drink and violence any more because I've accepted myself for who I am.'

NOTE

1.   A version of this chapter was published by Whurr Publishers in 2000 in *Violent Children and Adolescents: Asking the Question Why*, edited by Gwyneth Boswell.

REFERENCES

Ainsworth, M., Blehar, M., Waters, E. and Walls, S. (1978) *Patterns of Attachment: Assessed in the Strange Situation and at Home.* Hillsdale, NJ: Lawrence Erlbaum.

Beebe, B., Jaffe, J. and Lachmann, F.M. (1992) 'A dyadic systems view of communication.' In N.J. Skolnick and S.C. Warshaw (eds) *Relational Perspectives in Psychoanalysis.* Hillsdale, NJ: The Analytic Press.

Beebe, B. and Lachmann, F.M. (1992) 'The contribution of mother–infant mutual influence to the origins of self- and object representations.' In N.J. Skolnick and S.C. Warshaw (eds) *Relational Perspectives in Psychoanalysis*. Hillsdale, NJ: The Analytic Press.

Benjamin, J. (1995) 'Recognition and destruction: An outline of intersubjectivity.' In *Like Subjects, Love Objects: Essays on Recognition and Sexual Difference*. New Haven, CT: Yale University Press.

Boswell, G. (1996) *Young and Dangerous: The Backgrounds and Careers of Section 53 Offenders*. Aldershot: Avebury.

Boswell, G. (1998) 'Research-minded practice with young offenders who commit grave crimes.' *Probation Journal 45*, 202–207.

Bowlby, J. (1969) *Attachment and Loss Vol. 1, Attachment*. London: Pimlico.

Bowlby, J. (1973) *Attachment and Loss Vol. 2, Separation: Anger and Anxiety*. London: Pimlico.

Bowlby, J. (1979) *The Making and Breaking of Affectional Bonds*. London: Routledge.

Bowlby, J. (1980) *Attachment and Loss Vol. 3, Loss: Sadness and Depression*. London: Pimlico.

Bowlby, J. (1988) *A Secure Base: Clinical Applications of Attachment Theory*. Bristol: Arrowsmith.

Cain, A.C. and Fast, I. (1972) 'Children's disturbed reactions to parent suicide.' In A.C. Cain (ed) *Survivors of Suicide*. Springfield, IL: C.C. Thomas.

Casement, P. (1990) *On Learning from the Patient*. London: Routledge.

Cawson, P., Watton, C., Brooker, S. and Kelly, G. (2000) *Child Maltreatment in the United Kingdom*. London: NSPCC Publications.

Chapman, T. and Hough, M. (1998) *Evidence-Based Practice: A Guide to Effective Practice*. HM Inspectorate of Probation. London: Home Office Publications Unit.

Davies, J.M. and Frawley, M.G. (1994) *Treating the Adult Survivor of Childhood Sexual Abuse*. New York: Basic Books.

de Zulueta, F. (1993) *From Pain to Violence: The Traumatic Roots of Destructiveness*. London: Whurr Publishers.

Dicks, H.V. (1993) *Marital Tensions: Clinical Studies Towards a Psychological Theory of Interaction*. London: Karnac Books.

Downey, G., Khoun, H. and Feldman, S. (1997) 'Early interpersonal trauma and later adjustment: The mediational role of rejection sensitivity.' In D. Cicchetti and S.L. Toth (eds) *Development Perspectives on Trauma: Theory, Research and Intervention*. Rochester, NY: University of Rochester Press.

Fairbairn, W.R.D. (1996) *Psychological Studies of the Personality.* London: Routledge.

Fonagy, P. (1998) 'Moments of change in psychoanalytic theory: Discussion of a new theory of psychic change.' *Infant Mental Health Journal 19* (3), 346–353.

Fonagy, P. (1999) 'The male perpetrator: The role of trauma and failures of mentalization in aggression against women – an attachment theory perspective.' Unpublished paper given at the 6th John Bowlby Memorial Lecture, London, 20 February 1999.

Fonagy, P. and Target, M. (1998) 'An interpersonal view of the infant.' In A. Hurry (ed) *Psychoanalysis and Developmental Therapy.* London: Karnac Books.

Fonagy, P., Target, M., Steele, M., Steele, H., Leigh, T., Levinson, A. and Kennedy, R. (1997) 'Morality, disruptive behaviour, borderline personality disorder, crime, and their relationships to security of attachment.' In L. Atkinson and K.J. Zucker (eds) *Attachment and Psychopathology.* New York: Guilford Press.

Freud, A. (1993) *The Ego And The Mechanisms Of Defence.* London: Karnac Books.

George, C., Kaplan, N. and Main, M. (1984) 'Adult Attachment Interview (1st edition).' Unpublished manuscript, Department of Psychology, University of California at Berkeley.

Greenberg, M.T., Speltz, M.L. and DeKlyen, M. (1993) 'The role of attachment in the early development of disruptive behaviour problems.' *Development and Psychopathology 5*, 191–213.

Grossman, K.E. and Grossman, K. (1991) 'Attachment quality as an organiser of emotional and behavioural responses in a longitudinal perspective.' In C.M. Parkes, J. Stevenson-Hinde and P. Marris (eds) *Attachment Across the Life Cycle.* London: Routledge.

Herman, J.L. (1992) *Trauma and Recovery.* New York: Basic Books.

Herman, J.L. and van der Kolk, B.A. (1987) 'Traumatic antecedents of borderline personality disorder.' In B.A. van der Kolk (ed) *Psychological Trauma.* Washington, DC: American Psychiatric Press.

Holmes, J. (1993) *John Bowlby and Attachment Theory.* London: Routledge.

Holmes, J. (1996) *Attachment, Intimacy, Autonomy: Using Attachment Theory in Adult Psychotherapy.* New York: Jason Aronson.

Hurry, A. (1998) 'Psychoanalysis and developmental therapy.' In A. Hurry (ed) *Psychoanalysis and Developmental Therapy.* London: Karnac Books.

Kalmuss, D. (1984) 'The intergenerational transmission of marital aggression.' *Journal of Marriage and the Family 46*, 11–19.

Liotti, G. (1992) 'Disorganized/disoriented attachment in the etiology of the dissociative disorders.' *Dissociation 4*, 196–204.

Lyons-Ruth, K. and Jacobovitz, D. (1999) 'Attachment disorganization: Unresolved loss, relational violence and lapses in behavioural and attentional strategies.' In J. Cassidy and P.R. Shaver (eds) *Handbook of Attachment: Theory, Research and Clinical Applications.* New York: Guilford Press.

Mahler, M.S., Pine, F. and Bergman, A. (1985) *The Psychological Birth of the Human Infant: Symbiosis and Individuation.* London: Karnac Books.

Main, M. (1991) 'Metacognitive knowledge, metacognitive monitoring, and singular (coherent) vs multiple (incoherent) models of attachment: Findings and directions for future research.' In C.M. Parkes, J. Stevenson-Hinde and P. Marris (eds) *Attachment Across the Life Cycle.* London: Routledge.

Main, M. and Hesse, E. (1990) 'Parents' unresolved traumatic experiences are related to infant disorganized attachment status: Is frightened and/or frightening parental behaviour the linking mechanism?' In M. Greenberg, D. Cicchetti and E.M. Cummings (eds) *Attachment in the Preschool Years: Theory, Research and Intervention.* Chicago: University of Chicago Press.

Main, M., Kaplan, N. and Cassidy, J. (1985) 'Security in infancy, childhood, and adulthood: A move to the level of representation.' In I. Bretherton and E. Waters (eds) *Growing Points in Attachment: Theory and Research.* Monographs of the Society for Research in Child Development. Chicago: University of Chicago Press.

Main, M. and Weston, D. (1982) 'Avoidance of the attachment figure in infancy.' In C.M. Parkes and J. Stevenson-Hinde (eds) *The Place of Attachment in Human Behaviour.* London: Tavistock.

Maroda, K.J. (1991) *The Power of Countertransference: Innovations in Analytic Technique.* New York: John Wiley and Sons.

McDougall, J. (1985) *Theatres of the Mind: Illusion and Truth on the Psychoanalytic Stage.* London: Free Association Books.

McDougall, J. (1989) *Theatres of the Body: A Psychoanalytical Approach to Psychosomatic Illness.* London: Free Association Books.

Mitchell, S.A. (2000) *Relationality: From Attachment to Intersubjectivity.* Hillsdale, NJ: The Analytic Press.

Mollon, P. (1996) *Multiple Selves, Multiple Voices: Working with Trauma, Violation and Dissociation.* Chichester: John Wiley and Sons.

Nemiah, J.C. (1978) 'Alexithymia and psychosomatic illness.' *Journal of Continuing Education in Psychiatry (1978),* 25–37.

Peterfreund, E. (1983) *The Process of Psychoanalytic Therapy.* New York: The Analytic Press.

Pincus, L. and Dare, C. (1990) *Secrets in the Family.* London: Faber and Faber.

Roth, A. and Fonagy, P. (1996) *What Works for Whom: Limitations and Implications of the Research Literature.* New York: Guilford Press.

Sandler, J. and Sandler, A-M. (1998) *Internal Objects Revisited.* London: Karnac Books.

Schore, A.N. (1994) *Affect Regulation and the Origin of the Self: The Neurobiology of Emotional Development.* Hillsdale, NJ: Lawrence Erlbaum.

Settlage, C.F., Rosenthal, J., Spielman, P.M., Gassner, S., Afterman, J., Bemesderfer, S. and Kolodny, S. (1990) 'An exploratory study of mother–child interaction during the second year of life.' *Journal of the American Psychoanalytic Association 38,* 705–731.

Sifneos, P.E. (1973) 'The prevalence of "alexithymic" characteristics in psychosomatic patients.' *Psychotherapy and Psychosomatics 22,* 255–262.

Slade, A. (1999) 'Attachment theory and research: Implications for the theory and practice of individual psychotherapy with adults.' In J. Cassidy and P.R. Shaver (eds) *Handbook of Attachment: Theory, Research and Clinical Applications.* New York: Guilford.

Spezzano, C. (1993) *Affect in Psychoanalysis: A Clinical Synthesis.* Hillsdale, NJ: The Analytic Press.

Solomon, J. and George, C. (1996) 'Defining the caregiving system: Toward a theory of caregiving.' *Infant Mental Health Journal 17,* 183–197.

Stern, D.B. (1997) *Unformulated Experience: From Dissociation to Imagination in Psychoanalysis.* Hillsdale, NJ: The Analytic Press.

Stern, D.N. (1985) *The Interpersonal World of the Infant: A View from Psychoanalysis and Developmental Psychology.* New York: Basic Books.

Stern, D.N. (1998) *The Motherhood Constellation: A Unified View of Parent–Infant Psychotherapy.* London: Karnac Books.

Stern, D.N., Sander, L.W., Nahum, J.P., Harrison, A.M., Lyons-Ruth, K., Morgan, A.C., Bruschweiler-Stern, N. and Tronick, E.Z. (1998) 'The process of therapeutic change involving implicit knowledge: Some implications of developmental observations for adult psychotherapy.' *Infant Mental Health Journal 19* (3), 300–308.

Stoller, R.J. (1986) *Perversion: The Erotic Form of Hatred.* London: Karnac Books.

Tronick, E., Als, H., Adams, L., Wise, S. and Brazelton, T.B. (1978) 'The infant's response to entrapment between contradictory messages in face-to-face interaction.' *Journal of American Child Psychiatry 17*, 1–13.

Tyson, P. and Tyson, R.L. (1990) *Psychoanalytic Theories of Development: An Integration.* New York: Yale University.

van der Kolk, B.A. (1989) 'The compulsion to repeat the trauma.' *Psychiatric Clinics of North America 12* (2), 389–411.

van der Kolk, B.A. (1994) 'The body keeps the score: Memory and the evolving psychobiology of post-traumatic stress.' *Harvard Review of Psychiatry 1*, 253–265.

van der Kolk, B.A. and Fisler, R. (1995) 'Dissociation and the fragmentary nature of traumatic memories: Overview and exploratory study.' *Journal of Traumatic Stress 8* (4), 505–521.

West, M. and George, C. (1999) 'Abuse and violence in intimate adult relationships: New perspectives from attachment theory.' *Journal of Attachment and Human Development 1*, (2), 137–156.

Winnicott, D.W. (1974) 'Fear of breakdown.' *International Journal of Psycho-Analysis 1*, 103–107.

Winnicott, D.W. (1988) *Playing and Reality.* London: Penguin.

Part III

Institutional Issues

CHAPTER 5

Three Degrees of Security

Attachment and Forensic Institutions

Gwen Adshead

SUMMARY

Attachment theory can be a useful tool for understanding management problems in forensic institutions, where staff and residents are involved in long-term dependency relationships that involve both care and control. I discuss the relationship between attachment security and violence, and how the forensic institution needs to become a 'secure base'.

INTRODUCTION

Bowlby's theory of attachment as a developmental process was always envisaged as being clinical in its application (Bowlby 1988; Holmes 1993). However, there has been comparatively little attention to how attachment theory might be applied to ordinary psychiatric practice. Heard and Lake (1997) describe possible psychotherapeutic applications of attachment theory, and David Howe and colleagues (1999) have described its application to social work. In a previous paper I argued that some common but troubling management problems in psychiatry could be better understood using attachment theory (Adshead 1998). In this chapter I will take the same approach, but focus instead on the use of attachment theory for under-standing management issues in forensic institutions. The first part of the chapter reviews the literature on the relationship between attachment security and violence. In the latter part, I will try and apply this theory and related research to forensic clinical practice, by describing how pathological attachments influence the relationships between staff and patients, as they travel between conditions of low-, medium- and high-secure care. These three degrees of security reflect different states of insecurity in the minds of forensic patients, and present different challenges for staff who work in long-term residential secure units, from admission to discharge.

ATTACHMENT AND THE GENESIS OF VIOLENCE

Before considering the clinical aspects of attachment theory, I will briefly review how attachment theory can contribute to an understanding of how abnormal mental states increase the risk of violence. This is important clini-cally; if we think that attachment dynamics are influential in increasing the risk of violence, then they may also be relevant for therapeutic strategies that aim to reduce the risk.

Interpersonal violence includes a heterogeneous range of behaviours. Taking homicide as a (comparatively rare) example, each violently caused death subtly differs from another, although each is the product of multiple risk factors operating simultaneously. These risk factors are located in the individual and in the environment, at both the micro and macro levels, and may exert their influence by an interaction between individual and environ-ment – a point which is important for understanding violence within insti-tutions. A forensic patient's attachment experiences will therefore be only one risk factor for violence, both past and future. They may, however, be particularly important for understanding how the patient relates to both fellow patients and professional caregivers.

Although interpersonal violence is comparatively rare as a subset of criminal law breaking, the victims are disproportionately likely to be part of a violent offender's attachment network: a child, a parent, a partner or ex-partner. This is particularly so for violent offenders with mental disorder (Heads, Taylor and Lees 1997; National Confidential Inquiry 2001). Bowlby (1988) suggested that violence to attachment figures in the family tends to occur because any threat to the attachment relationship (such as loss or separation) can generate powerful feelings of anxiety and rage. Under-standing violence in the context of relationships may have implications for thinking about the risk of violent behaviour by patients in institutions, and towards whom it is directed.

Research based on attachment theory, which addresses the developmental consequences of early childhood trauma, may also contribute to understanding the genesis of violence in individuals. It is highly unusual for offender patients (either in prison or in hospital) to have had early childhood experience which would promote attachment security (Coid 1992; van IJzendoorn et al. 1997). Attachment security in childhood has a profound influence on the development of a child's theory of mind, that is, the capacity to imagine mental states in oneself or others (Fonagy and Target 1997). Such 'self-reflective function' is clearly relevant to the development of empathy, a capacity related to theory of mind, involving both cognitive and affective elements (Hoffman 2000). Failure of empathy is thought to be an important contributory factor in the commission of violence.

Disrupted and insecure attachments in childhood may be risky for other reasons. First, it is important to note that offender populations, including those in forensic psychiatric facilities, have usually had childhood attachment experiences that are not just insecure, but traumatic and terrifying. In one study, 80 per cent of mentally disordered offenders had suffered some form of abuse, neglect or exploitation in childhood (Coid 1992). These experiences include extremes of abandonment, terrorisation, cruelty and humiliation. Chronic and severe fear experiences in infancy and childhood have pathological effects on the developing brain, particularly in relation to arousal and mood regulation, and, perhaps importantly, the capacity to articulate distress (Schore 2001). These effects appear to be most pronounced in the right orbito-frontal cortex of the brain, an area which is the substrate for identity, choice-making, and interpreting interpersonal experience (Damasio 2000). Traumatic events in infancy or childhood can cause reduced neuronal development and impaired or disorganised formation of vital association networks; such neuronal impairment can interact with environmental disadvantage to increase the risk of severe violence in adulthood (Raine, Brennan and Mednick 1997).

Such findings from neurodevelopmental research are mirrored in studies of the effect of profound fear and terror experiences on adults who have suffered trauma. In adults, exposure to intense fear and helplessness is associated with disorders of mood regulation, threat perception, memory and arousal (DSM IV: American Psychiatric Association 1994). Key features of post-traumatic disorders include hyperarousal, increased sensitivity to threat, irritability and altered conscious awareness, all of which are risk factors for violence. At a psychological level, traumatic and fearful events in adulthood typically disrupt attachment networks, increasing feelings of isolation and anxiety. This isolation is, of course, more marked for forensic patients, who are physically separated from family ties and society as a whole when they are detained. Some research data exist which suggests that the commission of violent behaviour can itself act as traumatic stressor (Ford 1999).

These data demonstrate why the study of attachment processes may be particularly useful in understanding the genesis of violence in an individual detained in a secure custodial or therapeutic institution. I want now to look at these abnormal attachment patterns in more detail, and relate them to problems of living in the institution itself.

ABNORMAL ATTACHMENT PATTERNS IN OFFENDER POPULATIONS

The psychological manifestations of these early impairments may be detected in the ways that traumatised individuals experience and make attachment relationships of their own in adulthood, with peers, intimates or children. It may be helpful to give a highly abbreviated account of the different types of attachment pattern or representation in children and adults. (This is a huge topic, and interested readers are referred to Cassidy and Shaver 1999.)

Attachment theory argues that individuals form mental representations of attachment figures from childhood – what Bowlby called 'internal working models'. These representations (which include both conscious and unconscious elements) influence two significant interpersonal behavioural systems in adulthood: caregiving behaviours on behalf of others and care-eliciting for the self at times of threat (Solomon and George 1996).

There are different ways of measuring these representations; self-report scales may be used to assess more conscious experience of attachment style, whereas linguistic discourse analysis of transcribed attachment narratives may elicit more unconscious aspects. Most measures find a distinction between secure and insecure attachment representations or styles, and differentiate between several types of insecure attachment. An important feature of secure attachment is *coherence* of both language and thought (Main 1991), i.e. an individual's account of his attachment experiences and how they impact on the self is consistent, understandable, and does not contain lapses in logic or ordinary reasoning. In contrast, insecure attachment narratives are hard to follow, highly incoherent in terms of contradictions and inconsistencies, and leave the listener baffled and frustrated about who the speaker really is.

Three forms of insecure attachment in childhood have been described: avoidant, ambivalent and disorganised. Attachment theory postulates that attachment style in childhood predicts attachment style in adulthood, and there is supporting data for this hypothesis, especially in relation to insecure attachments (Waters *et al.* 2000). Avoidant attachment in childhood is associated with dismissing (D) attachment in adulthood; ambivalent attachment in childhood is associated with enmeshed (E) attachment in adulthood.

Disorganised attachment in childhood is particularly associated with the experience of being abused. Data about its long-term implications are still emerging. Disorganised attachment appears to be associated with controlling behaviour, increased mental disturbance and dissociation in adolescent samples. It seems likely that disorganised attachment in childhood may result in disorganised (CC) attachment in adulthood – a state of mind which has features of both enmeshed and dismissing states of mind, and which is highly incoherent. Disorganisation of attachment is also associated with dissociation phenomena, as if the individual has real difficulty in maintaining an even monitoring of conscious awareness of environmental reality, or a clear distinction between the internal world and the external world.

There is one further category of attachment representation associated with insecure attachment, namely unresolved (U) for loss or trauma. Theoretically based on data from attachment narratives, unresolved attachment has something in common with disorganised attachment, but the disturbance is more focused and less global in nature (Hesse 1999). It is possible to have mental aspects of secure attachment and yet still have some areas of unresolved attachment in relation to a bereavement or particular trauma.

There is now a significant published database available on the distribution of attachment representations in offenders (see Table 5.1). Perhaps the most important aspect of these data is that insecure attachment is a risk factor for violence, but only one among many. It is also clear that security of attachment is compatible with being a violent offender; and not all offenders have insecure attachment representations. However, the proportion of secure individuals is markedly reduced compared to non-clinical samples, which suggests that insecurity of attachment combines with other risk factors to trigger violent action.

Table 5.1: Attachment representations in normal and forensic populations (% distribution)			
Population	Secure (F)	Enmeshed (E)	Dismissing (D)	Unresolved (U) or Cannot Classify (CC)
Mothers (non-clinical)	58	18	24	19
Fathers (non-clinical)	62	16	22	Not available
Psychiatric patients	22	64	14	82
Forensic males (UK)	19	45	36	36
Forensic males (Dutch)	5	20	22	53
Forensic males (Swedish)	7	29	64	36
Forensic females (UK)	22	11	77	65

(Based on van IJzendoorn and Bakermans-Kranenburg 1996; van IJzendoorn et al. 1997; Adshead and Bluglass 2001; Frodi et al. 2001.)

Both dismissing and unresolved attachment patterns are over-represented among offenders compared to normal populations. Since a dismissing style is associated with attempts to negate or ignore affective distress in self or others, it is perhaps not surprising to find this pattern of attachment common in a group of people who have behaviourally demonstrated a capacity to ignore distress. It is likely that a dismissing state of mind is linked with a developmental failure of empathy, which implies some deficit of self-reflective function; it is hard to imagine the feelings of others if there is diminished capacity to think about one's own feelings. However, we know that not all violent offenders lack empathy all the time, so that more data is needed on the link between dismissing attachments and the regulation of empathic feelings.

The high level of unresolved trauma or loss is consistent with what is already known about childhood experience in the lives of offenders, and also suggests that there is some aspect of psychological experience which is still unmetabolised, or 'alive', in the mind of the offender. Because it is unresolved, it remains psychologically active, and can therefore influence behaviour. Evidence for this assertion comes from research into responses to the experience of traumatic stress. Survivors of trauma often find that unresolved feelings from the time of the trauma persist in the form of traumatic memories, and difficulties in speaking about the past. These unresolved mental elements (which are not always conscious) are often detectable in survivors' narratives of the past, in the form of language problems (Holmes and Brewin 2002).

ABNORMAL ATTACHMENT PATTERNS IN INSTITUTIONS: ADMISSION PROBLEMS

So far I have described how the experience of early childhood fear and adversity has an impact both on neuronal development in childhood, and on the development of abnormal attachment patterns of interpersonal behaviour. Now I want to argue that the abnormal attachment patterns described above are likely to be re-enacted in the offender's institution of residence. There are several facilitating factors that make this process happen (Box 5.1).

Box 5.1 Early problems of attachment in institutions

- index offence as attachment disruptor

- admission as high-threat situation

- early formation of toxic attachments

- institutional failure to contain

First, the offender is often an individual with reduced capacity to manage arousal and stress, particularly at times of threat. This reduced capacity is a result of the developmental pathology described above, and will be exacerbated by any additional mental disorder that the offender may suffer. The offender patient is therefore someone who is sensitive to threat, and reacts badly to it – especially attachment-related threat, such as abrupt losses or separations. It is also not uncommon for the index offence to represent a major disruption to attachment relationships; the patient/offender's victim is very likely to be someone to whom they were once closely attached.

Second (and related), admission to any forensic institution will be stressful and a source of threat to the inmate/patient. Admission itself implies a separation or dislocation from some known setting, and placement in a new surrounding, which is locked, unknown and may have frightening associations. 'Broadmoor', for example, is a name that for some conjures up an image of a very frightening place from which one will never emerge. Thus admission itself becomes a threat situation, which stimulates arousal in a person poorly able to manage stress. Threat situations stimulate attachment behaviours, and the offender patient will often early on seek out a figure to whom to attach, who best fits their pre-existing attachment representation.

At the admission stage, patients will draw on past attachment behavioural strategies to manage their sense of threat or fear. Here it is important to consider the importance of pathological or 'toxic' attachments (Adshead 2001). These are attachment patterns characterised by dismissing feelings of need or tenderness, and dissociation at times of threat; alternatively, they may be characterised by intense, extreme and unregulated feelings of love or hate, often combined with the experience of personal deadness or emptiness. Such toxic attachments are also associated with an acute sensitivity to discrepancies of power and control, so that other people are assessed in terms of their threat/control potential, or their vulnerability/exploitation potential. Hence in the early stages of admission to a long-stay institution, new patients are very likely to make toxic attachments to both staff and fellow patients, which mirror their previous experience of attachment relationships. If staff teams can be aware of this, then this admission period often provides useful information not only about the offender's attachment style, but also about how they are likely to relate to others in the future, and where therapeutic interventions may need to be targeted.

In the early stages, there may be aspects of the institution that are frank and overt reminders of previous attachment disruptions and insecurities. Many offender patients have been in institutional care before as a result of family failure and abuse, often for long periods and with multiple changes of carer. Child-care institutions can be abusive and neglectful, and cause damage not only directly by the infliction of abuse, but also indirectly by failing to offer a chance for repair. Sadly, we know that both prisons and forensic psychiatric establishments can also be places where abuse and neglect take place, and where punitive or humiliating strategies are used to reduce staff anxiety and keep order.

Finally, we need to consider the other meaning of admission for offender patients: the admission of what has happened and the experience of guilt. If we understand the commission of a violent offence, especially to an attachment figure, as a traumatic stressor, then we can expect the patient to be in a state of high anxiety in relation to thinking about the index offence. In post-traumatic stress terms, we can expect they will be avoidant, hyperaroused and irritable when it comes to talking about the index offence, even if it took place some time ago. The offence may still be 'live' in the mind of the patient, who is unlikely to be able to make any sort of admission until they feel secure and safe – which can hardly be expected in the early months after their arrival at a new place. A sense of shame (both conscious and unconscious) at admitting their past offences further increases anxiety, and may increase the risk of violence (Gilligan 1999).

REHEARSAL AND RE-ENACTMENT: 'ALL THE WORLD'S A STAGE'

I want now to think in more detail about toxic attachments in forensic institutions, in terms of patterns of relating, and choice of attachment figure. As
suggested above, different patterns of insecurity will be manifest in different
ways.

Individuals with a *dismissing* style may find it very difficult to engage in
therapy, or think about their offences, because they tend to dismiss feelings
of hurt and distress from their minds. They may be able to articulate a
history in a rather abstract way, but be inclined to dismiss unpleasant events
as 'all in the past'. Such men and women are heavily defended from experiencing distress, and may be reluctant to do so; and of course, the dismissing
style exists at a conscious level to protect them from feeling affects that they
cannot manage. It is a position best summed up by one patient: 'I was
oblivious to all feelings, emotion... The possibility of thinking'.

Although there is some evidence that dismissing patients can make
gains in therapy, this may only be because they have so far to go (Fonagy *et
al.* 1996). Other clinicians have been pessimistic about engaging dismissing
patients in therapy (Dozier *et al.* 2001). Dismissing patients may be overlooked by staff, or seem like 'model' patients, because they seem so
self-sufficient, and ask for very little.

Patients with a more *enmeshed* style of attachment pattern are likely to
form intense and volatile attachments to staff and patients. Several studies of
attachment and personality disorder have found a link between enmeshed
attachment and borderline personality disorder (Fonagy, Target and
Gergely 2000), so this pattern of intense but brittle attachment is not surprising. Staff can easily get caught up in these types of attachment patterns,
and this often results in splits in staff teams about a patient, with half the
team feeling a positive attachment to the patient, and the other half feeling
highly negative (Main 1957). Dissociative phenomena and experiential
emptiness tend to push the patient to seek a physical solution to affective
distress; this will often take the form of attacks on the body, such as eating
disorders, suicide attempts, or self-mutilation. Such attacks on the bodily
self also act as mute appeals or threats to professional caregivers, who can
easily respond with distress and anger (Adshead 1997).

Borderline personality disorder is also associated with early childhood
trauma, and *unresolved* attachment experience from both childhood and
adulthood may easily be re-enacted on the ward. Obvious sources of

re-enactment are losses and separations – for example, when a valued member of staff leaves. If this leaving is itself traumatic (for example, in the context of illness or death), then this can be a powerful stimulus of unresolved attachment feelings, with consequent effects on the coherence of thinking, and stability of mood.

Other institutional stimuli for unresolved trauma are experiences of further abuse or violence in the hospital or prison, shameful experiences and unplanned terminations of attachment. This last is not just another type of loss experience (although that aspect is important); abrupt terminations of treatment may also suddenly remove a source of affect and arousal regulation. For a person who manages affect and arousal badly, it is therefore *dangerous* to allow any form of therapy to be suddenly stopped, including psychological therapies. I emphasise this because abrupt terminations of therapy are not uncommon in secure institutions, where there is a high turnover of staff, or care is provided by trainees (Bostic, Shadid and Blotsky 1996).

Last, it is important to consider the patient's attachment to the institution. For some offender patients, the forensic institution is the first enduring attachment they have made in adulthood, and the only place where they may feel accepted or not out of place. This attachment is not without cost; it is painful to acknowledge that the only place one might feel 'at home', or feel one belongs, is in a maximum-security institution for people who have done terrible things to others. Moving on from the institution is potentially fraught with difficulty; the patient wants to move on from the shame and stigma of the forensic institution, but can only do this by leaving his 'secure base'.

At the same time, forensic institutions often behave in a highly irrational way towards patients with regard to discharge. A Catch 22 operates so that patients who express a wish to stay in maximum security are rarely allowed to do so, and are seen as trying to avoid independence. Quite what 'independence' would mean to someone raised in institutions is rarely discussed; nor is it clear why it would be such a bad thing to be dependent indefinitely. This issue is vital for teams to consider, because of the association with risk; offender patients will do whatever they have to do to feel secure psychologically, and if they are anxious about moving on from the hospital, they may act in such as way as to either sabotage the discharge, or engineer their own return.

INTERNAL AND EXTERNAL SECURITY: STAFF–PATIENT RELATIONSHIPS

Caregiving and care-seeking are manifestations of attachment behavioural systems that have the aim of promoting a sense of security in the individual. Forensic institutions also have an aim to promote security. There is therefore a powerful mirroring of language between attachment theory and the language of forensic systems. Forensic systems talk constantly about security: 'Is this place secure?', 'What do Security say?', 'He needs somewhere more secure'. Patients typically start with high degrees of security, and it is envisaged that they will 'need' less security later. What the psychotherapist is interested in is the psychological aspects of security, and how they may be matched or mirrored in the demands the patient makes on physical security. Therapeutic forensic services will also want to pay attention to the internal security of the patients' states of mind, and to the security of the minds of staff and the institution.

I want now to think about some of the attachment relationship factors that affect staff–patient relationships in institutions (Box 5.2). In any institution which has a caregiving function, we can expect staff and patients to relate to each other using the language of attachment, and the social constructions of attachment. These social aspects are important in Western cultures, where there is an emphasis on self-individuation and autonomy as mature attributes, and where dependence has negative connotations (Agich 1993). This stigmatisation of dependence is associated with a further factor promoting attachment relationships between staff and patients, namely, time.

---

*Box 5.2 Attachment factors
influencing staff–patient interactions*

- physical and psychological security needs: low, medium or high

- caregiving and care eliciting: normal and abnormal strategies by staff and patients

- time and duration of relationship between staff and patients

- patients have long-term disabilities (increased dependency needs) rather than brief periods of illness

Offender patients typically spend long periods of time in institutions, and do not move on to health quickly. Traditional Western medical accounts of illness (and illness behaviour) tend to presume a normal state of independence interrupted by a discrete, time-limited period of abnormality and dependence. Appropriate care-seeking and caregiving aim to restore normality and independence.

Such an illness model says little about the impact for the patient and the carer in those situations where there may be very little sense of 'normal' ever, and the patient is in a prolonged state of dependence with the caregiver. In such circumstances, the boundaries between patient and caregiver may be hard to maintain.

PATHOLOGICAL ATTACHMENT PATTERNS WITHIN INSTITUTIONS: ISSUES FOR STAFF

Everyone has an attachment narrative, and staff in forensic institutions are no different in this regard. Indeed, one of the crucial questions for staff, and those who recruit them, is 'What is it that draws you to work in a secure setting?' Of course, for some, the work setting may be simply a question of local geography, in which case, staff may need support to come to terms with the impact of caring for very disturbed patients (Winship 1995, 1998).

Other staff may be drawn to working in secure settings because of attachment issues of their own. They may have experienced disrupted attachments in childhood, or experience a conscious need to control others in adulthood – a style of relating which has been found to be associated with disorganised attachment in childhood. Bowlby (1980) originally suggested that 'compulsive caregiving' was a conscious response to insecure attachment, and deprivation of security. Staff may, then, re-enact attachment issues of their own with patients or colleagues, or find their own distressing experiences mirrored in the patients they care for.

There has been considerable research interest in the relevance of attachment theory for therapeutic relationships (Dozier and Tyrrell 1998; Rubino et al. 2000). There is some limited empirical support for the view that the success of therapeutic interventions is influenced by the therapist's own attachment style, and that therapeutic benefit is associated with more secure attachment styles and more coherence of thought and language in the therapist.

What these data suggest is that it will be beneficial for both staff and patients if the *staff's* needs for psychological security are met. Can we understand high rates of staff absenteeism, sickness and turnover as an attempt by staff to regulate their own needs for inner security? Could a lack of self-reflective function in the staff group, and institutional management system, help to explain the sad failures of care detailed in both Ashworth Enquiries? If we listen to the language of forensic systems, there is good reason to think that forensic institutions have real potential for becoming incoherent in their thinking. Here are some quotes from different groups of health care professionals in a forensic setting:

1.   (about a patient not coming to his therapy session): 'We can't move him because he's got a beard.'

2.   (about the institution's entry system): 'When I came in [the institution], I looked to see who was dead.'

3.   (on the door of the canteen): 'This building is alarmed.'

The uninitiated listener will not necessarily know that patients in the secure hospital cannot leave their wards if they do not resemble their security photograph; or that the names of deceased staff are put up on a noticeboard at the entry (or why); or that the last quote is probably not a description of the building's state of mind. It is perhaps enough to note that these quotes represent minor lapses in monitoring of language and thought which are associated with the incoherence of mind that goes with a lack of inner security.

MAKING A SECURE BASE IN FORENSIC INSTITUTIONS

I want to conclude by thinking about what it takes to make a forensic institution into a truly secure setting; one that provides a secure base for both its staff and its residents. To recap, the provision of a secure base which promotes secure attachments should theoretically result in the development of more coherent attachment relationships, improved affect and arousal regulation, and the development of the capacity to think not only about one's own mind, but also about the mental experiences of others. All of these would seem to be reasonable therapeutic objectives for forensic care planners.

I have outlined some of the features necessary for the provision of a secure forensic base in Box 5.3. Boundary creation and maintenance are an ordinary part of health care relationships; the boundaries of professional identity help to create therapeutic spaces, and keep separate those issues that belong to staff and those that belong to patients. Boundary maintenance is most important in forensic settings, because it helps to maintain safety for unregulated feelings, so that an individual session with the primary nurse is a good place to express some distressing affects, but the dining room is not. Of course, boundary crossings and violations are an essential feature of forensic work; all staff working in forensic settings have to create and maintain a boundary between their identities as therapists, who promote inner security, and their identities as custodians of external security. In this sense, they and the patients are always 'living on the edge' of a boundary.

Box 5.3 Means to creating a secure base
for attachment in forensic institutions

- setting and maintaining therapeutic boundaries
- supporting and supervising staff in boundary maintenance
- monitoring, naming and regulating affects for both staff and patients
- managing separation and losses; avoiding abrupt terminations
- facilitating effective mourning
- understanding anger as the result of anxiety, lowered threat perception and failure to regulate arousal
- damage limitation

Boundary maintenance is easier when there is time to think and reflect. If secure boundaries help to contain unregulated affects and arousal (in conjunction with psychotherapies and appropriate medication), then there needs to be adequate supervision and support time for staff to think about their work, and its impact on them emotionally. This is especially true for nursing staff who live with the patients for many hours at a time, unlike therapists or management who may spend very little time in direct face-to-face contact with patients. Providing care for the staff may have more beneficial effect on the feelings and experiences of patients than any direct therapeutic input – like the SureStart project for disadvantaged children, which targets the parents, rather than the children themselves.

A secure base encourages monitoring, naming and regulation of negative feelings, especially anxiety, threat perception and anger, using a portfolio of therapeutic interventions. A secure base is thoughtful about separations and losses of attachment figures, is active in preventing abrupt terminations where possible, and facilitates appropriate mourning. Bearing in mind that many residents in forensic institutions are damaged people, where repair is no longer possible, a secure base aims to prevent further damage, and help the patient to live with the damage they have caused. I often reflect, drawing on my experience in both secure settings and trauma clinics, that my forensic patients are like survivors of a disaster, where they were the disaster; and that the road back to some sort of coherent life is indeed a Via Dolorosa.

CONCLUSION

I hope that I have shown how attachment theory can help in understanding why people act violently to others, in understanding the problems they pose in hospital, and in creating truly secure therapeutic spaces. Among the many schools of psychotherapy, attachment theory is one of those with the most to offer forensic practice because, clinically and empirically, its main focus is on how human beings experience and seek security at times of threat and fear.

ACKNOWLEDGEMENTS AND DISCLAIMER

Thanks to Sameer Sarkar for the Bostic, Shadid and Blotsky reference; to Gary Winship for supervision; to the Broadmoor Library, who found the references; and to my secretary, Anne Kavanagh, for her work on the manuscript.

These are the views of the writer alone and do not represent the views of either the West London Mental Health Trust, or Camden and Islington Mental Health Trust.

REFERENCES

Adshead, G. (1997) 'Written on the body.' In E. Welldon and C. Van Velsen (eds) *A Practical Guide to Forensic Psychotherapy.* London: Jessica Kingsley Publishers.

Adshead, G. (1998) 'Psychiatric staff as attachment figures.' *British Journal of Psychiatry 172*, 64–69.

Adshead, G. (2001) 'Attachment in mental health institutions: A commentary.' *Attachment and Human Development 3*, 324–329.

Adshead, G. and Bluglass, K. (2001) 'Attachment representations and factitious illness by proxy: Relevance for the assessment of parenting capacity in child maltreatment.' *Child Abuse Review 10*, 398–410.

Agich, G. (1993) *Autonomy and long-term care.* Oxford: Oxford University Press.

American Psychiatric Association (1994) *Diagnostic and Statistical Manual Version 4.* Washington, DC: American Psychiatric Press.

Berlin, R. (1986) 'Attachment behaviour in hospitalised patients.' *Journal of the American Medical Association 255*, 3391–3393.

Bowlby, J. (1980) *Attachment and Loss Vol.3: Loss.* London: Hogarth. 1988 Edition, London: Pimlico.

Bowlby, J. (1988) 'Violence in the family as a disorder of attachment and caregiving.' In *A Secure Base: Clinical Applications of Attachment Theory.* London: Routledge.

Bostic, J., Shadid, L. and Blotsky, M. (1996) 'Our time is up: Forced terminations during psychotherapy training.' *American Journal of Psychotherapy 50*, 347–359.

Cassidy, J. and Shaver, P. (1999) *Handbook of Attachment: Theory, Research and Clinical Applications.* New York: Guilford.

Coid, J. (1992) 'DSM III diagnosis in criminal psychopaths.' *Criminal Behaviour and Mental Health 2*, 78–95.

Damasio, A. (2000) *The Feeling of What Happens.* London: Heinemann.

Dozier, M. and Tyrrell, C. (1998) 'The role of attachment in therapeutic relationships.' In J. Simpson and W.S Rholes (eds) *Attachment Theory and Close Relationships.* London: Guilford Press.

Dozier, M. Lomax, C., Tyrrell, C. and Lee, C.S. (2001) 'The challenge of treatment for clients with dismissing states of mind.' *Attachment and Human Development 3*, 62–76.

Fonagy, P., Leigh, T., Steele, M., Steele, H., Kennedy, R., Mattoon, G., Target, M. and Gerber, A. (1996) 'The relation of attachment status, psychiatric classification and response to psychotherapy.' *Journal of Consulting and Clinical Psychology 64*, 22–31.

Fonagy, P. and Target, M. (1997) 'Attachment and reflective function: Their role in self organisation.' *Development and Psychopathology 9*, 679–700.

Fonagy, P., Target, M. and Gergely, G. (2000) 'Attachment and borderline personality disorder: A theory and some evidence.' *Psychiatric Clinics of North America 23*, 103–122.

Fonagy P., Target, M., Steele, M. and Steele, H. (1997) 'The development of violence and crime as it relates to security of attachment.' In J. Osojsky (ed) *Children in a Violent Society.* New York: Guilford.

Ford, J. (1999) 'Disorders of extreme stress following war zone military trauma: Associated features of posttraumatic stress disorder or comorbid but distinct syndromes?' *Journal of Consulting and Clinical Psychology 67*, 3–12.

Frodi, A., Dernevik, M., Sepa, A., Philipson, J. and Bragesjo, M. (2001) 'Current attachment representations of incarcerated offenders varying in degree of psychopathy.' *Attachment and Human Development 3*, 269–283.

George, C. (1996) 'A representational perspective of child abuse and prevention: Internal working models of attachment and caregiving.' *Child Abuse and Neglect 20*, 411–424.

Gibson, L., Holt, J., Fondacaro, K., Tang, T., Powell, T. and Turbitt, E. (1999) 'An examination of antecedent trauma and psychiatric comorbidity among male inmates with PTSD.' *Journal of Traumatic Stress 12*, 473–484.

Gilligan, J. (1999) *Violence: Reflections on a Western Epidemic.* London: Jessica Kingsley Publishers.

Grey, N., Holmes, E. and Brewin, C. (2001) 'Peritraumatic emotional "hotspots" in memory.' *Behavioural and Cognitive Psychotherapy 29*, 367–372.

Haley, S. (1974) 'When the patient reports atrocities.' *Archives of General Psychiatry 30*, 191–196.

Heads, T., Taylor, P. and Lees, M. (1997) 'Childhood experiences of patients with schizophrenia and a history of violence: A Special Hospital sample.' *Criminal Behaviour and Mental Health 7*, 117–130.

Heard, D. and Lake, B. (1997) *The Challenge of Attachment for Caregiving.* London: Routledge.

Henderson, S. (1974) 'Care-eliciting behaviour in man.' *Journal of Nervous and Mental Disease 159*, 172–181.

Hesse, E. (1999) 'The Adult Attachment Interview.' In J. Cassidy and P. Shaver (eds) *Handbook of Attachment: Theory, Research and Clinical Applications.* New York: Guilford.

Hoffman, M.L. (2000) *Empathy and Moral Development.* Cambridge: Cambridge University Press.

Holmes, J. (1993) *John Bowlby and Attachment Theory.* London: Routledge.

Holtzworth Munroe, A., Bates, L., Smutzer, N. and Sardin, E. (1997) 'A brief review of the research on husband violence: Part 1. Maritally violent men versus non-violent men.' *Aggression and Violent Behaviour 2*, 65–99.

Howe, D., Brandon, M., Hinings, D. and Schofield, G. (1999) *Attachment Theory, Child Maltreatment and Family Support.* London: Macmillan.

Main, M. (1991) 'Metacognitive knowledge, meta-monitoring and singular (coherent) versus multiple (incoherent) models of attachment.' In C.M. Parkes, J. Stevenson-Hinde and P. Marris (eds) *Attachment Across the Life Cycle.* London: Routledge.

Main, T. (1957) 'The ailment.' *British Journal of Medical Psychology 30*, 129–145.

Marshall, W.L., Serran, G. and Cortoni, F. (2000) 'Childhood attachments, sexual abuse and their relationship to adult coping.' *Sexual Abuse: Journal of Research and Treatment 12*, 17–26.

National Confidential Inquiry (2001) *Safety First: Five-year Report of the National Confidential Inquiry into Suicide and Homicide by People with Mental Illness.* London: Department of Health.

Nelson, C. and Bosquet, M. (2000) 'Neurobiology of fetal and infant development: Implications for infant mental health.' In C. Zeanah (ed) *Handbook of Infant Mental Health.* 2nd edn. London: Guilford.

Raine, A., Brennan, P. and Mednick, S. (1997) 'Interaction between birth complications and early maternal rejection in predisposing individuals to adult violence: Specificity to serious, early onset violence.' *American Journal of Psychiatry 154*, 1265–1271.

Rubino, G., Barker, C., Roth, T. and Fearon, P. (2000) 'Therapist empathy and depth of interpretation in response to potential alliance ruptures: The role of the therapist and patient attachment styles.' *Psychotherapy Research 10*, 408–420.

Schore, A. (2001) 'The effects of early relational trauma on right brain development, affect regulation and infant mental health.' *Infant Mental Health 22*, 201–269.

Solomon, J. and George, C. (1996) 'Defining the caregiving system: Toward a theory of caregiving.' *Infant Mental Health Journal 17*, 183–197.

Sroufe, A. (1997) 'Psychopathology as an outcome of development.' *Development and Psychopathology 9*, 251–268.

van IJzendoorn, M. and Bakermans-Kranenburg, M. (1996) 'Attachment representations in mothers, fathers, adolescents and clinical groups.' *Journal of Consulting and Clinical Psychology 64*, 8–21.

van IJzendoorn M., Feldbrugge, J., Derks, F., De Ruiter, C., Verhagen, M., Philipse, M., van der Staak, C. and Riksen Walraven, J. (1997) 'Attachment representations of personality disordered criminal offenders.' *American Journal of Orthopsychiatry 67*, 449–459.

Waters, E., Hay, D. and Richters, J. (1986) 'Infant–parent attachment and the origins of prosocial and antisocial behaviour.' In D. Olweus, J. Block and M. Radke Yarrow (eds) *Development of Antisocial and Prosocial Behaviour.* New York: Academic Press.

Waters, E., Merrick, S., Treboux, D., Crowell, J. and Albersheim, L. (2000) 'Attachment security in infancy and adulthood: A 20-year longitudinal study.' *Child Development 71*, 684–689.

Winship, G. (1995) 'The unconscious impact of caring for acutely disturbed patients: A perspective for supervision.' *Journal of Psychiatric and Mental Health Nursing 2*, 227–231.

Winship, G. (1998) 'Intensive care nursing – psychoanalytic perspectives.' *Journal of Psychiatric and Mental Health Nursing 5*, 361–365.

CHAPTER 6

Forensic Mental Health Nursing

Care with Security in Mind

Anne Aiyegbusi

INTRODUCTION

In any formal sense, forensic mental health nursing remains a poorly defined discipline, lacking a discrete identity. Interestingly, previous attempts to define the primary tasks of forensic mental health nursing have tended to focus on legal and policy frameworks, mechanistic interventions or the logistical challenge that providing care to offender patients detained in custodial environments presents. This relatively circumscribed parameter is in contrast to the fact that within the wider field of mental health nursing, the relationship between nurse and patient has long been recognised as the primary therapeutic tool. The primary task is to provide assessment and enable positive mental health gains through the nurse–patient relationship.

Until very recently, little had ever been made of the interpersonal challenge inherent in the nursing role with forensic patients for whom the experience of profound early suffering, inflicted by primary carers, tends to be a common background characteristic. From clinical experience, it is clear that the forensic mental health population are largely people whose early childhood damage is repeated in adult life; only this time they are the perpetrators and not solely victims. Locating suffering outside of the self is an important method used by forensic populations to manage overwhelming affects. It is this pattern of interpersonal functioning that makes caring for forensic patients particularly challenging, as it is often the current carer who is made to suffer emotionally.

This chapter aims to shed light on the challenges presented to nurses in their task of managing positive therapeutic relationships with forensic patients. It will be demonstrated that an attachment theory framework can help to elucidate the interpersonal complexity that is central to clinical work with forensic patients, as well as providing a way of organising effective nursing interventions. Most critically though, examining the emotional impact on nurses, of working interpersonally with patients whose attachments are grossly disturbed, clarifies the reasons why an emotionally secure base is required, from where nursing care can be delivered.

Forensic mental health nursing – interpersonal complexity

Studies by Blackburn (1992, 1998) and Blackburn and Renwick (1996) reveal important implications for the nurse–patient relationship with mentally disordered offenders, whereby psychopathology is clarified from the perspective of patients' dysfunctional relationship styles. In social exchanges, mentally disordered offenders are likely to elicit interpersonal responses from other people which continually reinforce negative, dysfunctional expectations about what they will experience from human relationships (Blackburn 1992, 1998; Blackburn and Renwick 1996). For example, 'a hostile person expects hostile reactions from others and behaves in a way which gets them' (Blackburn 1992).

If relational disturbance is taken as the problem around which care is organised, there are a number of important implications for the practice of forensic mental health nursing:

- Powerful interpersonal dynamics occur within nurse–patient relationships in forensic settings. Patients' disadvantageous early life experiences with attachment figures shape their expectations of current caregivers.

- Positive change requires psychological therapy combined with structured, skilfully applied interpersonal interventions in the social environment.

- Dysfunctional interpersonal behaviours can have a *complementary* effect on others. The risk of perpetuating rather than discontinuing damaging styles of relating is therefore high.

- Forensic mental health nurses, with their conflicting roles of control and care, can too easily replicate their patients' relationships with abusive or neglecting early caregivers.

- The profoundly disturbed way that many forensic patients manage their intimate relationships can have an unexpected and negative effect on nurses' feelings and behaviour.

To focus on the nature of the nurse–patient relationship in forensic mental health care is to be forced to think about the pain, suffering and disempowerment of the victim in the patient, as well as the way in which others have been terrorised by the patient. Could this be one reason why it has been more acceptable within the specialty to focus, for example, on legal frameworks and mechanistic interventions? By not thinking about the patients' inner worlds and the impact their pasts will have on therapeutic relationships with nurses, a parallel process is defensively set up. The danger is that nurses go about the task of providing care in a way that ends up mirroring the type of non-thinking that is characteristic of the most difficult and disturbed forensic patients.

Menzies-Lyth (1988) has described how the social system of a hospital can be unconsciously organised for the purpose of defending against the anxiety of its members. The intense anxiety that is stirred up by the nature of the primary task cannot be thought about. Menzies-Lyth identifies a number of defensive strategies that are employed by services to avoid anxiety provoked by facing the nature of the primary task. These defences include the following:

- high sickness levels

- frequent changes of job

- ritualistic activities

- task allocation, avoiding the need to think about patients as whole people

- emotional detachment

- categorising patients and nurses to avoid thinking about individuality
- projecting irresponsible impulses onto junior colleagues and then punishing them harshly
- devaluing attachment
- reducing responsibility by forcing tasks upwards to superiors.

Menzies-Lyth's (1988) study was undertaken in a general hospital, but the same defences against pain, suffering and death that Menzies-Lyth observed in a general hospital can be witnessed in forensic settings. However, Cox (1996), writing about the high security psychiatric hospital, pointed out that the forensic setting has within it particular horrors that cannot be thought about. These emanate from the patients' inner worlds and have been externalised through their criminal behaviours. Cox describes how unspoken anxieties and fears occupy the unconscious life of the high security psychiatric institution and are defended against by a number of 'hyperconscious' strategies. These strategies may be understood as defences against the agony of knowing about 'the corpus of massed destructiveness and danger'.

Cox describes the therapeutic task for patients detained in a high security psychiatric institution as coming to terms with their fear and violence. For front-line clinical staff such as nurses, supporting patients may overwhelm their own 'psychological resources'. Such a painful outcome is particularly likely in the absence of appropriate training, supervision, and widespread acknowledgement of the primary task. In the face of the horror at the heart of nurse–patient relationships in forensic settings, it may come as no surprise that long-standing defences have been in place, forcing attention towards more practical and therefore emotionally manageable endeavours.

Attachment theory

Attachment theory is based on the seminal work of Dr John Bowlby, who studied the emotional impact on children of being separated from their primary caregivers, or of being subject to institutional care. Bowlby concluded that lack of maternal love during early life, through prolonged separation, abandonment or death, laid the foundations for subsequent mental ill health and personality disturbance (Bowlby 1951).

Bowlby's work unfolded into a distinct theory which holds centrally that an infant's attachment to its mother or primary caregiver is essential for survival and serves as the template for all future attachment relationships. Frameworks for managing relationships are internalised through early experience with attachment figures. Internal frameworks determine the following:

- internal working model for relationships with other people
- degree of emotional security in relationships with others
- a sense of whether others can be trusted with one's well-being, especially when sick or vulnerable
- esteem in relation to others
- capacity to deal with and recover from loss and stress
- quality of one's emotional life
- degree to which one is able to think about own and others' thinking
- capacity to self-soothe and regulate affect
- capacity to communicate in relationships
- degree of comfort with closeness.

ATTACHMENT REPRESENTATIONS

The Adult Attachment Interview (AAI: Main and Goldwyn 1998) is regarded as a particularly rigorous way of measuring attachment representations in adults. The attachment categories classified by the AAI are presented in Box 6.1, along with the way these styles may be observed in psychiatric patients.

Box 6.1 Attachment styles and their clinical manifestations

Secure
Characterised by self-confidence and the capacity to form stable relationships with others. Have 'good enough' capacities to manage their own distress, including making appropriate use of others as helpers. Securely attached patients are more likely to be compliant with medication and to disclose more of their symptoms (Dozier *et al.* 1990).

Dismissing
Characterised by dismissal of the importance of attachment relationships and of attachment experiences. People with a dismissing attachment style have difficulty understanding their own emotional needs or those of others. As a result, the likelihood of victimising other people is increased because they have diminished empathy. Because attachment related experience is not processed, these people defend themselves against memories of rejection or maltreatment by idealising the experiences or by dismissively denigrating them. Dismissing patients may have difficulty engaging with treatment at all, as they minimise or denigrate their own neediness, and tend to project their own distress onto others (Adshead 1998). Dismissing styles are over-represented in forensic populations (Adshead, this volume).

Preoccupied
Characterised by enmeshment in relationships with attachment figures, and a diminished sense of self. Preoccupied individuals manage their own distress by alternately drawing closer and withdrawing from people who might be able to help them. In psychiatric services, patients with a preoccupied style of attachment 'may get stuck, find it difficult to move on or act ambivalently towards offered care' (Adshead 1998). Preoccupied or enmeshed attachment is commonly found in those with borderline personality disorder and other disorders of mood.

Unresolved
This small category refers to people who have experienced loss or trauma that remains unprocessed or unresolved. The 'unresolved' category is over-represented in psychiatric populations, and is likely to be of particular significance in high-risk and difficult-to-manage patient groups (Fonagy 1998). Adshead (1998) describes how people with this style of attachment, when in contact with psychiatric services, 'may have difficulty in thinking about or managing the painful feelings aroused by treatment'.

Protection

Originally, Bowlby saw the central function of attachment as protection. Those who are vulnerable seek protection from perceived threat in the form of closeness and care from those who are stronger and able to provide it. Therefore, the first attachment relationship a person has is usually with their mother. Evidence of an attachment relationship is seen on the basis of attachment behaviour, which is at its most intense during infancy and early childhood. In the mother's presence the infant is calm and settled, but separation from her stimulates the attachment system, causing feelings of anxiety and anger. These feelings underpin the manifest attachment behaviour. Crying, reaching out and, if possible, physically following the mother, constitute the separation cry and proximity-seeking.

The function of attachment behaviour is to secure increased proximity or closeness to the mother or other attachment figure, and reduce anxiety in the face of threat. When the relationship is going well, the mother's own attachment system will be stimulated in response to her child's attachment behaviour. As a result, she will move closer and provide comfort, care and pleasurable stimulation, soothing the child's anxiety and anger, promoting a sense of emotional well-being and contentment on both psychological and physiological levels. When a child experiences threat or distress (such as feeling hurt, tired, hungry or cold), he or she will engage in more intense attachment behaviour than when comfortable and soothed. When frightened by alarming conditions such as the presence of a stranger, or when there is a threat to the attachment relationship, or when feeling is thwarted, the child will increase proximity to the mother with a high level of intensity (Bowlby 1969).

Affect regulation

In addition to its protective function, attachment is also 'inherently an emotional construct' (Sroufe 1995). Attachment relationships serve as powerful regulators of emotion. Sroufe points out that the caregiver initially interprets the infant's expressions of distress and other affective communications, attributes meaning and then responds with sensitivity. Responsive caregiving assuages negative affect, restoring equilibrium. By the second half of the first year of life, affect regulation is dyadic, with the infant actively participating in the process by seeking out the caregiver for soothing and assuagement of uncomfortable arousal. The infant achieves this by communicating its needs directly to the caregiver, who responds with the desired interaction. Thus, the infant and caregiver are tied together by an interpersonal system that centres on psychobiological attunement (Sroufe 1995). So, in young children, the separation cry and proximity-seeking function as methods of organising responsive care from an attuned 'other' for the purpose of emotional regulation as well as physical protection (de Zulueta 1993; Sroufe 1995; van der Kolk 1987). Developmentally, this process is essential for subsequent self-soothing later in life. In the face of tension and stress, confidence in the caregiver's capacity to modulate affect, by responsive, interpersonal interactions and by mediating with a threatening environment, is internalised. As Sroufe (1995) reminds us: 'From the level of brain physiology to the level of interpersonal and psychic functioning, that which is experienced becomes part of the self.'

Insecure childhood attachments

Children who have experienced an insecure relationship with their attachment figures are forced to find alternative methods of managing intense feelings of vulnerability. Some young children will cling 'hungrily' to emotionally unavailable or abusive attachment figures in an attempt to maintain some sense of safety in the direct face of inaccessibility or threat (Bowlby 1988; van der Kolk 1987). In cases of chronic rejection of a child's attachment behaviour by their carer, the child may shut down emotionally and thereafter remain in a state of 'aggressive detachment' (Bowlby 1973). Fonagy (1998) explains how children whose attachment figures are also their abusers strip their minds of any ability to think about their own feelings and the harmful intent of their abusive carers. According to Fonagy (1998), this is an important developmental antecedent, affecting the capacity of the most difficult psychiatric patients to think about their own states of mind in relation to those of others.

Violent action occurs in the absence of a sufficiently effective capacity to think. Instead of being able to process emotionally painful 'ideas and feelings' through thought, unpleasant bodily reaction is experienced (Fonagy et al. 1997). This process, or lack, is likely to offer some explanation for the violent actions that forensic patients engage in as part of their offending and sometimes thereafter during hospitalisation. Inability to think about the contents of others' minds means there is no inhibiting factor to prevent suffering from being inflicted on others (Fonagy *et al.* 1997).

When there is nothing to inhibit the infliction of suffering on another, when there is extreme anger that cannot be processed mentally, and when a grossly impaired ability to self-soothe exists in combination with these factors, there may be no buffer between experiencing overwhelming negative affect and discharging it in the form of violent action. (See Box 6.2.)

Box 6.2 'Attachment risk' factors for violence

- unresolved affects of overwhelming fear, distress or anger

- loss or threat of loss of attachment figure, who contains distress

- a new threat perceived

- absent or reduced capacity to regulate own affects in face of threat

- absence of other internal or external inhibitors to externalising affect

- previous use of physical solutions to threat

The secure base

Mary Ainsworth (1967) first used the term 'secure base' to describe the distance from the mother within which a child remains relaxed and confident to explore.

A successful secure base allows the child to develop:

- psychosocial relationships with others

- self-esteem, empathy and regard for the needs of others

- the ability to self-soothe and modulate arousal

- a capacity to hold others in mind and not feel entirely bereft in their absence

- the ability to stand back from difficult experiences and think about them.

Bowlby (1988) considered the provision of a secure base to be a fundamental task of parenting. The function of the secure base is to provide a soothing and validating premise from where children and adolescents can explore their surroundings and develop relationships with others. When fearful, anxious or sick, an individual can return to the safety of their secure base, confident of their needs being met and of being comforted and soothed. Thus, the secure base promotes in the young person an internalised sense of security, which enables exploration into the wider world. Holmes (1993) explains that 'the essence of the secure base is that it provides a springboard for curiosity and exploration'. Developmentally, the consistency of a secure base promotes, amongst other things, self-reliance, autonomy and the capacity to empathise or attune with other people, including those in distress (Bowlby 1988; van der Kolk 1987). The secure base is implicitly linked to security of attachment and secure states of mind by virtue of its function as a psychological distance regulator: 'When an individual (of any age) is feeling secure, he is likely to explore away from his attachment figure. When alarmed, anxious or unwell, he feels an urge towards proximity' (Bowlby 1988).

As a person matures, they are able to manage increasing amounts of time and distance away from their secure base. However, when stressed by fearful conditions, illness or the experience of loss, the proximity of the secure base is readily sought. As Bowlby (1988) points out, inaccessibility of the attachment figure may also lead to increased efforts to increase proximity. Importantly, the presence of the attachment figure and their capacity to provide unconditional support, should it be needed, promotes relaxation and confidence during periods of separation, and so mediates the ability to explore and wander from the secure base. This pattern of increasing independence when feeling secure, and proximity-seeking when feeling insecure, defines the secure base. Providing a secure base is emotionally rewarding for caregivers, functioning to further strengthen relational bonds. In adults, emotional proximity rather than close physical contact with a caregiver fulfils the secure base function. Holmes (2001) describes the secure base as 'the first and most important domain' of attachment theory and explains how the secure base can be understood as an internalised 'representation' of security in adults.

Adult attachment

When adults are sick, threatened, or suffering because of the loss of a relationship, attachment behaviour is also clearly observable. Confidence in others to meet one's emotional needs is determined by early experience of a tuned-in carer. A securely attached individual will find that the ability to self-soothe provides an effective method for managing unpleasant emotions. Should exceptionally stressful events be encountered, whereby negative affect threatens to overwhelm, the securely attached individual will engage in adaptive care-seeking with an expectation that their needs will be met through the support and comfort of an established, safe relationship.

When consistent, responsive, early caregiving has been absent, later confidence in other people meeting one's emotional needs will be undermined. The ability to self-soothe in the face of uncomfortable arousal will also be compromised. Instead, it is more likely that emotional need and vulnerability will be regarded as psychologically intolerable. There are a number of relational strategies that an insecurely attached individual might employ in an attempt to adapt to this position. Such strategies may include avoidance of intimacy or affection from others, or masochistically projecting one's own needs onto others and engaging in compulsive caregiving, regardless of the cost to self. Conversely, the more sadistic style would be to project neediness and vulnerability onto others and then attack it, regardless of the cost to others.

'Attention seeking' as an insecure form of adult attachment behaviour

The expressions of need through somatisation, violence, or emotional persecution of another are all defensive ways of trying to secure contact with others without risking rejection. The individual who expresses need through projection into external space has no conception of others as people who might respond warmly and supportively to her expression of need. Instead she uses these controlling tactics to force others to meet her needs, regardless of whether they are willing. Because there is no faith in others' capacity to care, there is an accompanying anxiety that drives behaviours that force approximations of caring input. It is this pattern, when engaged in by psychiatric patients, that leads their caregivers to experience them as 'attention seeking' and 'manipulative', because input is forced in an attempt by the patient to assuage anxiety. Caregivers may feel that they are being forced to 'give' emotionally long after their will to do so has been exhausted.

When an impaired capacity to self-soothe is combined with a tendency to negatively interpret the mental state of the other, a fear of intimacy, due to anticipated rejection from those who could potentially offer support and care, may be expected. In place of reliable relationships with other people, addictive behaviours, violence and self-injury are a risk. These dysfunctional strategies are among the behaviours that might be employed to manage uncomfortable emotion. When engaged in by incarcerated psychiatric patients, these are also behaviours that caregivers struggle to cope with. Again, caregivers' emotional input is gained both by indirect means and by force, for example, the repeated emergency situations that these patients bring about (Gorsuch 1998).

When the attachment figure is a source of danger

Fonagy (1998) has proffered a theory about the most disturbed psychiatric patients. At any given time, one can expect to find groups of the most disturbed psychiatric populations clustered in forensic services. Therefore Fonagy's thesis is of particular relevance to forensic mental health nurses. Fonagy suspects that the most disturbed psychiatric patients are likely to be those with no coherent strategy for attachment. Their early attachment experiences are likely to have involved a caregiver who has served as a source of both protection and fear. The situation facing the young child is synonymous with what George Orwell (1949) referred to as 'doublethink': '...[holding] two opinions which cancelled out, knowing them both to be contradictory and believing in both of them; [using] logic against logic...'

Thus, when faced with an abusive carer, a young child is confronted with a massive cognitive challenge. He is overwhelmed by fearful affects, which his internal psychological regulatory system is still too immature to manage. He turns to his primary attachment figure for containment, but finds that not only are they unavailable as a source of anxiety reduction, they are actually the source of his fear and distress. Since he cannot make sense of this situation, he adopts a strategy of not thinking and not feeling (Bowlby 1988). The non-thinking strategy enables the child to avoid having to negotiate 'doublethink'.

Most importantly, however, the child avoids the pain of having to think about his attachment figure's harmful intent towards him (Fonagy 1998). In not thinking, the child finds the only available method of separating the image of abuse from the image of the caregiver he turns to in times of threat. This childhood propensity for not thinking at times of stress is seen as the precursor to dissociation in adulthood. In addition to effectively blocking thought, early, severe abuse by primary carers also distorts the psychological functions of attachment that would normally underpin a person's capacity for healthy relationships later in life.

As Fonagy (1998) reminds us, threat stimulates the attachment system, producing a strong drive towards the caregiver. When the caregiver is the source of threat, an attempt may be made to deactivate the attachment system. This strategy undermines the development of attachment-oriented thinking. Failure to recognise one's own states of mind and those of other people is a long-term consequence. Where there is an inability to recognise what is in the mind, there is also a failure to understand the social behaviours that are based on states of mind. When a person has this kind of damaged internal framework for relationships, gross misinterpretations and distortions concerning self in relation to others, and vice versa, serve as the foundation for social interaction. Close interpersonal relationships are therefore difficult for these people to fathom. Attachment relationships are likely to be especially dangerous, serving to recreate the terror, pain and confusion of the earliest relationship, which will then need to be externalised. Rejection of and by attachment figures often follows. Clinical experience with some forensic patients suggests this pitiful drama is iatrogenic, and when repeated time and time again the emotional toll exacted is a breakdown in psychosocial functioning, leading to detention in a secure environment.

This pattern is in direct contrast to the secure individual who has developed with a sense of ease when thinking about her caregivers' states of mind. As a result, the secure individual is later both comfortable and competent within her relationships with others. Relationships enrich the life of the secure individual for whom internal security is reinforced. The grossly insecure adult who is violent may need a physically secure environment in the first instance, before gaining security of mind.

ATTACHMENT AND FORENSIC PATIENTS

Attachment theory has begun to influence the work of clinicians and researchers working with offender patients. Gorsuch (1998) studied a group of 'difficult to place' women offenders in the health care unit of Holloway Prison and noticed that 'all the women experienced a serious failure of care in their childhoods'. Gorsuch (1998) felt that the interpersonal dysfunction, including self-injury, which typified the way this population of women presented, could be understood from the perspective of damaged attachments and the women's maladaptive attempts to secure the proximity of carers. Gorsuch (1999) felt that the behaviour engaged in by this group of women offenders functioned as a futile attempt to get their anxiety and fear assuaged by their carers. Ironically, their attempts to secure care actually alienated them from formal psychiatric care and treatment. After studying the attachment characteristics of violent male offenders, Fonagy *et al.* (1997) proposed that damaged attachment systems mediate the inability to empathise with victims. In normal circumstances, empathy with the potential victim would inhibit the drive to harm.

Clinical experience with patients in forensic services soon brings with it recognition that the majority are victims as well as offenders. Histories of parental maltreatment, separation, abandonment, and tragedies such as the violent death of a parent during early childhood are commonplace in the backgrounds of these patients. Therapeutic relationships are frequently difficult to establish or sustain, especially as many are non-compliant with offered care and treatment; others do not seem to respond to relationships in the expected way, sometimes, for example, deteriorating immediately after a lengthy exchange which was thought to be positive by nurses. Others seem to destroy relationships, just as they appear to be going well.

Relationships between forensic patients in secure psychiatric services may be characterised by exploitation, envy and rivalry. In addition, the relationships around forensic patients are often difficult. Hence, team working may prove a challenging prospect, as conflicting but powerful emotions, linked to experiences with patients, make working together stressful.

Fonagy's (1998) thesis about the interpersonal functioning of people with severe personality disorders may provide a way of understanding the emotional challenges faced daily by forensic mental health nurses in their therapeutic work with patients. According to Fonagy (1998), failure to develop an autonomous sense of self is the corollary of experiencing abusive caregiving. Instead, part of the abusive caregiver is internalised. This in turn feels alien and persecutory. Projection is used in an unconscious attempt to be rid of this abusive part. In the context of hospitalised psychiatric patients, the disturbance is forced into their professional caregivers, who are then pressurised to feel and behave towards them as the original, early abusive caregivers did. For the professional caregiver, this sense of disturbance is emotionally difficult to manage. For the patient, it results in further failed care, which means they cannot make progress. If the professional cannot contain the patient's projections, a re-enactment of early abuse, neglect or rejection takes place. If the professional can contain the projections, the patient is left with the agonising, internal persecutor, which is likely to be unbearable, also preventing clinical progress. As Fonagy (1998) explains, this interpersonal process is what makes these patients 'difficult'.

Clinical example

Ruby is a twenty-eight-year-old woman who has been detained in a high security psychiatric hospital for ten years. She is the younger of two sisters born to alcoholic parents. Ruby was born three months pre-term and spent the first few weeks of her life in an incubator. Her mother was unable to bond with Ruby and rejected her. When Ruby was eight months old, she was admitted to hospital with fractured arms and suffering from malnutrition. At twelve months old, Ruby was placed with foster parents. In later years she reported that she had been severely physically abused by her foster mother and repeatedly sexually abused by her foster father from as far back as she could remember. Aged fourteen, Ruby ran away from home and lived rough until she was sixteen years old, when she was admitted to an acute psychiatric service. Ruby has subsequently told clinicians that she survived on the streets by prostituting herself. She has reported that she began to consume alcohol at the age of ten years in an attempt to feel 'better' emotionally. By the age of sixteen, Ruby had been consuming large quantities of alcohol and illicit drugs. Additionally, she had been regularly cutting herself and punching out windows from the age of thirteen. She was admitted to the psychiatric hospital under compulsory detention after taking an overdose of analgesic medication. She was initially taken to an accident and emergency department, where she assaulted a nurse who was attempting to perform a stomach washout.

While detained in the acute psychiatric unit, Ruby regularly cut herself, absconded in order to abuse substances, occasionally assaulted members of staff and other patients, and engaged in risky sexual activity with male patients. Attempts by key professionals to engage Ruby in a constructive programme of care failed. After she had spent eighteen months in hospital, Ruby was convinced that she would be discharged. She became increasingly aggressive and oppositional. She was referred for admission to the high security psychiatric hospital after setting fire to her bed and attempting to keep a member of nursing staff with her in the burning room. The nurse's arm was fractured by Ruby in attempting to prevent her from leaving the room. Luckily, nobody was fatally harmed in this incident. However, Ruby was convicted of arson with intent to endanger life, and attempted murder. She claimed not to have any memory of the incident that led to her convictions. She was detained in a high security psychiatric hospital for treatment of mental disorder. She was diagnosed as having borderline personality disorder, and legally classified as 'psychopathic'.

While detained in the high security psychiatric hospital without limit of time, Ruby gradually settled into the routine. She frequently expressed that she did not want to leave. Ruby's first few years in the hospital were characterised by her isolation from other people. She claimed to be at her happiest keeping herself to herself. As she did not present a disciplinary problem to the organisation, it was felt best to let her function in the way she found most comfortable. The only area of concern was when Ruby and a male member of staff were suspected of having a sexualised relationship. However, this was never proven.

After Ruby had been in the high security psychiatric hospital for a number of years, a new primary nurse was assigned to her care. The nurse was very keen to develop a therapeutic relationship with Ruby and spent a lot of time trying to get to know her. Initially, Ruby seemed to be avoiding the primary nurse's attempts to develop a therapeutic relationship, claiming not to be in the mood for questions, or that she was tired after attending her off-ward activities. When the primary nurse persisted, Ruby requested a change of primary nurse, stating that she did not like the one she had. Her request was declined, as the primary nurse felt she could work through the difficulties within the relationship. However, Ruby refused to discuss her feelings.

Approximately eight months into the relationship, Ruby began to write letters to her primary nurse explaining in detail her feelings of panic. She was able to describe how she experienced mounting anxiety and strong urges to get away whenever her primary nurse approached her. Ruby wrote that she was convinced that the primary nurse wanted something from her that she could not give. The letter-writing provided the primary nurse with a way into gaining a dialogue with Ruby. Over time, they were able to agree that Ruby's panic had more to do with how she had been treated in the past than with anything her primary nurse was likely to do to her. A care plan, agreed by Ruby, was implemented. The aim of the care plan was to address Ruby's panic symptoms. The intervention involved gradually increasing the duration of their one-to-one sessions at a pace Ruby could tolerate. This intervention was discontinued when Ruby could manage to engage with her primary nurse for an hour at a time.

For a few months, Ruby and her primary nurse appeared to be getting along very well, having apparently formed a positive, trusting relationship. Then, it was noted that Ruby had lost a substantial amount of weight. She resumed cutting herself and her attendance at off-ward areas reduced as she claimed to have symptoms of physical health problems. She was rushed to the general hospital with chest pains on a number of occasions. When her primary nurse returned from periods of leave, Ruby began to make threats to her. Her letter-writing, which was still relied upon as a way to communicate her feelings, assumed a different tone. She began to make threats to harm her primary nurse. Ruby's main complaint was that the primary nurse had broken her heart by enticing her into believing that she cared, and then had hurt her by leaving and not listening when she was trying to communicate her pain. When Ruby informed another member of staff that she was planning to take her primary nurse hostage, the primary nurse was rapidly moved from Ruby's ward and placed elsewhere in the hospital. After a period of initial disturbance, Ruby resumed her low profile within the hospital, keeping herself to herself and trusting nobody. Her former primary nurse was shattered by the experience and never again attempted to work so intensely or indeed professionally with patients diagnosed with severe personality disorder.

Discussion

Ruby's case is an example of how essentially good nursing care can go wrong, and of how difficult it is to make progress with patients whose early attachment experiences have included gross maltreatment by carers. In the case of someone like Ruby, who did not experience a protective caregiver to internalise, the nursing task will always be exceptionally difficult. One reason for this may be that models proven to be effective with less relationally disturbed individuals can be rendered void when applied in the forensic setting with individuals for whom vulnerability arouses intolerable and un-thought-about distress. The distress, which may be experienced concretely and bodily, can only be converted into actions, somatised, or projected onto somebody else – it cannot be processed mentally. Inevitably, the patients' current carers come to experience some of that distress too. Perhaps what differentiates effective from ineffective care and treatment is what current carers are then able to do with the emotional disturbance that their patients will inevitably attempt to force into them. In the case of Ruby, neither avoiding nor engaging enabled nurses as professionals to make positive therapeutic progress. Indeed, it may be argued that good, professional nursing care led to the rejection she feared. Thus a re-enactment of early trauma took place in the hospital setting within the nurse–patient relationship. However, Ruby was the victimiser as well as the victim this time.

On the face of it, the most effective therapeutic agent for Ruby is the high security psychiatric hospital, with the structure and physical containment offered. This is not unusual, and raises questions about the psychological function of secure units and hospitals for patients who have so little internalised security. Application of an attachment theory paradigm would have alerted professionals to the possibility that Ruby's attachment style included that of unresolved in relation to trauma. She had broken a nurse's arm, just as her mother had broken her arm during infancy. Throughout her life, she had not been able to manage a safe one-to-one relationship with a carer. Her early relationships were cruel and she had not been able to process any of her traumas through thought. Instead, they were re-enacted in the context of intimacy in which she was either victim or perpetrator.

The primary nursing model served to stir up for Ruby gross anger and fear that could not be contained within that relationship. The cruelty Ruby experienced at the hands of early carers had left her with an abusive part of herself that was turned inwards in self-damaging ways. Her internalised abusive carer was also evident in her persecution of the primary nurse. Relational patterns such as these are unlikely to be anticipated by nurses who, in accordance with traditional nursing models, expect good care to have the straightforward effect of enriching patients' lives in ways that serve to promote positive mental health gains. Ruby's primary nurse managed to withstand the initial rejection by Ruby, but when Ruby's insecurity escalated to the point where she could no longer think, basic nursing models did not prove robust enough to prevent a very painful process from ensuing, which resulted in the termination of the relationship, and therefore of any potential therapeutic work that Ruby and her primary nurse might have been able to engage in. It should also be noted that the primary nurse was emotionally shattered by the experience, which had a negative effect on her professionalism. It is in these challenging situations that an attachment framework can be of particular clinical value.

ESTABLISHING A SECURE BASE – THE MAIN TASK OF FORENSIC MENTAL HEALTH NURSING

Just as providing a secure base can be understood as the essential task of parenting (Bowlby 1988), it can also be a useful frame for specifying the essential task of forensic mental health nursing.

Establishing a secure base for patients involves the maintenance of both physical and interpersonal limits and boundaries. Along with the physical environment, interpersonal exchanges should be containing; therefore consistency, predictability and structure are important components to be included in both the physical and interpersonal environment. One important function would be to reduce the interpersonal chaos that often accompanies groups of forensic patients. Within this framework, clinical activity may take place.

When people have not been attuned to, early in life, there appears to be a repetitive process whereby they are easily misrepresented. This process operates in the service of maintaining the individual's insecurity. From the perspective of providing interpersonal care it may be worth considering the function of the secure base in adults – that is, more as the provision of emotional proximity than of close physical contact. Adshead (1998) describes how the secure base can offer 'affective containment and anxiety modulation by a multi-modal management strategy, which includes long-term psychological support, the appropriate use of the Mental Health Act, and appropriate medication.'

Particular interventions that nurses can offer in providing a secure base for patients include listening to what the patient is communicating. Listening may involve thinking about what the patient may actually mean, by processing their actual words and then feeding back an interpretation.

Case example

Max has been hospitalised for twenty years. He is known as a persistent and vexatious complainant. He bombards the hospital's complaints department to such an extent that they have a large backlog of unresolved complaints. This results in complaints then being made about the professionals who work in the complaints department.

Max's primary nurse, upon listening very carefully to the complaints made to him, noted that Max might as well be complaining about his own early deprivation and neglect by his parents. For example, Max seemed to be particularly aggrieved about the fact that nurses were supposed to care and that they had chosen a vocation, therefore, they should be caring, understanding and respectful at all times. Max felt that some nurses were abusing their vocation by being uncaring and more concerned about themselves than their patients. He was particularly offended by the fact that he had observed nurses 'slopping' the food from the food trolleys onto patients' plates and, on occasions, sitting with their feet up reading newspapers while ignoring patients.

Max had justified complaints to make. However, the extent to which he was inflamed when he felt his carers were not caring, but rather, neglectful and self-indulgent, suggests there might have been something in his background that, when reflected in his current environment, produced such anger.

Max's early life was characterised by severe neglect by his parents, who were chronic alcoholics. Max's parents placed their addiction at the centre of their lives, while their children were left to fend for themselves. They used child support money on alcohol. As a child, Max used to pray that God would make his parents look after his brother, sisters and himself properly. Similarly, he was writing to senior managers in the hope that they would make the ward nurses care for himself and his fellow patients properly.

Max's primary nurse was able to help Max think about what he was doing, what he was really angry about, and how he might move on from his impotent anger towards his parents, rather than engage in perpetual and futile conflict with the institution. It was agreed that a more productive way forward would be for patients and nurses on the ward to meet regularly and discuss concerns and complaints between themselves, attempting to resolve them at ward level, within the ward community. This enabled Max to do something constructive with his own grievances, and in negotiating with the nurses concerned he was actually empowered to produce a better standard of care for himself, rather than repeatedly attempting to force a positive outcome from a system that inevitably let him down.

THE MILIEU

In relation to the secure base, the therapeutic milieu requires careful thought and planning. The social environment of services may be regarded as an active treatment agent. This has tended not to be the case in forensic mental health services, where the role of those whose work primarily takes place in the social environment (i.e. nurses) has remained undefined. However, from an attachment theory perspective, there could be an emphasis on providing an interpersonal model of care whereby the overriding aim is to discontinue patients' maladaptive ways of relating by changing their negative expectations of relationships with others, especially with carers. However, it is very clear that in order to establish a secure base for patients, nursing staff also require a secure base. This section will focus on the secure base for nursing staff.

Secure base for nursing staff

In light of the emotional impact on forensic mental health nurses of managing therapeutic relationships with patients who are so interpersonally disturbed, it may be concluded that a priority for service provision is to ensure there is sufficient interpersonal support to enable this work to take place. Providing a secure base for nursing staff, from where they can think about, organise and implement their clinical work, is essential if a secure base is to be provided for patients.

Physical safety

A physically safe environment to work in is a fundamental requirement. Therefore, the locks, keys, alarms, and number of staff on duty at any given time have a role to play in the emotional sense of security that nursing staff experience.

Consistency

In order to have a secure base for staff, consistent relationships are required, so that a sense of connectedness to a team of supportive and trusted colleagues is developed. This may have implications for recruitment and retention in the case of some services where there is regular employment of agency or bank nurses to compensate for vacancies in permanent staffing complements.

Support

Support from the environment, from working practices and from professional and interpersonal relationships with colleagues, is vitally important. Support can be organised by setting up a framework of interventions that promotes a secure state of mind for nursing staff. To do so would require recognition of the emotional hard work that is central to the task of maintaining therapeutic relationships with forensic patients.

Because the psychopathology of many forensic patients is complex, opportunities to help ward-based nursing staff understand how to make sense of the way their patients present would be useful. Experience in forensic mental health services suggests that a short training programme followed by regular groups for reflection on individual patients, or on the milieu, can help nurses to think about their relationships with patients in a productive way. Presenting nurses with a paradigm and then supporting them in their task of implementing it enables them to enjoy the richness of clinical material, rather than feeling persecuted by it because they cannot fathom it.

Structured milieu

The structured and consistent programme constituting milieu therapy for patients provides a supportive way of working for staff. A sense of what to expect in the context of an agreed and organised way of working will help to reduce some of the anxiety and bewilderment that staff are likely to experience when the working environment is chaotic or unpredictable. By being with patients, nurses are able to observe and assess the patients' strengths as well as their pathology. In turn, the patients are not forced into a state of dependency that they cannot tolerate.

Consistent treatment process

A consistent treatment process applied by the team should also provide a means of support for staff, as well as offering therapeutic value to patients. By identifying the stages of recovery and agreeing a range of interventions, again, staff should know where they are with patients and be able to understand what their goals are without fear that they are doing the wrong thing. Also, colleagues should to some extent be able to monitor each other's work and pick up, in a supportive way, when avoidance takes place.

Education, training and development

Understanding the clinical agenda and having the skills to work with it obviously empowers staff and increases their sense of confidence. Learned helplessness, resulting from feelings that therapeutically nothing is being achieved for patients, is a major source of stress. Training can involve learning to contain powerfully toxic feelings, for example tolerating helplessness and the fact that, in the long term, the patient may not recover. What is important is that training is integrated with actual clinical practice and support.

Practices

In regard to ward management, forums enabling communication, expression and, most important perhaps, an opportunity for staff to influence the environment, need to be embedded in the working week. Staff meetings, as a medium for addressing domestic concerns, support the process of thinking and working through issues together.

Clinical communications systems are also important. However, in order for secure base principles to underpin the systems, a commitment to honest and open communication is essential. Aiming to face reality in a supportive and productive way represents an attempt to reverse the trend whereby anxiety prevents forensic mental health nursing staff from confronting their colleagues. Asking for help can also be impossible when anxiety about being seen as incompetent, and therefore a liability, overshadows all else. Therefore, a philosophy is required that recognises how the task of caring in a forensic context requires challenging as well as supportive interventions, and all learning and practices needs to reflect this.

Reflection as a routine part of the working day is also an important aspect of practice, with potential for being a means of support. In keeping with encouragement to think in the context of any traumatic material that impedes the capacity to think, regular reflection on work, patients, feelings and relationships within a supportive space is also an important component.

Self awareness
Identifying with the patient group in a forensic setting may be fraught with anxieties. However, it is clear that among members of nursing staff there will be people with attachment difficulties of their own. These difficulties are likely to be stirred up through working with the patient group. This makes it essential that the determined effort to provide a secure base for staff is included in the overall design of services.

CONCLUSION

In this chapter I have demonstrated how using attachment theory as an explanatory framework can help to understand some of the more challenging behaviours exhibited by patients in forensic settings. The task, then, of the forensic psychiatric nurse is to develop skills as a secure caregiver – a professional who can provide a secure base for patients so that they can learn to develop their own capacity to contain distress. Since all of us need others to relate to at times of stress and threat, those who manage forensic institutions need to give thought to the provision of a secure base for staff.

REFERENCES

Adshead, G. (1998) 'Psychiatric staff as attachment figures.' *British Journal of Psychiatry 172*, 64–69.
Ainsworth, M.D.S. (1967) *Infancy in Uganda: Infant Care and the Growth of Attachment.* Baltimore: Johns Hopkins University Press.

Blackburn, R. (1992) 'Criminal behaviour, personality disorder and mental illness: The origins of confusion.' *Criminal Behaviour and Mental Health 2*, 66–77.

Blackburn, R. (1998) 'Criminality and the interpersonal circle in mentally disordered offenders.' *Criminal Justice and Behaviour 25*, (2), 155–176.

Blackburn, R. and Renwick, S.J. (1996) 'Rating scale for measuring the interpersonal circle in forensic psychiatric patients.' *Psychological Assessment 8*, (1), 76–84.

Bowlby, J. (1951) *Maternal Care and Mental Health.* Geneva: WHO.

Bowlby, J. (1969) *Attachment and Loss Vol. 1: Attachment.* New York: Basic Books.

Bowlby, J. (1973) *Attachment and Loss Vol. 2: Separation.* New York: Basic Books.

Bowlby, J. (1988) *A Secure Base.* London: Routledge.

Cox, M. (1996) 'Psychodynamics and the Special Hospital "road blocks and thought blocks".' In C. Cordess and M. Cox (eds) *Forensic Psychotherapy: Psychodynamics and the Offender Patient.* London: Jessica Kingsley Publishers.

Dozier, M. (1990) 'Attachment organisation and treatment use for adults with serious psychopathological disorders.' *Development and Psychopathology 2*, 47–60.

de Zulueta, F. (1993) *From Pain to Violence: The Traumatic Roots of Destructiveness.* London: Whurr.

Fonagy, P. (1998) 'An attachment theory approach to treatment of the difficult patient.' *Bulletin of the Menninger Clinic 62*, (2), 147–169.

Fonagy, P., Target, M., Steele, M., Steele, H., Leigh, T., Levinson, A. and Kennedy, R. (1997) 'Morality, disruptive behavior, borderline personality disorder, crime, and their relationships to security of attachment.' In L. Atkinson and K.J. Zucker (eds) *Attachment and Psychopathology.* New York: Guilford Press.

Gorsuch, N. (1998) 'Unmet needs among disturbed female offenders.' *The Journal of Forensic Psychiatry 9*, (3), 556–570.

Holmes, J. (1993) *John Bowlby and Attachment Theory.* London: Routledge.

Holmes, J. (2001) *The Search for the Secure Base: Attachment Theory and Psychotherapy.* London: Routledge.

Main, M. and Goldwyn, R. (1998) 'Adult Attachment Scoring and Classification System.' Unpublished manuscript, University of California at Berkeley.

Menzies-Lyth, I. (1988) *Containing Anxiety in Institutions.* London: Free Association Books.

Orwell, G. (1949) *Nineteen-eighty-four.* (Reprinted 1989) London: Penguin.

Sroufe, A. (1995) *Emotional Development: The Organization of Emotional Life in the Early Years.* New York: Cambridge University Press.

van der Kolk, B.A. (1987) *Psychological Trauma.* Washington, DC: American Psychiatric Press.

CHAPTER 7

Finding a Secure Base

Attachment in Grendon Prison

Michael Parker and Mark Morris

The contribution of Bowlby's work to the understanding of mental life and to the psychologisation of social and policy discourse cannot be over-emphasised. His accounts are both intuitively compelling, and widely accessible. Despite widespread recognition and acceptance in developmental research, in some psychoanalytic circles attachment theory has apparently had less influence. One criticism that is levelled is the absence in the model of any account of the innate destructiveness of the child, either in fantasy or in reality.

In the application of Bowlby's ideas in forensic work, the issue of the role of the subject's destructiveness is brought into sharp relief. For example, attachment bonds are complicated where there has been a concrete loss of the attachment object, because he/she has been killed by the subject. In this chapter we hope to set out some thoughts on conflicted attachments as they manifest themselves in a therapeutic community prison setting. We shall first introduce the setting and then raise some general theoretical issues, before tracking the attachment process as it seems to occur in the clinical setting. This will be followed by an extended clinical example which illustrates some of the issues raised.

THE SETTING – GRENDON

Grendon Underwood is a 230-bed, all-male, high security B-category prison near Aylesbury which was opened in 1962, after considerable debate about what to do with 'psychopaths' in prisons. It consists of five discrete therapeutic communities of 40 or so residents each and an assessment-preparation unit for 25. The communities are modelled on the Maxwell-Jones Henderson model, with a standardised regime of a group every morning. Three days a week, residents attend a small group, and twice a week a large group 'community meeting'. Within the constraints imposed by the need for security, the activities of daily living are carried out by the community members, and are a potent focus for debate within the community. As far as possible, decisions about the community and the requests of individual residents are devolved to the community, although the staff group retains a right of veto.

The resident group is self-selected, in that they request transfer to Grendon in the face of strong, prison cultural opposition. Our requirements are that they have to be serving a sentence of four years or more (so that they will spend at least eighteen months with us); that the professionals to whom they are known think they are suitable; and that in the preliminary correspondence that is initiated, they demonstrate some capacity for psychological reflection, and at least superficial acknowledgement of responsibility for their crime.

Grendon's population is more disturbed on a variety of indices than the residents of other prisons; about 50 per cent currently are 'lifers', usually meaning they have been found guilty of murder; and about 30 per cent are in prison for a sex offence. Almost all are in prison for offences against the person, and about 25 per cent of receptions score highly on the Hare psychopathy checklist – denoting severe psychopathy. Diagnostically, 70 per cent have a personality disorder, and 60 per cent meet DSM criteria for more than one – most commonly antisocial, paranoid and borderline, in that order.

Anecdotally, Grendon works with many of the prison 'faces' of yesterday – the people whose behaviour has been difficult to contain, who have been involved in disturbances, taking hostages, and so on. They often describe a life where intimidation and violence have been their means of psychological and physical survival, both in life and then in prison.

The staff group in each community consists of 12 prison officers, a probation officer, a psychologist and a community therapist. When you walk in, the prison buildings (or 'wings') feel a bit like an old style psychiatric hospital ward, with the nursing role carried by the officers. The officers are the front line staff, with a shift pattern that covers through the week, and also in terms of being more available for the residents. Instead of the traditional and ritualised nursing care work, however, the officers have the task of standard 'prison craft' to carry out. There is a tight regime of cell searches, security checks, drug tests and other operational tasks that conflict directly with their caring, sympathetic role as social therapists. This dilemma is illustrated by the fact that while on duty, a prison officer has the custodial authority of a police constable, in which role he or she is also required to facilitate or co-facilitate the small groups, and other psychotherapeutic work.

The community staff team is clinically managed by the community therapist, whose task it is to facilitate the psychodynamic work. This is achieved with a structure of 'feedback' meetings following the morning's groups. The notion of 'feedback' is quite important. After each small group, the community briefly meets as a large group to hear a précis of what has happened in each; in the community meetings proper, the agenda includes time for participants in the other activities (art therapy; psychodrama; cognitive programmes) to 'feed back' the content of these sessions. There is a rolling programme of assessments and reviews of the community membership by the staff group, and the gist of these discussions is 'fed back' to the community. This emphasis on the sharing of information explicitly attempts to counter the pervasive culture of secrecy and intrigue of many families of origin, and by default the prison culture, as well as promoting a sense of community and reducing risk.

ATTACHMENT AND PSYCHOPATHY

Cleckley's classical description of psychopathy expanded the concept previously captured by such terms as 'moral insanity' and 'manie sans délire' (Cleckley 1988). The apparent cruelty and duplicity of the psychopath has increasingly been understood in terms of empathic failure – an inability to perceive the suffering of the victim. In extreme circumstances, it would seem that most people are capable of this sort of switching off of empathy, as illustrated by documented human cruelties, ranging from massacres in Rwanda to the ability of health care professionals to inure themselves to the patient's suffering during a painful medical procedure. Closing down empathy in this way is presumably a spectrum, with some individuals finding it easier than others. At the far end of the spectrum are those individuals who rarely if ever are pained or touched by the suffering of another, who might best be called psychopaths. Freed from the discomfort and guilt of causing suffering, the psychopath does that which amuses or occupies him, oblivious to the trauma caused to victims. Meloy (1988) distinguishes this form of violence from 'catathymic' violence, where, for example, a violent incident occurs as an unexpected explosion of rage, for which there is guilt, or at least a recognition of wrong afterwards. To psychopaths proper, the victims (and all of us) are merely objects or playthings, there for their amusement.

Given the cruelty of the violence perpetrated by psychopaths, it is not surprising that the term has come to be used as a term of abuse, and people so labelled can generate genuine fear and loathing among the professionals who have to work with them. Given the strength of these feelings, psychodynamic theories of explanation for understanding the problem are not particularly well received, nor widely used. An early Freudian 'Civilisation and its discontents' model, with its account of the ubiquity of psychopathic tendencies tied down by the flimsy mores of civilised culture, flies in the face of society's important need to project its own repressed evil intention onto the 'evil men' behind the prison wall. Likewise, the Kleinian emphasis on destructiveness and the death instinct, which locates psychopathy firmly in each and every one of us, limits its popularity.

The perspectives of Bowlby and Winnicott start from a different point of view, suggesting that the problem might not be an innate aspect of the human condition, but rather might be caused by some form of developmental trauma. For Winnicott (1956), the thief steals something because he feels he deserves something. The thief deserved a loving mother, who was denied him, so he takes something else as a substitute. Murray Cox (1982) describes a patient who 'took a life, because he needed one', which illustrates an extreme example of this notion. If the crime of paedophilia is the destruction and distortion of a child's development by exploiting a pseudo-trust as a vehicle to intrude sexuality, the abuser often enacts nothing more than a repetition of his own experience. Many sex offenders' lives have been disabled by abusers who did to them what they do to others.

Perhaps they feel they 'deserve' a child's innocence, or 'deserve' to betray the trust because this was their experience.

Bowlby proposed an attachment model of psychopathy in his paper 'Forty-four juvenile thieves' (1946), where he identified 14 boys who were 'affectionless psychopaths'. This model would propose psychopathy as a condition where a capacity for a reciprocal affectionate bond has not developed, and in consequence, neither has a need or a wish to establish affectionate contacts with people. This represents a shift of emphasis from the dominant meta-psychological understanding of psychopathy to one that conceptualises psychopathy as a failure of empathy (Blair 1995). For the Bowlby model of the psychopath, whether or not the perpetrator empathises with the suffering of the victim is irrelevant. If the basic pathology of the psychopath is that he is affectionless, then there is no motivation for him to strive for an affectionate connection with people in general, or the victim in particular.

A basic prerequisite for the formation of affectionate bonds to another would require some acknowledgement of the existence and experience of that person. This connection between attachment, empathy and other-perception is explored by Fonagy (1999). In brief, the task of the developing child is to learn to think about thinking – to be able to reflect on her own emotions and mental states, and those of others. Parents who are narcissistically identified with their children – who have difficulty seeing the child as a psychologically independent individual – do not themselves think of the child as having an independent mind, and so do not allow the child the mental space to develop this 'reflective capacity'. Clearly there is a link between an extreme lack of a reflective capacity, and the empathetic failure mentioned above.

Bowlby and Winnicott studied psychopathy in passing, and Freud's work was more from a sociological perspective, as much concerned with the evil of civil breakdown and war. The most authoritative psychodynamic writing on psychopathy comes from Meloy (1992), who argues an attachment model. In brief, he argues that for psychopaths the experience of parenting or early life is so traumatising for the child that a defensive, violent and macho 'shell' is built up which maintains an illusion that the individual simply does not need anyone. This 'psychopathic shell' model is congruent with the clinical experience of being faced with a rather intimidating person who after considerable effort can be reached psychodynamically, and who as a result dissolves away into an infantile and vulnerable, childlike state. While fleeting initially, the ability to observe and be aware of the underlying vulnerability provides a secure foundation for understanding both the need for and nature of the psychopathic attitude as a defensive structure, and for future therapeutic work.

However, this account can be criticised on the grounds that (a) many children have traumatic lives and do not become psychopaths, and (b) the notion that serial killers are simply created by unpleasant mothering is facile. A counter-argument is that Meloy's model is dynamic, not static. Development offers opportunities as well as risks, so that the proto-psychopath will experience a series of opportunities to change – to become attached to objects who will not abuse. These invitations to intimacy will themselves become a threat, which needs to be ruthlessly put down. For example, if, after a childhood of abuse, a proto-romance begins with a partner, any threat to the relationship may generate huge anxiety linked to those earlier traumas. The need to obliterate the unconscious anxiety is mirrored in a conscious impulse to obliterate the partner, who may have to be killed off as ruthlessly as the threat of vulnerability. This only needs to become a repetition-compulsion pattern to create a serial killer.

THE DEVELOPMENT OF A REAL ATTACHMENT IN GRENDON

Cynics would argue that Grendon's main task is completed before the prisoner arrives. A classic story is of a 'likely lad' – a doughty prisoner who protests against the prison authorities (physically, or legally with complaints and litigation) and is active in prisoner groups and gangs. On the umpteenth visit to the prison segregation unit, and if he can feel sadness, he wonders about the extent to which his own actions contribute to the situation he is in. This point is critical because it can lead to the beginning of thinking that his situation is to some degree his own responsibility: not the judge's fault, or the barrister's fault, or the co-defendant's or the partner's or the 'grasser's' fault – but his own. The penny drops that he himself might be actively con-tributing to his difficult situation. Furthermore, he realises that if he behaved differently, this would materially change his current situation.

The critical point might be one of many things – receiving a long sentence; a life experience such as the death of a relative; the conviction of a friend or family member. One of these gives pause, and triggers some reflection. Grendon then builds on this. Central to the assessment process is an effort to establish that there is something of this sort of proto-acceptance of responsibility.

The initial phase: 'illusory attachment'

Some acceptance of responsibility is only half the story. There is often another agenda, which sees coming to Grendon simply as a means of 'conning' the system. Prisoners say the right things to get in, but then retain a flinty resistance to any further insight. They can use psychological skills of duping and misleading, acquired over many years, to give the impression of therapeutic work and making progress, while in reality maintaining a safe distance from the real contact that the therapeutic process invites them into. This idealised and artificial initial phase can be abruptly brought to a halt if the duplicity is too great, and if the therapeutic work is actively sabotaged; for example, by bringing in drugs, which might result in discharge. This phase illustrates what Meloy calls the 'apparent attachment'. The person might make real strides in terms of reducing violent or self-harming behaviour, and there is a temptation to take this at face value, but it is very difficult to gauge the real nature of the attachment until something goes wrong. For example, an issue stirs someone up to an outburst, or there is security intelligence which contrasts with the clinical picture – such as with drugs. On these occasions, there is a fleeting opportunity to see the gulf between the avowed security of attachment, and the actual security – or lack of it.

Second phase: 'angry attachment'

The second phase is more real. Inmates begin to transfer their challenging of the environment from purely the enactment realm to the verbal realm also. The hostility and rage resulting from childhood attachment experiences re-emerge and are transferred onto the setting and the staff group. Staff are bitterly attacked for their hypocrisy in declaring an interest in helping inmates, yet maintaining security within a prison setting; or for having the opportunity to go home in the evening. Staff may be accused of providing a poor standard of therapy, or insufficient therapy, and when genuine and inevitable mistakes are made, they can be viciously attacked and pilloried.

The response of the staff group, however, is different to the response of the primary attachment objects, and this heralds the third phase. In the inmates' life to date, the violent attachments that they have developed will have been reciprocated in kind. Most adults to whom they have become violently and intimately attached will, at some time or another, have attacked or abused them, as their primary attachment figures did, thus completing a further cycle of violence. They therefore unconsciously anticipate that staff to whom they are attached are going to attack them. Indeed, one of the most difficult things for staff to bear in the work is an inmate driven to distraction by the wish to elicit an abusive response. He seems terrified of an alternative, and ups the stakes logarithmically to trigger the abusive response that he is familiar with, and that he apparently needs to preserve his sanity.

However, the professional task is to ensure that the abuse is, as far as possible, not returned. The staff group acts with restraint and fairness, while acknowledging their limitations as carers. In short, the staff group attempts to be 'good enough' as attachment objects for the prisoners. Sometimes (too frequently) the acting out reaches a level that simply cannot be tolerated, and inmates have to be moved to a more secure setting, but contact with the therapeutic group is not severed, and there is often the option of return in negotiation with the staff team.

Third phase: a 'secure base'

This third phase represents the realisation by the inmate that their staff group, or their community, represents something different, something that they have not experienced before – a secure base. This realisation forms slowly, that the staff group and the community can to some degree be trusted.

This realisation is fraught with testing out. There is a terror that the community and the staff group on whom the individual now depends are outside the control of the individual's manipulations. For most prisoners, manipulation and control of the object have been ways to maintain inner security, and now there is an awful process of retrospective insight into the meaning of what has gone before: however naughty they were as children, they didn't deserve to be beaten; and also, whatever their victim did, they didn't deserve what the prisoner did to them.

In many ways, the tumbled account of personal and offending history that emerges in the therapeutic process can obscure the state of the attachment relationship, similar to the way that suspicion, hostility or fake enthusiasm did in the first phase. But little by little, the attachment grows, as it is tested out in the reactions of the staff group. This process might be similar to Ainsworth's observations of infants exploring their environment as if they are attached to mother by elastic, maintaining an optimum distance.

However, the depth of the attachment seems to remain hidden, emerging as a genuine dread of the ending of therapy and either release or transfer to another prison. Prisoners are fearful that they will have changed in such a way that they will be unable to function back in a normal prison environment, that they will have softened in such a way as to make them vulnerable. In fact, from a developmental perspective, strings are being added to their bow, rather than being removed. It is true that they may have developed the capacity to tolerate levels of vulnerability that were not possible before, but this represents a developmental progression rather than amputation of a set of skills needed to survive in different environments. Anecdotally Grendon graduates make better use of whatever resources are around, facilitating their rehabilitation.

This fear of moving on may be evident in daily behaviour and anxieties which articulate the fear of impending loss of the attachment figures. One way of understanding intensive psychoanalytic treatment is that in some way it 're-parents' patients, and, along these lines, the Grendon community might be thought of as 're-familying' prisoners. For a number, the process of taking leave of a prison 'family' to whom they have become attached is extremely hard. To separate from the first 'family' who has sat and listened to the realities and fantasies of crime and not been entirely rejecting is simply too much, and suicidal ideas can emerge. Modern psychodynamic perspectives on suicide emphasise the murderousness of the act, and the violence that the suicide victim is perpetrating on their surroundings. Undoubtedly, rage at leaving Grendon contributes to the likelihood of suicide in this way, but there seems to be more to it. There is a rational element to these suicidal fantasies. The accounts of some of these men are so horrendous, with themselves as both victims and perpetrators, that to juxtapose them with the imperfect but good enough environment and life that a Grendon community provides seems impossible. For some of them, not only is their Grendon community the closest thing to a family and friends that they have ever had: it is the only home or psychic possession they have ever had. Having experienced a sense of belonging, there is nothing beyond it. In the concrete world in which these men live, the task of working towards an understanding that they 'take their community with them' as a resolution of mourning is somewhat difficult – but that is a further, long process.

One interesting feature of this process is that there may be a difference between the object of transference and the eventual attachment figures. It seems as though in the initial two phases, a very strong transference relationship is established to the prison as a whole. The cathexis seems to be to 'Grendon' rather than to specific staff roles or individuals, or even to the particular community that the individual is a member of. This is explicable in a number of ways, and especially by the fact that the culture of the prison is very different to others that inmates will have experienced, and quite pervasive. Staff talk about the 'Grendon way' of managing issues and resolving problems, and the therapeutic approach and organisational culture seem to be bounded by the concrete walls of the prison. Attachments, however, as they tentatively develop, are different. The secure base that emerges to some degree in the third phase is not Grendon as a whole, which is too amorphous and abstract. Instead it is composed of various specific structures and aspects of the work – the inmate's small group; their own community; individual members of staff and fellow inmates. The process of grieving and preparation for departure is about these things that have come to have genuine meaning and relevance in the inmate's life, rather than the more abstract notion of a whole prison culture.

Some of these issues can be followed in this extended clinical example of a Grendon inmate's therapeutic progress.

CLINICAL EXAMPLE

Rene, a young, second-generation West Indian man, grew up with Mother working long hours as a nurse and Father unemployed, drinking and smoking cannabis regularly, and staying out often and returning at unpredictable hours of the day or night. Rene describes Father as beating him savagely and verbally abusing him; he was afraid of him. He has one sister, one stepbrother and two stepsisters. From the age of seven to nine he was sent to stay with his uncle, Father's brother, to enable Mother to work. He described being sexually abused by this uncle from age eight to nine, but feeling afraid to say anything to Mother or Father for fear of being beaten. At age 15 he left home as fast as he could, as he 'could not wait to get out'.

He set up home with his girlfriend Miriam when he was sixteen and she seventeen, and they quickly had a baby girl. Rene began to be violent with Miriam, possessive, and would not let her leave the relationship on pain of severe violence. On one occasion Rene was so violent towards Miriam that she had to be hospitalised with a broken nose. Their relationship ended when he went to prison, and she later died of a heroin overdose that he has come to regard as his fault, and for which he feels guilty.

From age fifteen to thirty he committed many armed robberies, burglaries and thefts, and sold drugs. He developed a lifestyle in which he describes having to be in control, and in his words, 'if there's any abusing to be done I had to be doing it, not anyone doing it to me.' This self-generated behaviour represented to him a means of being in control, and specifically of preventing abuse, which he describes being aware of at the time he was engaged in committing criminal acts. His index offence is armed robbery for which he is serving a long sentence of seventeen years. He has described gaining considerable pleasure from making others suffer and experience humiliation and is currently particularly attentive and alert when the issue of forced sexual intercourse is being discussed. His own experiences of abuse, when discussed by him in therapy, still leave him so angry and disturbed that he says he would like to do serious 'damage' to others by way of immediate ego-syntonic restoration: it makes him feel better. Prior to his sentence his behaviour appeared to be worsening and he was becoming more careless about how he committed his crimes. The intervals between crimes were shortening and he described feeling that he was out of control. He described feeling out of balance if not committing crimes at sufficiently frequent intervals.

The initial pattern of attachment Rene made with staff on the Wing was characterised by his powerful, aggressively delivered and repetitive insistence that others listen to him until he had said all that he had to say, however many repetitions that might involve, and without interrupting him or contradicting him. He had to have his say absolutely about anything he chose and he would shout and yell, gesticulate and wave his arms until staff or fellow inmates had listened. This behaviour seemed primarily aimed at staff, and when he had clearly broken the rules and was caught, he would teasingly offer his backside to us in mock submission and with a wicked grin on his face, asking to be punished, but in a sexually ambiguous way, as though searching for proof either way of whether staff or others would pick up his unconscious invitation to punish or abuse. The invitation to fulfil the countertransference enactment was clearly evident. It was pointed out to him and attempts made to bring this potentially self-destructive behaviour to awareness, and so to an end.

Rene searched for the rules and expectations of behaviour most carefully and attempted to comply in the presence of staff, but out of staff's sight he would engage in taking drugs with his peers and intimidating others on the landings, obeying the prison codes for armed robbers who rule the roost with whatever force or persuasion it takes to do so. He led a double life, appeared to want to change, but found this difficult to do. Particular pressure was placed on him by his black peer group, who saw him as deserting them; and he was insulted with all imaginable comments indicating sell-out and submission to white people in order to anger and provoke him back into defiance, rule breaking, delinquency, and identifying with the 'brothers' once again. He told us repeatedly that he did not want to return to a life of crime and that he liked it when rules were clear.

Grendon appears to provide the role of father/superego/rule-enforcer to which Rene currently responds with understanding and appreciation. He has invited his therapist to punish him in a combination of teasing and testing ways – but also managed to say, 'I don't want to leave, is that bad? I feel safe here: I've never felt safe before.' Initially it was very difficult for him to leave behind the old patterns of behaviour that he was used to. His loyalty was severely divided and he was under great stress while apparently having to behave in two different and competing ways.

Rene began by engaging with us in the illusory relationship (Meloy 1992), telling us what he thought we wanted to hear, while behaving in the old, criminal way when out of our sight: threatening, intimidating, talking about guns, drugs and women in ways suggesting he wanted to be involved once again in crime. After being sent away on what used to be called a 'lie down', a period of three months away from Grendon in another B-category prison (seen as a punishment), he returned and has succeeded in changing his overall behaviour in a major way. He has formed an attachment to 'the Wing', as he calls it, and to some staff individually. As one clear way of demonstrating this, he adopts anti-drugs attitudes and is a voice in the community, articulating pro-Wing attitudes. He now tends to be a main pro-social Wing culture carrier and spokesperson in Wing meetings, dis-agreeing with fellow inmates if necessary and representing the Wing rather than the inmate culture.

It is hoped, when this process is evident in behaviour on a consistent basis, that internalisation of the new pro-social objects has taken root, and currently this shows itself in Rene's regularly asking about the rules and why they are important, and wanting reminders about them – as though he wants to ensure that the solid base he is discovering is in reality as secure as it seems. A factor in changing that leaves him exposed and vulnerable is the act of abandoning old ways of behaving.

Recently, Rene has become more dependent on staff: closer to us and seeking out assurance that we think that he is doing well and is on course to change. This has an anxious quality that suggests he is not engaged in an illusory relationship with us, but in a more anxious process of allowing himself to be in a different emotional zone in which he is not so exclusively in omnipotent control of his objects. He fondly remembers an ex-inmate who was a strong culture carrier and, in his middle phase on A-Wing at Grendon, was closely aligned with the staff perspective.

The working assumption is that with a sufficient degree of intern-alisation of new objects, and new ways of relating, Rene will be enabled to leave with clear enough non-criminal objects in place. These will have been sufficiently practised at Grendon that they constitute firm alternatives to the original criminal codes to which he was formerly attached, and provide suf-ficient learned new behaviour to enable change to be sustained.

Detachment and leaving is an important phase and time in therapy, and much anger and anxiety can accompany the final stages. It is common for men to revert to previous forms of behaviour and appear to regress. At Grendon one of the most commonly discussed sources of anxiety concerns men returning to C-category or other B-category establishments where they fear once again feeling unsafe and needing to revert to previous patterns of behaviour, such as putting on tough fronts, or considering being strategi-cally violent to prevent being taken advantage of by others. There is a firm hierarchy of behaviour and signals men understand well, and this is described as a major preoccupying anxiety with men in prison, since it takes up a great deal of thinking time in preparing the necessary front or appear-ance in order not to be seen as weak.

The ideal solution posed for Grendon inmates is that they progress through the system and either leave Grendon as free men, or move onwards to open conditions (D-category establishments). In open conditions, they face less risk of either being provoked into behaviours they do not want, or simply having to face more aggressive posturing behaviour that is said to characterise B- and C-category prisons.

Leaving Grendon forms a core part of the working-through process. One of the staff's main tasks is to avoid collusion with enactments and destructiveness on the part of inmates which replicate old patterns of destructive behaviour yet again. Staff must be particularly vigilant to avoid being tempted into a punitive countertransference response to such behaviour. We would argue that most aggressive behaviour prior to transfer is not indicative of regression and deterioration but more akin to a last gasp of the repetition compulsion, and should be partly understood as such.

Rene's position is that he still has a significant period of time to serve in prison and he can be viewed as being in the middle phase of his stay: the practising phase. However, the process of finding somewhere to live, and non-criminal contacts as sources of support on discharge, has already been started, and eventually, when his risk level has been reduced, he will be able to have short visits out into the community (release on temporary licence, in which he can begin to re-acclimatise to life in the community). Currently his behaviour has considerably calmed and modified, and he is less inclined to test staff by trying to provoke a response. He is, if anything, rather more thoughtful and far less histrionic: he has not lost his temper or shouted and lost control for more than six months. He is attempting, slowly and painfully, to form a relationship with his daughter, who is angry with him for his criminal lifestyle and his being absent for all of her life as a child and teenager. Fortunately, he no longer says that he never wants to leave, as was the case nine months ago when he told us that Grendon was his home. He now 'can't wait to leave' when thorough care arrangements are in place and his discharge date is reached.

CONCLUSIONS

In this paper we have reviewed some of the psychodynamic ideas about psy-chopathy, and explored the utility of the attachment model for understand-ing the work of a prison therapeutic community. We have argued that over a long and intense process of therapeutic community work, the apparent and duplicitous attachment of the psychopath might first evolve into a more clearly hostile or ambivalent attachment, and subsequently a more genuine attachment may ensue. Follow-up data on recidivism suggests that if men can make a 'secure' attachment to Grendon, then they have an increased chance of internalising that security, so that they and others may be safer.

REFERENCES

Blair, R.J.R. (1995) 'A cognitive developmental approach to morality: Investigating the psychopath.' *Cognition 57*, 1–29.

Bowlby, J. (1946) *Forty-four Juvenile Thieves: Their Character and Home Life.* London: Balliere Tyndall and Cox.

Cleckley, H. (1941) *The Mask of Sanity.* St. Louis, MO: C.V. Mosby Co. (Fifth edn. 1988.)

Cox, M. (1982) 'I took a life because I needed one: Psychotherapeutic possibilities with the schizophrenic offender-patient.' *Psychotherapy and Psychosomatics 37*, 96–105.

Fonagy, P. (1999) 'The male perpetrator: The role of trauma and failures of mentalisation in aggression against women – an attachment theory perspective.' The 6th John Bowlby Memorial Lecture.

Meloy, J.R. (1988) *The Psychopathic Mind: Origins, Dynamics and Treatment.* Northvale, NJ: Jason Aronson.

Meloy, J.R. (1992) *Violent Attachments* Northvale, NJ: Jason Aronson.

Winnicott, D. (1958) 'The antisocial tendency.' In *Collected Papers: Through Paediatrics to Psychoanalysis.* London: Tavistock.

Part IV

Research Data

CHAPTER 8

Attachment Representations and Factitious Illness by Proxy

Relevance for Assessment of Parenting Capacity in Child Maltreatment

Gwen Adshead and Kerry Bluglass

SUMMARY

The assessment framework document indicates a need to assess parenting capacity in parents involved in child protection procedures. Parenting capacity includes an assessment of the parents' own experience of parenting as a child. In this chapter we present data from a pilot study of attachment representations in a sample of mothers exhibiting factitious illness by proxy behaviours. We suggest that attachment representations can help to explain how such mothers fail to care for their children, and argue that attachment theory generally is helpful for understanding how normal and abnormal caregiving behavioural systems develop. We conclude that it is useful to understand child maltreatment, at least in part, as a failure of caregiving in the parent as a result of parental insecurity of attachment.

> *All happy families resemble one another; each unhappy family is unhappy in its own way.*
>
> Leo Tolstoy, *Anna Karenina*

BACKGROUND

The Working Together guidelines make it clear that detailed assessment of the capacity to parent a child is an essential part of investigations into cases of alleged maltreatment or neglect (Department of Health *et al.* 1999). Dimensions of parenting capacity are described in the Framework for Assessment of Children in Need (Department of Health *et al.* 2000), and include the capability to provide basic care, emotional warmth, stability and boundaries. The framework document also notes that the parents' own past experience may be relevant for the assessment of parenting capacity.

In this chapter we will suggest that attachment theory offers a useful way of conceptualising how parents' own experience of being cared for as children by their own parents may influence their capacity to parent their child. Rather than focusing only on actual parenting behaviours, attachment theory provides an account of how parents think about being parents and caregivers, and what the role of caregiver means to them – which may in turn help to understand failure of caregiving by parents. Further, we may be able to use this information to provide interventions which specifically address parental difficulties in care provision. This chapter is based on our clinical experience as experts preparing reports on adults who have mistreated their children, and as researchers in the area of factitious illness by proxy (FIP), also known as Munchausen's syndrome by proxy. To support our argument, we will present some data from a pilot study of attachment representations in mothers who have exhibited this type of behaviour.

ATTACHMENT THEORY

Attachment theory covers a huge literature and only a brief review will be provided here. As described by Bowlby (1969, 1980), attachment theory offers an account of how early childhood experience with caregivers influences the development of models of interpersonal relating, and relationships with others in adulthood. Bowlby argued that experiences with caregivers, especially at times of distress or perceived threat, were internalised by the infant as internal psychological representations ('working models'), and manifested as an organised system of behaviour (i.e. attachment behaviours) which the infant could use to regulate distress and anxiety. Drawing on primate studies, Bowlby argued that successful (or 'secure') working models of attachment relationships with caregivers in infancy resulted in healthy and successful social behaviours in adulthood.

In contrast, insecure attachment in infancy could result in highly unsuccessful adult functioning. Non-human primate studies found that monkeys whose attachments were disrupted by lengthy early separation from carers or a lack of social interaction demonstrated abnormal social, sexual and parenting behaviour. Specifically, they demonstrated abnormal behaviours such as self-mutilation, unprovoked attacks on more dominant adults (which usually resulted in their being attacked and either seriously wounded or killed) and, relevant for this paper, attacks on their own offspring.

According to Bowlby, adult interpersonal behaviours are mediated by an individual's internal working models of relationships, which form as a result of early attachment experiences. These models are mental representations with both cognitive and affective elements, both conscious and unconscious. They are especially active in relationships between a carer and a cared-for person, where there is a dependent relationship that involves a discrepancy of power, and where the cared-for person is vulnerable without the carer. Positive attachment experience is associated with the development of secure internal working models of a carer (Bowlby 1969), what Kraemer (1992) has called a 'caregiver icon'. Solomon and George (1996) have suggested that a mature internal working model of the self as a parent is essential for being the type of caregiver the child will experience as a 'secure base'; in a more recent paper, they describe how maternal failures in caregiving at times of stress are associated with insecure working models of attachment in adults (Solomon and George 1999).

MEASURING WORKING MODELS OF ATTACHMENT

Later researchers have studied ways of examining these internal working models, or attachment representations, both in adults and children. In children, attachment representations have been studied using the Strange Situation paradigm, in which a child's response to separation from the mother and contact with a stranger are assessed (Ainsworth et al. 1978). In adults, mental representations of attachment have been studied using a variety of questionnaires and interviews, of which the best known is probably the Adult Attachment Interview (AAI: George, Kaplan and Main

1996). The AAI is a semi-structured interview which invites subjects to provide a narrative about their early attachment experiences, as they remember them. The interview is taped, transcribed and rated by a trained rater, according to a manual.

In normal non-clinical groups of adults, insecure attachment occurs in about 40 per cent of any sample (van IJzendoorn and Bakermans-Kranenburg 1996). Insecurity can occur in different forms, the most well described being either a 'dismissing or avoidant' attachment style or 'enmeshed/preoccupied'. Dismissing (D) individuals, as the term suggests, tend to dismiss the importance of attachment matters from their lives, and emphasise the importance of independence and personal strength. They may have little to say about attachment figures, either past or present. In contrast, preoccupied or enmeshed (E) individuals tend to speak at length about their closest relationships, but in an incoherent and confused way. They may be angrily or fearfully preoccupied with their early attachment figures, and often seem to have very little sense of their 'voice' in the narrative.

In addition to these two insecure attachment styles, individuals who have experienced significant trauma or bereavements in their lives may show evidence of lack of resolution to such events. Unresolved distress manifests itself in the narrative as incoherent or confused material. Where this incoherence is confined to one part of the text, narratives are rated Unresolved (U), and where it is global it is rated Cannot Classify (CC: Hesse 1999). Narratives are rated for both resolution of trauma and security, so that it is possible for individuals to be both secure/insecure and unresolved. The point here is that individuals who are unresolved for trauma or loss may have difficulties in thinking coherently when memories of these events are recalled.

ATTACHMENT REPRESENTATIONS IN MALTREATING PARENTS

It is widely accepted that attachment relationships between children and parents are a crucial area for assessment and intervention in child protection (Cleaver *et al.* 1999; Howe *et al.* 2000). This acceptance is based on a large body of empirical evidence which shows that child maltreatment causes disruption to attachment relationships between children and their parents, with both short-term and long-term effects on children's psychosocial development (Cicchetti and Rogosch 1994; Morton and Browne 1998).

There have been comparatively fewer studies of maltreating parents' own internal models of attachment. Crittenden (1996), reviewing the literature, argues that parents' representational models of their own attachment are a 'critical cause' for child maltreatment. Some representative studies are described below.

DeLozier (1982) describes severe attachment insecurity in a group of abusive mothers, compared with non-abusive mothers. She found that these women had experienced not only repeatedly disrupted attachments as children; they had also been subject to repeated threats of violence. Mitchell (1990) found similar results in a study of physically abusive Hispanic mothers: not only were there high levels of attachment insecurity; there was also a very high prevalence of early bereavement and trauma in their histories. Lyons-Ruth and Block (1996) also found a link between the severity of a mother's own history of trauma, and withdrawn or hostile behaviour towards her child.

Crittenden, Partridge and Claussen (1991) used the AAI to study attachment in parental couples where there had been child maltreatment by either mother or father. They found much greater proportions of insecure attachment in the maltreating group compared to non-maltreating parents. The most common insecure attachment style was the dismissing style (D). It is interesting to compare this finding with studies of attachment representations in perpetrators of other types of violence, which also show greater proportions of dismissing-insecure style (Allen, Hauser and Borman Spurrell 1996; Rosenstein and Horowitz 1996). Fonagy et al. (1997) have suggested that antisocial behaviour and dismissing style may be linked through failure to develop the capacity to think about self or others, which in turn affects the capacity for empathy.

These attachment studies of maltreating parents indicate a profound difficulty associated with the caregiving behavioural system. Specifically, these data suggest that the parent's own insecurity of attachment results in decreased capacity to care for a dependent child; and further, that because of the insecurity of the internal working model of attachment relationships, parent–child interactions which would normally stimulate appropriate caregiving behaviour fail to do so. These data seem to indicate that instead of caregiving behaviours, the parent responds with anxiety, rejection, anger and hostility, or detachment.

What could the mechanism be for this failure of caregiving? George (1996) has argued that child attachment, parental attachment and parental caregiving are all types of internal working model, linked at the level of representation and defensive process. She emphasises both the conscious, cognitive aspects of these models, and the less conscious, defensive aspects, particularly attributions and evaluations of the self and other in relationship. We suggest that key features of a parent–child relationship which might activate the internal working model of caregiving are those situations characterised by (a) heightened dependency needs in the other, and (b) either perceived or real differences in power and vulnerability between the caregiver and the care receiver.

Attachment theory suggests that the normal caregiver, with a balanced, coherent and flexible model of caregiving, responds to such situations with increased caregiving behaviour. Equally, at times of stress and distress, the securely attached dependent care receiver increases care-eliciting behaviours. Instead, for maltreating parents, it seems as though perceived distress in the child is interpreted and experienced as a threat to the caregiver. Normal caregiving is deactivated, perhaps by the experience of unmanageable affects of anxiety, fear, or anger. George (1996) describes failed caregiving in terms of rejection, uncertainty and helplessness. However, this account does not describe those situations where the caregiver is frankly hostile and cruel to the child: where something about the perception of neediness stimulates something dangerous in the caregiver towards dependent others. Such a pathological response to the perception of need would be more likely where the parent has experienced fear or threat experiences in the past which are either dismissed from consciousness, or conscious but associated with great anxiety.

FACTITIOUS ILLNESS BY PROXY AND ABNORMAL CARE ELICITING

Using this model, we reasoned that FIP behaviours might be better understood as abnormal caregiving behaviour, and that attachment theory might therefore offer a useful perspective. FIP behaviours may also be understood as abnormal care-eliciting behaviour by the mother on behalf of the child, i.e. the mother is herself activating an attachment behavioural system in relation to professional caregivers, such as GPs, nurses, health visitors, etc. FIP behaviours include repeated presentation to doctors, false accounts of symptoms, fabrication of symptoms, and symptoms induction, which may be life-threatening. The child (usually an infant) is repeatedly presented to professional carers as 'sick' by mothers who appear caring and concerned. They may interact with professional carers (both nurses and doctors) in either apparently pleasant and involved ways, or sometimes in preoccupied and hostile ways. A key feature seems to be the relationship between the 'sick' child, the 'caring' mother, and the professional carers, who control access to treatment and alleviation of distress (Eminson 2000).

These mothers have previously been described as attempting to gain attention or care for themselves through their children (Meadow 1977). Schreier and Libow (1993) and Welldon (2001) argue that the mother uses the child to form a perverse relationship with the doctor. Bools, Neale and Meadow (1994) found that 65 per cent of a sample of these mothers had a diagnosis of personality disorder (mainly borderline type), and an equally high proportion had histories of childhood abuse.

We reasoned that the mother–child relationship in FIP indicates two disorders of the attachment system: first, the mother's own failure to care for the child, and the active induction of threat or distress to the child; and second, an abnormal pattern of relating to, and eliciting care from, professional caregivers. The mother appears to 'need' the child to be 'ill', and therefore close to her; at the same time, she 'needs' to involve professional carers to witness her care and involvement, and to elicit care on behalf of her child.

Using an attachment theory perspective, we hypothesised that the mother's attachment system was highly disorganised, both in terms of caregiving to the child, and care-eliciting from others. These mothers appear to be heightening the child's attachment to themselves by making the child ill, and simultaneously undermining the attachment by inflicting pain and distress on the child. They also enact the same pattern of heightened attachment to professional carers, while at the same time undermining professional attempts to help by sabotaging treatment.

DATA FROM A CLINICAL SAMPLE

By using an attachment measurement in the clinical assessment of mothers who have exhibited FIP behaviour, we could begin to explore the hypotheses described above, which might then allow for more formal empirical testing in the future. We have carried out the AAI with 26 mothers referred for medico-legal assessment in the context of child care proceedings. These are therefore a highly selected sample of detected mothers, who are further selected for psychiatric assessment; these sources of sampling bias are an essential difficulty in research into FIP. The mothers are asked for their consent to the interview as part of the medico-legal assessment, and consent to use the unidentifiable, anonymised data was obtained from the legal representatives.

The referred mothers have shown a range of FIP behaviours, from excessive consultation with the family doctor, to poisoning or smothering behaviours. In two cases the child died as a result of the behaviours. The mean age of the mothers was 27; most of the children were under two years of age. No standardised diagnosis was made but all received a full clinical assessment by a psychiatrist in addition to the AAI.

We have found very high proportions of insecure attachment style in this group (88%), i.e. twice the proportions found in normal samples. In this insecure group the most common pattern was the dismissing pattern, which occurred in 77 per cent of the sample. This over-representation of the Dismissing category is similar to that found in Crittenden's study of maltreating parents, and van IJzendoorn's study of male antisocial personality disorder (van IJzendoorn *et al.* 1997).

We also found a very high prevalence (65%) of the Unresolved for trauma or bereavement (U) classification. In normal, non-clinical samples of mothers, the proportion of the U-category is 17 per cent. Half of the women did give histories of childhood abuse (either sexual or physical, or both); interestingly, a significant minority also gave histories of trauma in adulthood, such as exposure to domestic violence or rape.

From an attachment perspective, we would hypothesise that for some women with unresolved trauma reactions and experience of early childhood adversity, their caregiving capacity is disorganised from an early age, so that dependency needs in others arouse both anxious and hostile affects. This internal working model of caregiving may be encapsulated and buffered by intelligence and social constructions of gender role which depict women as naturally caring. Some of these women may even become competent professional carers (such career choices have been found to be over-represented in some studies of FIP).

However, thoughts of conception, or an actual pregnancy, can destabilise the internal working model and break down the protective encapsulating mechanism which has enabled the woman to maintain successful interpersonal functioning. The dependency needs of the child, and the disparity of power between the mother and the child, stimulate feelings of panic, helplessness and hostility. An external carer is sought to provide attachment security, but the dynamics of dependency and power disparity are then played out with the health care professionals also.

It may be that FIP behaviour is specifically stimulated where there has been experience of chronic illness, and later death from that illness, within the family while the parent is growing up. This might affect the parent directly if she suffered illness in childhood, so that caregiving became associated with illness (Craig *et al.* 1993); alternatively, illness and subsequent death in a sibling or grandparent could affect security of attachment, either directly by the impact on family dynamics at the time, or indirectly where there was unresolved grief as a result of the loss. Further research could explore these historical aspects of the parent's own childhood in more detail. There is also a need for comparison data on attachment representations of parents of children who actually suffer from chronic, life-threatening illness. Finally, more careful analysis of FIP parents' unresolved responses to childhood trauma (especially violence) may help us to understand why some parents respond to their children's vulnerability with aggression and hostility. There is no question that some FIP behaviour is cruel and hostile (Adshead *et al.* 1999); in this sense, therefore, FIP resembles other types of child maltreatment, and should be understood as such (Jureidini and Donald 2001).

CONCLUSION

Based on the evidence reviewed above, it seems reasonable to conclude that the capacity to parent might be better formulated as a capacity for caregiving; and that this caregiving capacity is strongly influenced by the parents' own attachment representations of caregiving and care-eliciting. Attachment theory therefore provides empirical support for the transgenerational influence of childhood experience into adulthood, so powerfully described by Fraiberg *et al.* (1975) as the 'ghosts in the nursery'.

We have found that assessment of attachment representations in abusive parents is helpful for the assessment of parenting capacity because it offers a specific focus on the mother's own experience of being cared for and what she understands by the concept of 'being parented'. As George (1996) suggests, what we are looking at is the mother's own cognitive model of how an adult caregiver relates to a dependent and needy child. An attachment-based interview allows for questioning about areas which are germane to FIP, such as being cared for when ill, what happened when the parent sought help or care from her own carers, and histories of family illness of bereavement. We have also found that it may indicate possible foci for therapeutic work. For example, where there is evidence of unresolved grief or trauma, it may be that parenting capacity could be enhanced by a specific psychological intervention.

There are some practical difficulties in using the AAI, which requires a lengthy and expensive training to rate reliably. It is also unwieldy, insofar as it has to be taped and transcribed (which can take several hours) and then rated (which usually takes between two and four hours, depending on its length). There are other measures of attachment which may be more convenient to administer and rate, including self-report measures. However, most attachment researchers argue that the AAI is optimal because it has good psychometric properties, and because of the detailed material that it generates. We would also argue that in the context of child protection assessments, it is useful to have use of an interview where there are no easily apparent 'right' answers.

One of the other problems with most attachment measures is that they only result in a categorisation of 'secure' or 'insecure'. It is clear that we need better and more complex data about attachment representations and failures of caregiving. Although insecure attachment may well be a risk factor for failed caregiving, it is not sufficient to be causal, and especially not predictive. It is possible to have an insecure model of attachment in mind, and still be a good enough parent; it also appears that it is possible to have a secure state of mind with regard to attachment, and still maltreat your child. Such findings emphasise the importance of multifactorial risk assessment in any case of child maltreatment; attachment representations will only reflect one aspect of a complex problem. However, it is an aspect which may have meaning for maltreating parents (Howe *et al.* 2000).

Rather than rely on simply categorising people as 'insecurely attached', we may need to gather more data about the nature and quality of the insecurity, and importantly, how and when it has manifested itself at different stages in the individual's life history. It may be useful to think about taking a caregiving history from parents which would actually begin in childhood, so that one looked at earliest experiences of caregiving with siblings, pets, or elderly relatives. Gender role development may be important here, since successful caregiving to others is one aspect of the successful stereotype for Western women in particular.

The category of 'insecure' is not only insufficient: it is also too crude to do justice to the many types of failed caregiving that we see. In this sense, Tolstoy was right; there are perhaps many ways to be an unhappy, failing caregiver within a family. Attachment theory can give us better ways to talk and think about them.

ACKNOWLEDGEMENTS

We are grateful to the two anonymous reviewers who provided helpful feedback and suggestions. We also thank Anne Kavanagh for secretarial assistance.

REFERENCES

Adshead, G., Brooke, D., Samuels, M., Jenner, S. and Southall, D. (2000) 'Maternal behaviours associated with smothering.' *Child Abuse and Neglect* 24, 9 1175–1183.

Ainsworth, M., Blehar, M., Waters, E. and Wall, S. (1978) *Patterns of Attachment: A Psychological Study of the Strange Situation.* Hillsdale, NJ: Erlbaum.

Allen, J.P., Hauser, S. and Borman Spurrell, E. (1996) 'Attachment theory as a framework for understanding sequelae of severe adolescent psychopathology: An 11-year follow-up study.' *Journal of Consulting and Clinical Psychology* 64, 254–263.

Bools, C., Neale, B. and Meadow, R. (1994) 'Munchausen Syndrome by Proxy: A study of psychopathology.' *Child Abuse and Neglect* 18, 773–788.

Bowlby, J. (1969) *Attachment and Loss Vol.1: Attachment.* London: Hogarth Press.

Bowlby, J. (1980) *Attachment and Loss Vol.3: Loss.* London: Hogarth Press.

Cicchetti, D. and Rogosch, F. (1994) 'The toll of child maltreatment on the developing child.' *Child and Adolescent Psychiatric Clinics of North America 3,* 759–776.

Cleaver, H., Unell, I. and Aldgate, J. (1999) *Children's Needs – Parenting Capacity.* London: The Stationery Office.

Craig, T.K., Boardman, A.P., Mills, K., Daly-Jones, O. and Drake, H. (1993) 'The South London Somatisation Study Part I: Longitudinal course and the influence of early life experience.' *British Journal of Psychiatry 163,* 579–588.

Crittenden, P. (1996) 'Research on maltreating families: implications for intervention.' In J. Briere, L. Berliner, J. Myers, T. Reid, C. Jenny and C.T. Hendrix (eds) *The APSAC Handbook on Child Maltreatment.* Thousand Oaks, CA: Sage.

Crittenden, P., Partridge, M. and Claussen, A. (1991) 'Family patterns of relationship in normative and dysfunctional families.' *Development and Psychopathology 3,* 491–512.

DeLozier, P. (1982) 'Attachment theory and child abuse.' In C.M. Parkes and J. Stevenson-Hinde (eds) *The Place of Attachment in Human Behaviour.* London: Tavistock.

Department of Health/Home Office/Department of Education and Employment (1999) *Working Together to Protect Children.* London: The Stationery Office.

Department of Health/Department of Education and Employment/Home Office (2000) *Framework for the Assessment of Children in Need and Their Families.* London: The Stationery Office.

Eminson, M. (2000) 'Background.' In M. Eminson and R.J. Postlethwaite (eds) *MSBP Abuse: A Practical Approach.* London: Butterworth Heinemann.

Fonagy, P., Target, M., Steele, M., Steele, H., Leigh, T., Levinson, A. and Kennedy, R. (1997) 'Morality, disruptive behaviour, borderline personality disorder, crime and their relationship to attachment.' In L. Atkinson and K. Zucker (eds) *Attachment and Psychopathology.* London: Guilford.

Fraiberg, S., Adelson, E. and Shapiro, V. (1975) 'Ghosts in the nursery: A psychoanalytic approach to the problems of impaired mother–infant relationships.' *Journal of the American Academy of Child Psychiatry 14,* 387–421.

George, C. (1996) 'A representational perspective of child abuse and prevention: Internal working models of attachment and caregiving.' *Child Abuse and Neglect 20,* 411–424.

George, C., Kaplan, N. and Main, M. (1996) 'Adult Attachment Interview protocol.' Unpublished manuscript, Department of Psychology, University of Berkeley, CA.

Hesse, E. (1999) 'The Adult attachment Interview: historical and current perspectives.' In J. Cassidy and P. Shaver (eds) *Handbook of Attachment: Theory, Research, and Clinical Applications.* New York: Guilford Press.

Howe, D., Brandon, M., Hinings, D. and Schofield, G. (1999) *Attachment Theory, Child Maltreatment and Family Support.* London: Macmillan.

Jureidini, J. and Donald, T. (2001) 'Child abuse specific to the medical system.' In G. Adshead and D. Brooke (eds) *Munchausen's Syndrome by Proxy: Current Issues in Assessment, Treatment and Research.* London: Imperial Press.

Kraemer, G.W. (1992) 'A psychobiological theory of attachment.' *Behavioural and Brain Sciences 15,* 493–511.

Lyons-Ruth, K. and Block, D. (1996) 'The disturbed caregiving system: Relations among childhood trauma, maternal caregiving and infant affect and attachment.' *Infant Mental Health Journal 17,* 257–275.

Meadow, R. (1977) 'Munchausen's Syndrome by Proxy: The hinterland of child abuse.' *Lancet 2,* 343–345.

Mitchell, M. (1990) 'Attachment antecedents and socio-cultural factors in hispanic mothers' physical abuse of their children.' In K. Pottharst (ed) *Research Explorations in Adult Attachment.* New York: Peter Lang.

Morton, N. and Browne, K. (1998) 'Theory and observation of attachment and its relation to child maltreatment: A review.' *Child Abuse and Neglect 22,* 1093–1104.

Rosenstein, D.S. and Horowitz, H.A. (1996) 'Adolescent attachment and psychopathology.' *Journal of Consulting and Clinical Psychology 64,* 244–253.

Schreier, H. and Libow, J. (1993) *Hurting for Love: Munchausen by Proxy Syndrome.* New York: Guilford.

Solomon, J. and George, C. (1996) 'Defining the caregiving system: Towards a theory of caregiving.' *Infant Mental Health Journal 17,* 183–197.

Solomon, J. and George, C. (1999) 'The caregiving system in mothers of infants: A comparison of divorcing and married mothers.' *Attachment and Human Development 2,* 171–190.

van IJzendoorn, M. and Bakermans-Kranenburg, M. (1996) 'Attachment representations in mothers, fathers, adolescents and clinical groups: A meta-analytic search for normative data.' *Journal of Consulting and Clinical Psychology 64,* 8–21.

van IJzendoorn, M., Feldbrugge, J., Derks, F., de Ruiter, C., Verhagen, M., Philipse, M., van der Staak, C. and Riksen-Walraven, J. (1997) 'Attachment representations of personality disordered offenders.' *American Journal of Orthopsychiatry 67*, 449–459.

Welldon, E. (2001) 'The extraordinary case of Mrs H.' In G. Adshead and D. Brooke (eds) *Munchausen's Syndrome by Proxy: Current Issues in Assessment, Treatment and Research.* London: Imperial Press.

CHAPTER 9

Violence and Attachment

Attachment Styles, Self-regulation and Interpersonal Problems in a Prison Population

Thomas Ross and Friedemann Pfäfflin

SUMMARY

In this study, attachment styles, self-regulation and interpersonal problems in a group of 31 imprisoned violent offenders were assessed. The offenders had been convicted of at least one violent crime against another person, and served a prison sentence of at least three years.

In order to assess attachment styles, self-regulation and interpersonal relations, a semi-structured attachment interview, the Adult Attachment Prototype Rating (*Erwachsenen-Bindungsprototypen-Rating*, EBPR: Strauß and Lobo-Drost 1999) was applied. Using the same methods, two comparison groups of non-violent men, consisting of 22 prison service trainees and 21 members of two Christian congregations were investigated. Self-regulation processes were measured with the Narcissism Inventory (Deneke and Hilgenstock 1989) and interpersonal problem areas were assessed with the Inventory of Interpersonal Problems (IIP-D: Horowitz, Strauß and Kordy 1994).

Attachment styles in violent offenders differed from those of the comparison groups. The offender group displayed less secure attachment styles, less emotional attachment to others, and more instability in relationships. These differences were accompanied by a stronger wish for personal autonomy in the offender group. With respect to self-regulation processes, the only difference that was found between the offender group and the prison service trainees was in terms of an individual's experience of social isolation. As expected, the congregation members turned out to be much more identified with the norms, regulations, and ideals of society. Contrary to expectation, most interpersonal problem areas did not differ across the investigated groups.

THEORETICAL BACKGROUND

Attachment theory is very promising for the forensic field for two main reasons: first, it provides the framework for a developmental perspective of violent behaviour; and second, it helps to better understand normal and pathological relationship formation in an interpersonal context. Research informed by attachment theory has considerable explanatory power for known risk factors of violent behaviour such as the genesis of personality disorders (Adshead 2001; Fonagy 1999; Fonagy et al. 1997a; van IJzendoorn et al. 1997). Attachment theory also promotes an understanding of psychotherapeutic processes with offenders and the accompanying peculiarities and problems. Bowlby's concept of cognitive-emotional representations of relationship experiences (Bowlby 1988) has shown that the patient's responsiveness to relationships in therapeutic settings is a function of his/her mental representation of close relationships. This mental representation determines whether a patient is capable of building a trusting relationship with another person in general, or, in a therapeutic setting, whether he/she is able to establish a fruitful working alliance with the therapist. Therefore, it is not far-fetched to claim that the forensic field will benefit from the introduction of attachment concepts into theoretical discussion about the aetiology and genesis of violent acts on the one hand, and into forensic psychotherapy on the other. As early as 1946 Bowlby described forensic implications of his theory (Bowlby 1946), but after decades of research on non-clinical and clinical populations, the first systematic attempts to apply attachment theory to the *aetiology of violent crime* emerged only a few years ago.

In terms of attachment theory, violent behaviour is a serious relational disorder. In order to understand these disorders, the following theoretical aspects of attachment theory are important (Lyons-Ruth and Jacobovitz 1999, p.541):

- the presence of an attachment behavioural control system
- the role of anger in that control system
- the operation of both intersubjective and intrapsychic mechanisms in channelling the experience and expression of attachment-related affects, as well as the fear, anger, and unregulated physiological arousal resulting from frustration of attachment goals
- the intergenerational transmission of relational patterns.

Negative affect displayed due to impulse control deficits can be of high relevance for the forensic field. Anger is a natural response to frustration, and serves as an important communicative signal to the attachment partner that something is wrong. When anger does not elicit an adequate interpersonal response, ideally in the form of sensitive responsiveness, the negative affect may increase to an extent with which the individual can no longer cope. Behavioural organisation may break down or take increasingly deviant forms as communication fails to achieve its goal. In Bowlby's terms, a person would undergo a transition from the 'protest' to the 'despair' phase, in the absence of an adequate substitute (Bowlby 1980). According to attachment theory, the genesis of violent behaviour can be traced back to a long-lasting succession of inadequate behavioural responses by caregivers to an infant's attachment needs.

In the absence of adequate regulation of negative affect in interpersonal situations (which is usually related to an elevation of physiological arousal), various intersubjective, intrapsychic and physiological compensatory mechanisms are set in motion, resulting in maladaptive, contradictory, or controlling behavioural and mental organisation, according to Lyons-Ruth and Jacobovitz (1999), who posit that 'violence in intimate relationships can be one outcome of such a deviation in the organization of attachment relationships, and one in which great intensity of positive longing, anger, and fear may be combined with a lack of felt security, lapses in attention, dysfluent communication, and unregulated arousal' (Lyons-Ruth and Jacobovitz 1999, p.542).

Perhaps the most detailed and thoughtful attempt to put forward an attachment theory of violent behaviour stems from Fonagy *et al.* (1997b). The theory is based on the assumption that early emotional deprivation and traumatic experiences are related to the occurrence of violent crime.

According to attachment theory, individuals internalise their experience with caregivers, forming an internal representation of self and others (Bowlby 1969, 1973, 1980, 1995). These representations are referred to as *internal working models*. These models organise expectations regarding the availability and responsiveness of attachment figures. As a core element of the personality structure, internal working models are thought to affect the individual's appraisal of social situations. They are dynamic in nature, integrating affective, behavioural and cognitive experiences to a general expectancy of interpersonal relations, which constitute the attachment representation of a person (Bretherton and Munholland 1999). On a behavioural level, attachment representations are referred to as attachment styles, reflecting behavioural correlates of attachment experiences. As to the question of whether the quality of internal representations corresponds directly to the quality of attachment styles, more empirical clarification is needed. An important clinical assumption of the nature of internal working models is that they only develop adequately in a supportive social environment. Depending on the quality of this environment, different attachment representations develop as a result of internalised relationship experiences.

Internal working models are conveyed and modulated by the caregiver's interactional behaviour toward the infant (parental style). According to attachment theory, the capability of the caregiver to perceive emotional signals or desires of the child, and to interpret and respond to them accordingly (sensitive responsiveness) is regarded as an important precondition for adequate emotional development (Bowlby 1969, 1973, 1980). Thus, internal working models are supposed to have a major impact on an individual's ability to respond adequately to emotionally loaded social signals, and to communicate constructively with others.

Apart from sensitive responsiveness and maternal sensitivity, Fonagy *et al.* (1997a, b) stress the role of an individual's mentalising capacity as a precondition to peaceful interaction with a given social environment. The capability to recognise mental states of others and to understand them in terms of affect and cognition is ultimately related to the ability to reflect on one's own mental states (reflective self-function) and to integrate them into a coherent system of action (self-evaluation). The infant develops this capability through an emotionally stable, predictable and loving interactional process with its primary attachment figure. According to Fonagy *et al.* (1997b), there are at least four ways in which a failure of mentalisation can lead to moral disengagement, facilitating the emergence of violent behaviour. First, those with reduced ability to recognise the mental states of others will also have an impaired sense of identity. This may be a source of substantial discomfort, but also results in reducing a person's sense of responsibility for his or her own actions. Second, building on the assumption that mentalising capacity is essentially important for anticipating the consequences of an action on the mind of victim and observer, limitations upon mentalising might permit the individual to disregard or at least misrepresent the psychological effects of an act on others. Third, further related processes may facilitate the devaluing or dehumanising of the victim, and consequently treating other people like physical objects. Fourth, the limitations of metacognitive capacity may result in enhanced volatility of the mental representation system, within which ideas may be readily reconstructed and actions misinterpreted. Unacceptable behaviour may thus be reconstrued as acceptable in a selective and self-serving manner.

   Parental style, sensitive responsiveness, and mentalising capacity are the cornerstones for an individual's development of a coherent system of self (Fonagy and Target 1996). Mentalising capacity and the development of a coherent self may have an inhibiting influence on violent actions (Levinson and Fonagy 1999).

Empirical findings

Fonagy's theoretical assumptions are corroborated by a series of empirical results. There seems to be a link between insecure attachment and antisocial personality disorder (Rosenstein and Horowitz 1996). Six out of seven adolescent patients were classified as 'dismissing', the seventh as 'preoccupied'. Ward, Hudson and Marshall (1996) investigated two groups of rapists (n = 30) and child molesters (n = 55) compared to violent (n = 32) and non-violent offenders (n = 30) with no prior sex offence. Insecure attachment representations prevailed in all groups, ranging from 60 per cent (non-violent offenders) to 90 per cent (violent offenders). Sixty-seven per cent of the rapists and 78 per cent of the child molesters were insecurely attached. While the rapists were mostly classified as dismissive, the child molesters had more ambivalent or enmeshed attachment classifications. In a study conducted by van IJzendoorn *et al.* (1997) on 40 forensic psychiatric patients suffering from personality disorders, autonomous classifications were found to be almost absent (5%) while the combined *unresolved/cannot classify* groups accounted for over 50 per cent of the sample (53% *unresolved/cannot classify*, 22% *dismissing*, and 20% *enmeshed/preoccupied*). However, criminal offenders were not more likely than other clinical groups to display *unresolved* or *cannot classify* states of mind, but the severity of the personality disorder was related to the unavailability of attachment figures in their childhood. In another study, 22 patients with mental disorders were investigated (Levinson and Fonagy 1999). The authors reported 8 (36%) *unresolved* and 14 (64%) *preoccupied* attachment classifications.

Taking the empirical evidence about violent offenders and their attachment representations into account, it seems evident that there is an association between insecure attachment and the emergence of personality disorders and violent behaviour. However, specific attachment representations of violent offenders or different offender types have not yet been identified. In all studies cited above, attachment representations were assessed with the Adult Attachment Interview (AAI: George, Kaplan and Main 1985). This is a semi-structured interview measuring intrapsychic representations of early attachment experience, using discourse analytic techniques. It does not take into account the behavioural domain (the attachment style) of interpersonal relationships. As yet, there are no studies published about attachment styles of violent offenders.

OBJECTIVE AND HYPOTHESES

Drawing on these considerations, the purpose of this study was to learn whether there are attachment styles in violent offenders which can be distinguished from those found in a sample of non-violent subjects. The comparison groups consisted of men with no police registration prior to investigation, and would in theory have a low probability of committing a violent offence. It seemed reasonable to compare an offender sample with non-violent samples in order to find out about specific violence inhibitors that might even be different to those in the average population.

We expected the offender group to display more insecure attachment styles than both comparison groups. We hypothesised that the following group differences would emerge: more insecure relationship structures, a greater wish for personal autonomy, and more emotional detachment from others in the offender group compared to both non-violent samples.

With respect to intrapsychic self-regulation, we hypothesised characteristic differences between the offender group and both comparison groups. The offender group was expected to show 'classic' narcissistic strategies of self-regulation, more fantasies of greatness, a strong yearning for praise and recognition, and more aggressive devaluation of significant others. Generally, the offenders were thought to be less identified with the norms and values of society.

Furthermore, we expected to find more and qualitatively different interpersonal problems across the groups. The offenders were expected to experience more problems than the non-violent groups as a result of a relatively high preponderance of a dominant interpersonal style and hostile aggression.

METHOD

Sample

Three groups were recruited: 1. violent offenders; 2. prison service trainees; 3. members of two Christian congregations. All participants were male.

Violent offenders

Thirty-one offenders detained in four South German prisons were investigated. Recruitment criteria were as follows:

- at least one violent offence against another person, as listed in the German Penal Code, including homicide, physical assault, sexual assault, robbery, extortion, abduction, and arson
- prison sentence of at least three years.

Procedure

The prison service staff were informed about goals, design and process of the study. They then briefly informed all offenders meeting the recruitment criteria. The recruitment process was monitored and commented on by the academic staff. After all participants were screened, an appointment was scheduled. The participants were informed of their voluntary status, that they could withdraw at any time, and that their responses were confidential. Consent forms were reviewed and signed, and subjects were paid 20 DM for their participation.

The investigation took between three and four hours, and a combination of interview and self-report measures were used. (Some measures were taken which are not reported in this chapter.)

Prison service trainees

Twenty-two prison service trainees working in two South German prisons were recruited. The training officer, who had previously been informed, provided information about the study. Full information was given prior to investigation and consent forms were signed. Participation was voluntary.

Members of Christian congregations

The second comparison group consisted of 21 members of two Christian charismatic congregations in South Germany. The charismatic movement within the Protestant church is characterised by enthusiasm and perfectionism with respect to the contents of the Bible. Believers claim to experience the blessings of Christian charismas such as the action of the Holy Spirit. A central element of their religious faith is a strong belief in spiritual reincarnation and christening through the Holy Spirit (Gasper, Mü ller and Valentin 1990; Hollenweger 1971). Detailed information about goals, design and basic assumptions of the study was provided to the leading circle of the congregations. Subsequently, all male congregational members were contacted and invited to participate. Appointments for interviews were made and data collection took place at the participants' homes. All subjects volunteered and written consent was obtained.

On theoretical grounds, we postulated that both comparison groups had in common a strong bond to authority, which serves as a cognitive organiser providing a psychological source of comfort and security. What

God does for religiously committed individuals, might for prison staff be provided via the relatively unambiguous world of a hierarchically structured institutional context.

There is empirical evidence that, from an attachment theory perspective, authority-prone behaviour can be construed as a search for a 'safe haven'. Kirkpatrick and Shaver (1992) and Kirkpatrick (1997, 1998, 1999) developed a dynamic model, which describes religious behaviour as a function of basic interpersonal experiences with primary caregivers. Two main hypotheses were proposed:

(a)   *compensation hypothesis:* Many individuals may turn to God or other authorities as substitute or surrogate attachment figures. The central idea of this hypothesis is that the belief in authorities may compensate for either negative or deficient attachment experiences with primary attachment figures. It is in these cases that a search for an alternative and more adequate attachment figure seems likely to be initiated, and consequently that individuals are likely to turn to a substitute attachment figure, reflecting an underlying wish for psychological structure and emotional security.

(b)   *correspondence hypothesis:* Individual differences in belief systems and experiences run parallel to individual differences in mental modes and attachment styles. Individuals who possess positive or secure generalised mental models of self and of attachment figures may be expected to view authorities in similar terms.

Sample characteristics

Age

The average age was 36.1 years (SD = 9.4) for the offender group , 30.7 years (SD = 6.9) for the trainees and 36.5 years (SD = 7.7) for the congregation members. The offenders and congregation members were significantly older than the trainees (U-Tests, exact statistics: group comparison offenders × trainees, $p<0.05$; congregation members × trainees, $p<0.01$; offenders × congregation members, ns).

Educational achievement and professional qualification
The offender group held lower educational qualifications (group compari-son offenders × trainees p<0.05; offenders × congregation members p<0.01, Mann-Whitney U-Tests) and had lower professional qualifications (offenders × trainees p<0.001; offenders × congregation members p<0.001, Mann-Whitney U-Tests) than the comparison groups.

The offender sample (n = 31) was imprisoned for the following offences: murder and manslaughter (27.8%); physical injury (11.1%); sexual offences (19.4%); robbery (36.1%); arson (5.6%). The average number of prison sentences (n = 27) was M = 2.4 (SD = 2.99) and the average number of convictions (n = 30) was M = 6.2 (SD = 6.45).

Attachment styles

Attachment styles were assessed with the Adult Attachment Prototype Rating (EBPR: Strauß and Lobo 1997; Strauß and Lobo-Drost 1999). The EBPR is essentially based on the Pilkonis Prototype Rating, which was first applied on a group of depressive patients (Pilkonis 1988) and subsequently used for the diagnosis of other patient groups, such as anxiety patients. The EBPR is a semi-structured clinical interview designed to assess the biography of an individual, focusing on interpersonal behaviour and rela-tionships. It consists of three basic elements: 1. interview, 2. prototype rating, 3. self-report scale. The EBPR assesses: behavioural styles in attach-ment situations; causes of a specific behaviour of an individual; past and present quality of interpersonal relationships; characteristic similarities with parents; loss of a close person in childhood, adolescence or adulthood; other important relationships; and the causes of short- or longlasting relationships.

In the prototype rating (Strauß and Lobo-Drost, Version 1.0 1999) seven attachment prototypes, each of which corresponds to one of the main attachment categories *secure, ambivalent* or *enmeshed/preoccupied*, and *dismiss-ing* (Adult Attachment Interview (AAI) George *et al.* 1985) are differentiated. A fourth category has been added, consisting of both *ambivalent* and *dismiss-ing* features. Prototype 1 – 'secure features' (as defined in the EBPR) corre-sponds to the *secure* category of the AAI; Prototype 2 – 'excessive depend-ency', Prototype 3 – 'borderline features' and Prototype 4 – 'excessive care' refer to *ambivalent* or *enmeshed/preoccupied* attachment strategies; Prototype 5 – 'obsessive-compulsive features', Prototype 6 – 'defensive separation' and

Prototype 7 – 'lack of interpersonal sensitivity' are best reflected by the *dismissing* category of the AAI.[1]

The interviews were rated by two specifically trained independent raters and the inter-rater reliability was good, the intra-class coefficients for all prototypes ranging from r = 0.56, Prototype 2 and r = 0.80, Prototype 1.

Self-regulation

The Narcissism Inventory tackles different theoretically relevant aspects of the organisation and regulation of the narcissistic personality system. The inventory is based on psychoanalytic theory on the structure of the self-system or the narcissistic personality system. The 163 items were factor-analysed and resulted in a series of homogeneous scales reflecting four main dimensions.

- *The threatened self* is reflected by a grave instability of the self-system. In its negative pole it may be fragile, anxiety-ridden, and threatened by a loss of control over affect and impulse.

- *The narcissistic self* is represented by regulation patterns which reflect important aspects of a narcissistic personality. Its characteristics are: a high level of egocentrism, proneness to insult, overestimation of self, and a strong wish for narcissistic gratification.

- *The idealistic self* has a self-regulation pattern that is characterised by a manifest or latent anxiety to experience disappointment or insult in object relations.

- *The hypochondriac self* focuses on its own body, which is experienced and used as if it was an object.

In order to interpret the dimensions, a model was proposed, describing narcissistic personality features as a self-regulating intrapsychic system.

Subjects are required to determine on a five-point Likert scale whether a given statement applies 'not at all; a little; partly yes, partly no; mostly; definitely'. The Narcissism Inventory was validated using a large clinical sample of n = 1,277. Cronbach's alpha varies between 0.71 and 0.94 across the 18 scales (Deneke and Hilgenstock 1989).

Interpersonal problems

The Inventory of Interpersonal Problems (IIP-D: Horowitz *et al.* 1994) is based on Sullivan's (1953) and Leary's (1957) interpersonal circumplex model of behaviour, stemming from the long tradition of interpersonal concepts in clinical psychology, psychotherapy and personality theory. According to the model, interpersonal behaviour can be displayed in a two-dimensional semantic space. The dimensions are affiliation (hostility vs. love) and control (dominance vs. submission). In eight scales, different interpersonal problem areas are tackled: too autocratic/dominant, too quarrelsome/competitive, too dismissive/cold, too introverted/socially avoidant, too insecure/submissive, too exploitable/compliant, too solicitous/friendly, and too expressive/obtrusive.

On a five-point scale, subjects are requested to rate the extent to which a given interpersonal problem applies to them, using the ratings: not, little, average, quite, very. The 127 items are divided into two subgroups. The first group (78 items) refers to the individual perception of interpersonal behaviour and experience. The second (49 items) looks at frequent experiences and behaviours in interpersonal situations. The retest reliability of the IIP-scales is between 0.81 and 0.90. Cronbach's alpha ranges from 0.36 to 0.64 (n = 1333; Horowitz *et al.* 1994, p.25).

RESULTS

Attachment styles

In order to examine group differences, two-group comparisons were calculated.[2] The attachment styles of the offender group differed significantly from those of both comparison groups (offenders × trainees p05, offenders × congregation members $p > 0.01$, Fisher's exact test). Trainees and congregation members did not differ in terms of their attachment styles.

Prototype rating

Fisher's exact test for this distribution was significant ($p < 0.01$). The means of Prototypes 1, 3, 4, 6 and 7 differ significantly between the three groups. In order to identify the groups accounting for the differences, Mann-Whitney U-Tests were calculated. Probabilities (p) and effect sizes (ES) for the group differences are provided.

Table 9.1 Expert rating of attachment styles (Kruskal-Wallis
H-Tests, Monte-Carlo Method, 10,000 samples). Means (M),
standard deviations (SD) and probability level (p)

Proto-type	Offenders (n = 31)		Trainees (n = 22)		Congregation members (n = 21)		
	M	SD	M	SD	M	SD	p
P1	3.39	2.01	1.59	1.18	1.62	0.92	≤0.001
P2	4.65	2.27	3.59	1.22	3.81	2.02	ns
P3	3.13	1.65	5.41	1.68	4.48	1.60	≤0.001
P4	5.39	1.43	4.32	1.36	4.19	1.03	<0.01
P5	2.94	1.46	2.23	0.87	2.14	0.79	ns
P6	3.74	1.83	5.23	1.38	5.57	1.29	≤0.001
P7	4.78	2.01	5.64	1.73	6.19	1.03	<0.05

P1: secure features   P5: obsessive-compulsive features
P2: excessive dependency   P6: defensive separation
P3: borderline features   P7: lack of interpersonal sensitivity
P4: excessive care

Note: The results were calculated on the basis of the interview and the prototype rating.

The *offender group* scored lower[2] than the *trainees* in prototype P1, 'secure features' (p<0.001; ES = −1.05); P2, 'excessive dependency' (p<0.05; ES = −0.56); P4, 'excessive care' (p<0.01; ES = −0.76); and P5, 'obsessive-compulsive features' (p<0.05, ES = − 0.57). They scored significantly higher in P3, 'borderline features' (p<0.001; ES = +1.37) and P6, 'defensive separation' (p<0.01; ES = +0.90). Contrary to our expectations, the group difference did not become significant in Prototype 7, 'lack of inter-personal sensitivity'.

The *offender group* scored lower than the *congregation members* in Prototype P1, 'secure features' (p<0.001; ES = −1.06); P4, 'excessive care' (p<0.001; ES = − 0.93); and P5, 'obsessive-compulsive features' (p<0.05;

ES = − 0.65). They scored higher in Prototype P3, 'borderline features' (p<0.01; ES = +0.83); P6, 'defensive separation' (p<0.001, ES = +1.12); and P7, 'lack of interpersonal sensitivity' (p<0.01; ES = +0.84).

The *trainee group* was rated significantly lower than the *congregation members* in Prototype P3, 'borderline features' (p<0.05; ES =−0.57). All other U-Tests failed to reach significance on a p<0.05 alpha level.

Table 9.2 Selected scales of the Narcissism Inventory (Kruskal-Wallis H-Tests, Monte-Carlo Method, 10,000 samples) – Mean (M), standard deviations (SD) and probability level (p)

Scale (dimension in brackets)	Offenders (n = 29)		Trainees (n = 20)		Congregation members (n = 19)		
	M	SD	M	SD	M	SD	p
AIV (D1)	22.14	9.46	21.50	8.15	19.05	8.28	ns
SOI (D1)	25.52	8.62	21.35	7.01	21.00	6.41	ns
GRS (D2)	28.21	7.61	29.40	6.49	29.26	5.37	ns
GLB (D2)	23.86	8.17	25.90	5.37	27.53	5.50	ns
NAW (D2)	23.62	7.75	24.10	7.56	20.11	5.02	ns
SIS (D2)	25.79	9.24	26.35	7.32	30.05	5.60	ns
AUI (D3)	30.83	8.12	35.20	7.59	32.16	4.36	ns
OBA (D3)	30.86	7.68	26.65	7.91	23.69	6.52	<0.01
WEI (D3)	31.67	6.88	35.64	6.82	38.80	6.08	<0.01
NAK (D4)	16.14	7.31	16.80	6.63	15.68	6.16	ns

AIV: loss of affect and impulse control
SOI: social isolation
GRS: greatness
GLB: greed for praise and recognition
NAW: narcissistic rage
SIS: longing for ideal self object
AUI: autarky ideal

OBA: devaluation of object
WEI: value ideal
NAK: narcissistic gain
D1: threatened self
D2: 'classic' narcissistic self
D3: idealistic self
D4: hypochondriac self

Self-regulation[3]

U-Tests were calculated in order to test for effects between the groups, with respect to four variables: object devaluation (OBA), value ideal (WEI), social isolation (SOI), and greed for praise and recognition (GLB).

Table 9.3 Probability level (p) and effect sizes (ES) – Object devaluation, value ideal, social isolation and greed for praise and recognition

	Offenders × trainees		Offenders × congregation members		Trainees × congregation members	
	p	ES	p	ES	p	ES
Object devaluation	ns	− 0.54	≤0.001	− 0.99	ns	− 0.41
Value ideal	ns	− 0.58	≤0.001	+ 1.08	ns	+ 0.49
Social isolation	<0.05	− 0.52	<0.05	− 0.58	ns	− 0.05
Greed for praise and recognition	ns	+ 0.28	<0.05	+ 0.51	ns	+ 0.30

The offenders and the congregation members differed significantly with respect to the scales 'devaluation of object' and 'value ideal'. The offenders felt more socially isolated than both comparison groups. The congregation members scored higher in the scale 'greed for praise and recognition' than the offender group.

Interpersonal problems

Kruskal-Wallis H-Tests on all IIP-D scales (Monte-Carlo Method, 10,000 samples) yielded no statistically significant difference between the three groups with respect to different interpersonal problem areas, except for the scale 'too quarrelsome/competitive' (offenders n = 29, M = 10.93, SD = 4.28; trainees n = 20, M = 8.95, SD = 3.72; congregation members n = 15, M = 6.47, SD = 2.97, p<0.01) and the affiliation dimension (offenders M = 1.40, SD = 3.86; trainees M = 3.02, SD = 3.54; congregation members M = 4.70, SD = 3.70, p<0.05). As some of the comparisons failed to reach statistical significance only by a margin, U-Tests for group comparisons were calculated.

The offender group scores significantly higher than the congregation members in the scale 'too quarrelsome/competitive' ($p<0.001$, ES = -1.17) and the dominance dimension ($p<0.05$, ES = -0.76), and significantly lower in the affiliation dimension ($p<0.01$, ES = $+0.92$). The trainees described themselves as more dominant than the congregation members ($p<0.05$, ES = -0.61) but neither of these groups differ from the offenders on that measure.

DISCUSSION

We postulated that violent offenders would show a higher proportion of insecure attachment than both comparison groups. The expected differences between the offender group and the comparison groups in terms of relationship organisation, emotional attachment to others, and desire for personal autonomy were confirmed. With respect to attachment styles, there were no differences between trainees and congregation members. Surprisingly, we found a high percentage of secure attachment styles in the offender group (35% secure, 19% ambivalent, 19% dismissing, and 26% mixed-insecure). Taking into consideration that the investigation took up to four hours per person and demanded a great deal of intellectual and communicative abilities, there might be a positive bias in the offender group toward a high level of social functioning, which in turn might have evolved as a result of relatively secure attachment experiences across the life cycle.

The percentage of secure attachment classifications is still much higher in the comparison groups (trainees 77% secure, congregation members 81% secure attachment classifications).

It should also be noted that these findings differ clearly from clinical studies using the EBPR. This is especially true for the proportion of secure attachment classifications. Lobo (1997) published a study in which treatment effects in 22 patients following long-term in-patient psychotherapy were investigated with respect to their attachment styles. Forty-seven per cent were categorised insecure-ambivalent, 24 per cent insecure-dismissing, and another 24 per cent mixed-insecure. Only one patient was classified secure. The Pilkonis Prototype Rating, which is the precursor of the EBPR, was first applied with depressive patients (Pilkonis 1988). In order to predict therapeutic outcome after a six-month follow-up period, Pilkonis *et al.* (1991) tried to relate attachment characteristics of 40 depressive patients to personality disorders. Twenty-three per cent of the patients were rated insecure-dismissing, 25 per cent insecure-ambivalent, 28 per cent mixed-insecure, and 25 per cent could not be classified. All patients with insecure-ambivalent attachment, 44 per cent of the insecure-dismissing, and 64 per cent of the patients with mixed-insecure attachment classifications suffered from a personality disorder. In another clinical study Pilkonis *et al.* (1995) recruited a sample of 152 patients who received treatment for an affective and anxiety disorder. Only four patients were securely attached. Sixty-three (43%) were classified insecure-ambivalent, 25 (17%) insecure-dismissing, and 60 (41%) mixed-insecure.

Neither the offender group nor the comparison groups are similar to clinical in-patients in terms of quality of attachment styles and interpersonal problems. On the contrary: taking a closer look at the offender group, it seems largely to reflect the findings reported for the attachment status of any socio-economically disadvantaged sample, regardless of the presence of problems with social adjustment or adequate social behaviour (Mickelson, Kessler and Shaver 1997; van IJzendoorn and Bakermans-Kranenburg 1996). Taking into consideration that most violent offenders come from low-income families, this is not surprising.

The differences between the groups are largely due to the high percentage of 'secure' attachment classifications in the comparison groups, which is higher than the data on normal samples suggest (Mickelson *et al.* 1997; van IJzendoorn and Bakermans-Kranenburg 1996). On theoretical grounds, important elements of attachment security are the predictability of reactions and the reliability of attachment figures in the social environment, structuring and determining the function of the internal working model. Within their highly structured social environments, the interpersonal interactions of comparison groups are to a large extent reliable and predictable. It seems reasonable to suppose that the emotional stability which is thereby conveyed (in the sense of a 'secure base'), and which is linked to the expectation of physical and psychological freedom from injury, accounts for the major difference in attachment security across the three investigated groups.

Self-regulation

As suggested by the literature on self-regulative processes of offenders (Bateman 1996; de Zulueta 1996; Fonagy 1996; Kernberg 1975, 1992), differences between the groups were anticipated with respect to intra-psychic narcissistic regulative processes such as fantasies of greatness, the self-ideal, and a profound wish for praise and recognition, combined with a devaluation of significant others. Furthermore, it was expected that the groups would differ in their capability to control affect and impulse and in their feeling of social isolation. This hypothesis was partly confirmed. The offenders devalued others more often than the congregation members and were less attached to a societal value system. However, these differences did not show in a comparison between the offender group and the trainees. Religious persons may largely concur with social norms, and stress the importance of well-functioning social contacts (Spilka and McIntosh 1997; Wulff 1997). Surprisingly, however, there was no statistically significant group difference concerning the experience of social isolation; this was not to be expected, considering the fact that the degree of freedom to form and maintain social contacts is limited for incarcerated offenders. However, a closer look at the data reveals differences in the expected direction. U-Tests showed that, if compared with only one of the comparison groups, offenders experience more social isolation than each respective comparison group.

There was no evidence for a diminished ability of offenders to control their own reactions as a consequence of experienced disappointments and insults (Hollander and Stein 1995; Webster and Jackson 1997). Considering the fact that participation in the study required a minimum of three hours' intensive work, it is likely that the offenders who participated performed a self-selection with regard to high frustration tolerance. Interestingly, the congregation members scored significantly higher than the offender group in the scale 'greed for praise and recognition', which is one of the scales reflecting the dimension of the classic narcissistic self. High scores on this scale indicate a profound wish for narcissistic gratification without delay, a need for praise and a grandiose self-portrayal. This result clearly supports Kirkpatrick's compensation hypothesis as to why individuals become strong believers in a personal God.

It should be noted that none of the investigated groups reflect the norm in terms of self-regulation processes. A series of Wilcoxon-Tests resulted in

significant differences between the offender group and a small sample of
healthy men (n = 16, Deneke and Hilgenstock 1989). The offender group
scored lower in the scale 'autarky ideal' (p<0.001) and higher in the scales
'loss of affect and impulse control' (p<0.01), 'narcissistic rage' (p<0.01),
'object devaluation' (p<0.001) and 'narcissistic gain' (p<0.05).

The trainees scored higher than the norm sample in the scales 'loss of
affect and impulse control' (p<0.01), 'greed for praise and recognition'
(p<0.01), 'narcissistic rage' (p<0.05), 'object devaluation' (p<0.05), and
'narcissistic gain' (p<0.01), and the congregation members scored lower in
the scale 'autarky ideal' (p<0.001) and higher in the scales 'greed for praise
and recognition' (p<0.01), 'value ideal' (p<0.01), and 'longing for ideal self
object' (p<0.001).

While the differences for the offender group seem to be consistent with
what one would expect, it is obvious that the two comparison groups are not
representative of the norm population either. The scales in which differences were found between the trainees and the norm group largely correspond to those found between the offender group and the normal group,
but the effect sizes are a little smaller. The congregation members differ
from the norm group mainly with respect to scales reflecting the classic narcissistic self, indicating their longing for an omnipotent, powerful and stim-
ulating self object.

Interpersonal problems

Except for the scale 'too quarrelsome/competitive', there were no differences between the offender group and the comparison groups. Although
there is no clear statistical support for the main hypothesis, a trend may still
be visible, as two scales, 'too autocratic/dominant' and 'too dismiss-
ive/cold' (both of which are elements of the dominance dimension),
scraped past the statistical alpha level of p<0.05 (p =0.06). The offenders
described themselves as more dominant than the congregation members, in
the sense of hostile dominance, and consequently they scored lower on the
affiliation dimension. It might be the case that friendly and peaceful
behaviour plays an important role in the social value system of congregation
members and will thus be reinforced within the religious community. This
might lead to a subsequent internalisation of a friendly communication
ideal and low overt hostility levels. This interpretation is further supported
by their high scores in the scales 'too insecure/submissive' (M = 12.00,

SD = 4.09; offenders M = 10.97, SD = 5.27; trainees M = 9.60, SD = 5.14), 'too solicitous/friendly' (M = 12.53, SD = 2.64; offenders M = 11.97, SD = 5.58; trainees M = 11.85, SD = 5.51) and 'too exploit-able/compliant' (M = 13.73, SD = 3.35; offenders M = 11.72, SD = 5.22; trainees M = 11.00, SD = 5.96).

The trainees, too, score higher in the dominance scale than the congregation members, but there is no difference from the offender group (p<0.05). With respect to the group comparison offenders × trainees, the hypothesis is therefore rejected.

A comparison with the scale means of the normative sample (n = 1,335, Horowitz et al. 1994) yielded significantly higher means in the offender group on the scale 'too quarrelsome/competitive' (Wilcoxon-Test, p<0.05) as compared to the norm sample. While this finding supports our expectations, significantly lower scores of both comparison groups on the scales 'too dismissive/cold' (p<0.01) and 'too quarrelsome/competitive' (comparison: congregation members × normative sample, p<0.01) again indicate that the comparison groups are not representative. Both groups consist of individuals who perceive themselves as low in aggression, friendly and level-headed. It is debatable how far this self-image reflects social desirability or reaction formation within their social reference system. It is plausible to assume that conflict-prone interpersonal styles are unacceptable for both prison service trainees and congregation members, so it would seem that aggressive impulses must therefore be collectively repressed. Furthermore, it is likely that a high level of social control inhibits the behavioural expression of aggressive and violent impulses and therefore leads to a reduced probability of violent acts among socially controlled individuals.

Some of the differences between this and other studies of attachment might be explained by the heterogeneous methodological access to the subject. The assessment methods used for the identification of attachment in adult subjects differ largely between studies, ranging from a variety of attachment interviews based on expert ratings, and self-report scales with different theoretical underpinnings. In this study we used the EBPR, which is different to both the AAI and self-report scales in terms of analytic criteria. Due to the different research foci one cannot expect a high degree of correspondence between the two interviews. While the EBPR highlights behavioural representations of attachment reflected by narrative content, the AAI, using discourse analysis as a research technique, focuses on the coherence of the narrative and stresses the manner of reporting attachment-relevant experiences and intrapsychic coping mechanisms.

In general, it is an important future challenge for attachment researchers to unify the approaches to measuring attachment, or to explain which construct they wish to measure using a certain type of research instrument.

Regarding the results of this study, the question of possible predictive validity of attachment styles for the future prediction of violent behaviour must be raised. Longitudinal studies measuring attachment styles, in combination with known risk factors for violence, are required.

NOTES

1.   EBPR and AAI measure different dimensions of attachment. While attachment styles measured with the EBPR relate to manifest (observable and conscious) aspects of attachment behaviour displayed across the life cycle, attachment representations measured with the AAI reflect different states of mind (unconscious) with regard to early attachment relations and experiences (see Ross, in this volume).

2.   The EBPR analysis requires a ranking of the seven prototypes according to their degree of importance. The most prominent attachment prototype is ranked one; the lowest, seven. For the depiction of the results, this logic has been followed. Thus, the range of the figures (means) ranges from one (very high rating) to seven (very low rating).

3.   Sample sizes differing from n = 31 offenders, n = 22 prison service trainees and n = 21 congregation members in the self-report questionnaires (Narcissism Inventory and Inventory of Interpersonal Problems) are due to large proportions of missing data in some data sets, which were subsequently excluded from statistical analysis.

REFERENCES

Adshead, G. (2001) 'Personality disorder and disordered parenting: A perspective from attachment theory.' *Persönlichkeitsstörungen, Theorie und Therapie 5*, 81–89.

Bateman, A. (1996) 'Defence Mechanisms: General and forensic aspects.' In C. Cordess and M. Cox (eds) *Forensic Psychotherapy: Crime, Psychodynamics and the Offender Patient.* London, Bristol: Jessica Kingsley Publishers.

Bowlby, J. (1946) 'Forty-four juvenile thieves. Their characters and home life.' *Journal of Psychoanalysis 25*, 1–57, 207–228.

Bowlby, J. (1969) *Attachment and Loss. Vol.1 (Attachment)*. New York: Basic Books.

Bowlby, J. (1973) *Attachment and Loss. Vol.2 (Separation: Anxiety and Anger)*. New York: Basic Books.

Bowlby, J. (1980) *Attachment and Loss. Vol3. (Loss)*. New York: Basic Books.

Bowlby, J. (1988) 'Developmental psychiatry comes of age.' *American Journal of Psychiatry 145*, 1–10.

Bowlby, J. (1995) 'Bindung: Historische Wurzeln, theoretische Konzepte und klinische Relevanz.' In G. Spangler and P. Zimmermann (eds) *Die Bindungstheorie: Grundlagen, Forschung und Anwendung*. Stuttgart: Klett-Cotta.

Bretherton, I. and Munholland, K.A. (1999) 'Internal working models in attachment relationships. A construct revisited.' In J. Cassidy and P.R. Shaver (eds) *Handbook of Attachment. Theory, Research, and Clinical Applications*. New York: Guilford.

Deneke, F.W. and Hilgenstock, B. (1989) *Das Narzißmusinventar*. Bern: Huber.

de Zulueta, F. (1996) 'Theories of aggression and violence.' In C. Cordess and M. Cox (eds) *Forensic Psychotherapy: Crime, Psychodynamics and the Offender Patient*. London: Jessica Kingsley Publishers.

Fonagy, P. (1996) 'The significance of the development of metacognitive control over mental representations in parenting and infant development.' *Journal of Clinical Psychoanalysis 5*, 67–86.

Fonagy, P. (1999) 'Attachment, the development of self, and its pathology in personality disorders.' In J. Derksen and C. Maffei (eds) *Treatment of Personality Disorders*. New York: Kluwer Academic/Plenum.

Fonagy, P., Steele, H., Steele, M., Mattoon, G. and Target, M. (1995) 'Attachment, the reflective self, and borderline states. The predictive specificity of the Adult Attachment Interview and pathological emotional development.' In S. Goldberg, R. Muir and J. Kerr (eds) *Attachment Theory: Social, Developmental, and Clinical Perspectives*. New York: The Analytic Press.

Fonagy, P. and Target, M. (1996) 'Personality and sexual development, psychopathology and offending: Crime, psychodynamics and the offender patient.' In C. Cordess and M. Cox (eds) *Forensic Psychotherapy*. London: Jessica Kingsley Publishers.

Fonagy, P., Target, M., Steele, M. and Steele, H. (1997a) 'The development of violence and crime as it relates to security of attachment.' In J.D. Osofsky (eds) *Children in a Violent Society.* New York: Guilford.

Fonagy, P., Target, M., Steele, M., Steele, H., Leigh, T., Levinson, A. and Kennedy, R. (1997b) 'Crime and attachment: Morality, disruptive behavior, borderline personality, crime, and their relationships to security of attachment.' In L. Atkinson and K. Zucker (eds) *Attachment and Psychopathology.* New York: Guilford Press.

Gasper, H., Mü ller, J. and Valentin, F. (1990)*Lexikon der Sekten, Sondergruppen und Weltanschauungen.* Freiburg: Herder.

George, C., Kaplan, N. and Main, M. (1985) 'The Adult Attachment Interview.' Unpublished manuscript. University of California, Berkeley.

Hollander, E. and Stein, D. (1995) *Impulsivity and Aggression.* Toronto: Wiley.

Hollenweger, W. (1971) *Die Pfingstkirchen.* Stuttgart: Klett-Cotta.

Horowitz, L.M., Strauß, B. and Kordy, H. (1994) *Manual zum Inventar zur Erfassung interpersonaler Probleme (IIP-D).* Weinheim: Beltz-Test-Gesellschaft.

Kernberg, O.F. (1975) *Borderline Conditions and Pathological Narcissism.* New York: Aronson.

Kernberg, O.F. (1992) *Aggression in Personality Disorders and Perversion.* New Haven, CT: Yale University Press.

Kirkpatrick, L.A. and Shaver, P.R. (1992) 'An attachment-theoretical approach to romantic love and religious belief.' *Personality and Social Psychology Bulletin 18,* 266–275.

Kirkpatrick, L.A. (1997) 'An attachment-theory approach to the psychology of religion.' In B. Spilka and D.N. McIntosh (eds) *The Psychology of Religion.* Boulder, CO: Westview Press.

Kirkpatrick, L.A. (1998) 'God as a substitute attachment figure: A longitudinal study of adult attachment style and religious change in college students.' *Personality and Social Psychology Bulletin 24,* 961–973.

Kirkpatrick, L.A. (1999) 'Attachment and religious representations and behavior.' In J. Cassidy and P.R. Shaver (eds) *Handbook of Attachment: Theory, Research, and Clinical Applications.* New York: Guilford.

Leary, T. (1957) *Interpersonal Diagnosis of Personality.* Chicago: Ronald Press Company.

Levinson, A. and Fonagy, P. (1999) 'Criminality and attachment. The relationship between interpersonal awareness and offending in a prison population.' Paper presented at the 8th Annual Meeting of the International Association for Forensic Psychotherapy, May 7–9, Sheffield, UK.

Lobo, A. (1997) 'Entwicklung und Erprobung eines Verfahrens zur Erfassung von Erwachsenenbindungsprototypen.' Unpublished masters thesis, University of Bielefeld, Germany.

Lyons-Ruth, K. and Jacobovitz, D. (1999) 'Attachment disorganization: Unresolved loss, relational violence, and lapses in behavioural and attentional strategies.' In J. Cassidy and P.R. Shaver (eds) *Handbook of Attachment. Theory, Research, and Clinical Applications.* New York: Guilford.

Mickelson, K.D., Kessler, R.C. and Shaver, P.R. (1997) 'Adult attachment in a nationally representative sample.' *Journal of Personality and Social Psychology 73*, 1092–1106.

Pilkonis, P.A. (1988) 'Personality prototypes among depressives: Themes of dependency and autonomy.' *Journal of Personality Disorders 2*, 144–152.

Pilkonis, P., Heape, C., Proietti, J., Clark, S., McDavid, J. and Pitts, T. (1995) 'The reliability and validity of two structured diagnostic interviews for personality disorders.' *Archives of General Psychiatry 52*, 1025–1033.

Pilkonis, P.A., Heape, C.L., Ruddy, J. and Serrao, P. (1991) 'Validity in the diagnosis of personality disorders: The use of the LEAD standard.' *Journal of Consulting and Clinical Psychology 3*, 46–54.

Rosenstein, D. and Horowitz, H. (1996) 'Adolescent attachment and psychopathology.' *Journal of Clinical and Consulting Psychology 64*, 244–253.

Spilka, B. and McIntosh, D.N. (eds) (1997) *The Psychology of Religion: Theoretical Approaches.* Boulder, CO: Westview Press.

Strauß, B. and Lobo-Drost, A. (1999) 'Das Erwachsenen-Bindungsprototypen-Rating (EBPR) Version 1.0'. Unpublished manual.

Sullivan, H.S. (1953) *The Interpersonal Theory of Psychiatry.* New York: Norton.

van IJzendoorn, M.H. and Bakermans-Kranenburg, M.J. (1996) 'Attachment representations in mothers, fathers, adolescents, and clinical groups: A meta-analytic search for normative data.' *Journal of Consulting and Clinical Psychology 64*, 8–21.

van IJzendoorn, M.H., Feldbrugge, J.T., Derks, F.C., de Ruiter, C., Verhagen, M.F., Philipise, M.W., van der Staak, C.P. and Riksen-Walraven, J.M. (1997) 'Attachment representations of personality-disordered criminal offenders.' *American Journal of Orthopsychiatry 67*, 449–459.

Ward, T., Hudson, S.M. and Marshall, W.L. (1996) 'Attachment style in sex offenders: A preliminary study.' *Journal of Sex Research 33*, 17–26.

Webster, C. and Jackson, M. (1997) *Impulsivity: Theory, Assessment, and Treatment.* New York: Guilford.

Wulff, D.M. (1997) *Psychology of Religion: Classic and Contemporary.* (2nd edn.) New York: Wiley.

CHAPTER 10

Attachment Representations and Attachment Styles in Traumatized Women

Franziska Lamott, Natalie Sammet and Friedemann Pfäfflin

INTRODUCTION

Women are frequently exposed to violence. In Germany, one in seven women has been a victim of sexual violence at least once in her life (Wetzels and Pfeiffer 1995). According to estimates of the Federal Ministry for Family, the Elderly, Women and Youth (Bundesministerium f ür Familie, Senioren, Frauen und Jugend, 1998) violence is acted out in every third partnership in Germany. These data illustrate how common aggression and violent behaviour are, especially so within intimate relationships. Most women tolerate this violence for shorter or longer periods until they finally succeed in leaving their partner. On average, this occurs only after six to seven futile attempts at separation (Dransfeld 1998). Some succeed in separating only after taking refuge in shelters for battered women, once – or even repeatedly. Five years after the establishment of the first shelter for battered women in London in 1971, similar institutions were founded in Berlin and Cologne in 1976. According to a survey by the German Parliament, there were 435 such institutions in Germany in 1998, which sheltered approximately 45,000 women (and their children) per year (Deutscher Bundestag 1999).

Women are, however, not only victims. Sometimes they are perpetrators too. As compared to men, their crime rate is much lower. To give some figures: in Nigeria 3 per cent of the registered crime was committed by women, in the Netherlands 8 per cent, and in Japan 19 per cent (Feest 1993). According to German police statistics the female crime rate amounts to approximately 20 per cent, but only about 15 per cent of the women are finally sentenced, mostly for offences against property; and only about 4 per cent of female perpetrators end up as detainees in either a prison or a secure forensic psychiatric hospital (Feest 1993; Nowara 1993; Rasch 1999). These latter have usually committed serious crimes, e.g. manslaughter or murder of their own child or partner. The victims of women who kill are largely (approximately 85%) close relatives, partners, husbands, and children (Müller 1996), as compared with 50 per cent of the victims of men. While 56 per cent of the men who kill already have previous convictions of various kinds, this is only true for 14 per cent of the women (Müller 1996).

The aim of the studies presented here was to compare attachment representations and attachment styles of women who had killed and been sentenced either to imprisonment (Sample 1) or to detainment in a secure psychiatric hospital (Sample 2), with a third sample of women who escaped further victimization by their partners by taking refuge in a shelter for battered women (Sample 3). It was hypothesized that they differed in the amount of earlier traumatization experienced, and that their ways of conflict resolution would mirror different attachment patterns.

SAMPLES

As all the studies were exploratory ones, it was neither intended nor was it possible to draw representative samples. The investigators had to rely on support from the respective authorities of prisons and secure psychiatric hospitals as well as on the co-operation of the staff within all institutions involved. A precondition for participation for all three samples was sufficient knowledge of German, a conviction of murder or manslaughter (for Samples 1 and 2), or having taken refuge in a shelter for battered women (for Sample 3). All participants received a remuneration of 20 euros.

Sample 1 consisted of 23 women who served a prison sentence for murder or manslaughter and who had agreed to participate after having been informed by a female staff psychologist. All 23 women addressed agreed to participate.

Sample 2 consisted of 14 women detained in a secure psychiatric hospital by court order as a result of having killed another person and not being fully responsible for their criminal act due to one of the (mostly psychiatric) conditions provided for such circumstances in the criminal code. Recruitment of participants was much more difficult as compared with the prison setting: only 17 of the 20 women addressed agreed to participate and only 14 completed the investigation. Two who initially co-operated felt too burdened by the re-confrontation with their histories, and one woman turned out to be insufficiently fluent in German to comprehend the questions in the interview and questionnaires.

Sample 3 consisted of 14 women who had taken refuge in shelters for battered women. Participation rates were lowest in this group. The staff of 19 out of 20 shelters for battered women had agreed to co-operate and encourage clients to participate in the study, yet they were not very successful. Different from the women in Samples 1 and 2, who lived under safe and steady conditions in either a prison or a psychiatric hospital, the women in Sample 3 were particularly struggling to find solutions for their actual conflicts, so that most of them refrained from participating in a research project from which they could not expect immediate relief for their burdens.

METHODS

Samples 1 and 2 were interviewed with the Adult Attachment Interview (AAI, George, Kaplan and Main 1986), and Sample 3 with the German version of the Adult Attachment Prototype Rating (*Erwachsenen-Bindungsprototypen-Rating* (EBPR), Strauss and Lobo 1997; Strauss, Lobo-Drost and Pilkonis 1999), a semi-structured interview drawing on Pilkonis's (1988) prototypes of attachment styles (cf. Ross and Pfäfflin in this volume). The AAIs as well as the EBPRs were transcribed from the video- and/or audiotapes and rated by qualified raters.

In addition, the German versions of the Trauma Symptom Checklist (TSC-33, Briere and Runtz 1989), the Symptom Checklist (SCL-90, Derogatis 1994), and the Inventory for Interpersonal Problems (IIP-D,

Horowitz, Strauss and Kordy 1994) were applied. The test data are not reported here, as the purpose of this contribution focuses on attachment patterns. (For further details see Lamott and Pfäfflin 2001 and Sammet 2000.)

RESULTS

Demographic data

Most of the women in Samples 1 and 2 were married and had mothered children. All but five (14%) of their victims were close persons, either husbands or partners; this was the case for all but two of the 23 prisoners in Sample 1. Two of Sample 1 had killed their own children (as most of the women in Sample 2 had done). Eleven (48%) of the women in Sample 1 had acted with an accomplice, whereas all in Sample 2 had acted on their own account. Of the women in Sample 2 who were detained in a secure psychiatric hospital, 64 per cent were diagnosed as schizophrenic (ICD-10, F20); 14 per cent as suffering from an affective disorder (ICD-10, F30); 14 per cent as suffering from a specific personality disorder (ICD-10, F60.31); and 7 per cent as suffering from a mental disorder due to general medical conditions (ICD-10, F00.9).

Experience of violence

When comparing the types and amount of violence experienced by the women of all three samples, no statistically significant difference was found in the sum total of violence experienced. They had suffered various forms of sexual and other violence from their parents, their partners, and from other sources. Traumas experienced in childhood were widespread, mainly child sexual abuse, often committed by a father or stepfather, and later continued by a husband or partner.

Experience of loss of significant others

Fifty-seven per cent of the women in Sample 1, 71 per cent of the women in Sample 2, and 71 per cent of the women in Sample 3 had lost a significant other, usually a parent, during childhood.

Experience of trauma

Experiences of violence and of the loss of a significant other are, or at least may be, traumas in themselves. It is worth mentioning, however, that most women in both Samples 1 and 2 had experienced their own criminal acts as additional traumas.

Attachment representations, Samples 1 and 2

Attachment representations as measured by the three main classifications (F = secure; Ds = insecure-dismissive; E = insecure-enmeshed) are equally distributed over the combined total of Samples 1 and 2:

    F   (n = 10)   31%

    Ds   (n = 10)   31%

    E   (n = 12)   38%

The distribution is, however, unequal when Samples 1 and 2 are compared. In Sample 1 (prison), in total 'only' 58 per cent were classified as insecure (Ds 26% plus E 32%), and in Sample 2 (psychiatry), 85 per cent (Ds 39% plus E 46%) (see Table 10.1).

Attachment status, Samples 1 and 2

When taking into account the additional categories U (unresolved, traumatized; Gloger-Tippelt and Hofmann 1997) and CC (cannot classify; Hesse 1996), the picture looks quite different: in Sample 1 (prison) only 26 per cent were categorized as secure (F), 11 per cent as Ds, 1 per cent as E; but 42 per cent as U and 16 per cent as CC. The respective numbers for Sample 2 were F 1 per cent, Ds 29 per cent, E 14 per cent, U 14 per cent and CC 36 per cent. (See Table 10.2.)

Attachment styles and attachment status, Sample 3

In sample 3, 35.7 per cent of the women were classified as secure, 64.3 per cent as insecure (mainly insecure avoidant). When taking into account the additional categories U (unresolved, traumatized) and CC (cannot classify), the picture again looks quite different: 21 per cent were classified as F, 38.5 per cent as Ds or E, but 42.9 per cent as U and 7.1 per cent as CC. The differences are largely due to the different methods used for the analysis of attachment styles (EBPR) and attachment status (AAI). For further discussion of methodological issues see Ross, in this volume.

Table 10.1 Attachment representations in different groups of women

	Normal mothers*	Female perpetrators	Subgroups of perpetrators		Clinical groups*
			Prison	Psychiatry	
	n = 584	n = 32	n = 19	n = 13	n = 439
F	338 (58%)	10 (31%)	8 (42%)	2 (15%)	55 (13%)
Ds	139 (24%)	10 (31%)	5 (26%)	5 (39%)	180 (41%)
E	107 (18%)	12 (38%)	6 (32%)	6 (46%)	204 (46%)

* *Results of the meta-analysis by van IJzendoorn and Bakerman-Kranenburg (1996)*

F = autonomous

Ds = dismissing

E = preoccupied

Table 10.2 AAI main classifications and attachment status

	AAI main classifications and attachment status	Prison	Psychiatry	Total
		n=19	n=14	n=33
F	Autonomous	5 (26%)	1 (7%)	6 (18%)
Ds	Dismissing	2 (11%)	4 (29%)	6 (18%)
E	Preoccupied	1 (5%)	2 (14%)	3 (9%)
U	Unresolved/ disorganized	8 (42%)	2 (14%)	10 (31%)
CC	Cannot classify	3 (16%)	5 (36%)	8 (24%)

In describing their relationships with their parents, the women who had killed their husbands (mostly Sample 1) characterized their mothers as much more loving than their fathers, albeit weak. In most cases, these mothers were unable to protect their daughters and frequently were themselves victims of violent husbands. The fathers were described as harsh and dominant, often violating physical and sexual boundaries. It was, however, remarkable that these fathers were often also idealized, which would indicate a rather ambivalent representation of the fathers.

In contrast, mothers who had killed their own children (mainly in Sample 2) characterized their fathers as much more loving than their mothers. The mothers were predominantly described as dismissing, cold and depressed. It seemed as if the motherly representation was 'void' or 'empty'.

DISCUSSION

The three samples of women differ clearly in a number of respects. Criminologically, Samples 1 (prison) and 2 (psychiatry) seem to be similar in as much as both groups consist of women who have killed another (usually, a close) person. The women in Sample 3 avoided a criminological escalation by taking refuge in a shelter for battered women.

There are also differences from a psychiatric point of view. The women in Sample 1 stood trial without a clinical psychiatric diagnosis and therefore were sent to prison, while the women in Sample 2 were regarded as not fully responsible for their actions owing to a psychiatric diagnosis, and were therefore sent by a court decision to a secure psychiatric clinic for treatment.

As regards trauma histories, the women in Sample 1 had mostly suffered physical and sexual abuse during their childhood, whereas the women in Sample 2 were for the most part traumatized by the death of significant others during their childhood or by a depressive and suicidal mother.

Attachment representations and attachment styles differed among the three samples. As compared to the data drawn from the meta-analysis of van IJzendoorn and Bakerman-Kranenburg (1996), all three samples clearly show a smaller proportion of the F classification than 'normal mothers', and Sample 2 (psychiatry), not surprisingly, comes closest to the data for 'clinical groups'.

Applying the five-category AAI classification system to further analyse the data, one of the most striking results of the studies was the high percentages of the categories U and CC in all three samples (see Table 10.2). While the U category captures a limited breakdown of the narrative, usually within the context of memories of specific traumas, it is still possible to identify one of the main representations (F, Ds, E) within a specific narrative by a person with unresolved traumatic experience. The CC category, by contrast, captures a total breakdown of discourse strategies throughout the narrative. Hesse (1996) introduced the CC classification, but it should not be used as a classification just for 'leftover' parts that cannot be specifically classified. Instead, we suggest using it as a sign for fragmentation of the narrative, and so giving it the specific designator 'fragmented' or 'FRAG'. For clinical examples see Chapter 3 (in this volume) by Lamott *et al.*

CONCLUSIONS

Insecure attachment representations, and especially unresolved traumatic experiences, seem to promote the development and maintenance of psychic disorders, namely those of the borderline type, all the more when those who inflicted the traumas were significant others, e.g. father or mother. Under such circumstances identification with the aggressor may become one of the predominant defence mechanisms and result in violent behaviour against the self or against others. Frequently, it may also have an impact on the choice of a partner. When interpersonal conflicts end in a deadly disaster, it seems obvious that there was an underlying lack of reflective function and ability for constructive conflict solution. Results from attachment and psychotraumatological research may contribute to a better understanding of such processes, and help therapists and other agents who are in charge of traumatized persons to reflect on the models for violent behaviour and to create the conditions for understanding and alternative types of action.

REFERENCES

Briere, J. and Runtz, M. (1989) 'The Trauma Symptom Checklist (TSC-33) Early data on a new scale.' *Journal of Interpersonal Violence 4*, 151–163.

Bundesministerium f ür Familie, Senioren, Frauen und Jugend (1998)*Frauen in der Bundesrepublik Deutschland.* Berlin: Schriftenreihe des BMFSFJ Nr. 9435.

Derogatis, L.R. (1994) *SCL-90–R (Symptom Checklist 90–R): Administration, Scoring and Procedures Manual.* Minneapolis: Computer Systems Inc.

Dransfeld, G. (1998) 'Gewalt in der Partnerschaft – Frauenhausarbeit in Deutschland.' *Theorie und Praxis der sozialen Arbeit 49*, 148–152.

Deutscher Bundestag (1999) *Drucksache 14/849*, 27 April 1999.

Feest, J. (1993) 'Frauenkriminalität.' In G. Kaiser, H.-J. Kerner, F. Sack and H. Schellhoss (eds) *Kleines Kriminologisches Wörterbuch.* 3rd. edn. Heidelberg: C.F. Mü ller.

George, C., Kaplan, N. and Main, M. (1986) 'Adult Attachment Interview Protocol.' Unpublished manuscript, University of California at Berkeley.

Gloger-Tippelt, G. and Hoffmann, V. (1997) 'Das Adult Attachment Interview: Konzeption, Methode und Erfahrungen im deutschen Sprachraum.' *Kindheit und Entwicklung 6*, 161–172.

Hesse, E. (1996) 'Discourse, memory and the Adult Attachment Interview: A note with the emphasis on the emerging "cannot classify" category.' *Infant Mental Health Journal 17*, 4–11.

Horowitz, L.M., Strauss, B. and Kordy, H. (1994) *Manual zum Inventar zur Erfassung interpersoneller Probleme (IIP-D).* Weinheim: Beltz.

Lamott, F., Fremmer-Bombik. E. and Pfäfflin, F. (2003) 'Fragmented attachment representations.' (In this volume.)

Lamott, F. and Pfäfflin, F. (2001) 'Bindungsrepräsentationen von Frauen, die getötet haben.' *Monatsschrift füör Kriminologie und Strafrechtsreform 84*, 10–24.

Müller, H. (1996) *Menschen, die getötet haben.* Opladen: Westdeutscher Verlag.

Nowara, S. (1993) 'Psychisch kranke Straftäterinnen.' In N. Leygraf, R. Volbert, H. Horstkotte and S. Fried (eds) *Die Sprache des Verbrechens. Wege zu einer klinischen Kriminologie.* Stuttgart: Kohlhammer.

Pilkonis, P.A. (1988) 'Personality prototypes among depressives: Themes of dependency and autonomy.' *Journal of Personality Disorders 2*, 144–152.

Rasch, W. (1999) *Forensische Psychiatrie.* 2nd edn. Stuttgart: Kohlhammer.

Ross, T. (2003) 'Attachment representation, attachment style or attachment pattern? Usage of terminology in attachment theory.' (Chapter 2 in this volume.)

Ross, T. and Pfäfflin, F. (2003) 'Violence and attachment: Attachment styles, self-regulation, and interpersonal problems in a prison population.' (Chapter 9 in this volume.)

Sammet, N. (2000) 'Frauen mit Gewalterfahrungen: Bindungsmuster und Lösungsversuche.' Dissertation, University of Ulm.

Strauss, B. and Lobo, A. (1997) 'Das Beziehungsprototypenverfahren von Bindungsqualitäten im Erwachsenenalter nach Pilkonis.' Unpublished manuscript.

Strauss, B., Lobo-Drost, A.J. and Pilkonis, P.A. (1999) 'Einschätzung von Bindungsstilen bei Erwachsenen – erste Erfahrungen mit der deutschen Version einer Prototypenbeurteilung.' *Zeitschrift föür Klinische Psychologie, Psychiatrie und Psychotherapie 47,* 347–346.

van IJzendoorn, M.H. and Bakermans-Kranenburg, M.J. (1996) 'Attachment representations in mothers, fathers, adolescents, and clinical groups: A meta-analytic search for normative data.' *Journal of Consulting and Clinical Psychology 64,* 8–21.

Wetzels, P. and Pfeiffer, C. (1995) 'Sexuelle Gewalt gegen Frauen in öffentlichen und privaten Raum.' Ergebnisse der KFN-Opferbefragung 1992. Forschungsbericht des Kriminologischen Forschungsinstituts Niedersachsen e. V. (Nr. 37), im Auftrag des BMFSFJ.

Conclusion

A Matter of Security

Gwen Adshead and Friedemann Pfäfflin

It seems clear that attachment theory is a paradigm that has real meaning and utility in forensic psychiatry and psychotherapy. Its utility lies not only in the explanation it offers of the severe psychopathology that we see in forensic work, but also in the ways that it offers ways of thinking about treatment. For an example of the former, we have Lamott and colleagues' work on fragmented attachment representations, which offers a convincing explanation for the range of dissociated and psychotic states that trouble our patients so frequently. In terms of therapy (which Bowlby himself emphasised as being of prime importance), both Paul Renn's and Anne Aiyegbusi's chapters provide practical ways of trying to match up internal psychological security with security and safety in the external world – a therapeutic goal that no forensic clinician can ignore.

WHAT PRICE SECURITY?

There is more to be said about the meaning of attachment theory for forensic psychiatry and psychotherapy. First, we want to think effectively about the capacity to be distressed – most clearly expressed in this quote about Ophelia in *Hamlet*: 'She spoke as one *incapable* of her own distress' (emphasis added). To us, this suggests that the capacities to experience one's own distress and to manage it effectively are acquired and are clearly related to effective secure attachment. An infant in distress at times of threat seeks proximity to his caregiver, and feels soothed and contained. A coherent internal working model of that soothing and containing relationship needs to be internalised in order to enable the child to manage his own affects and arousal safely. Fonagy (in this volume) offers a compelling account of how failure in mentalisation of such representations might operate in people who are violent. What it means is that those who are violent live in an unsafe world *all the time*; and forensic workers, and indeed all those who have an interest in the study and prevention of violence, need to appreciate this. Nothing can be taken for granted, especially in the context of the therapeutic alliance (Sarkar 2002). This fundamental lack of security also means that there are patients who need maximum security for their own psychic safety, as well as that of others; it may also explain why some forensic patients find it impossible to leave secure institutions, and indeed do all they can to stay there. In fact, we might hypothesise that, rather than acting criminally from an unconscious sense of guilt (Freud 1912), they act from an unconscious need to achieve security for themselves and to protect their internalised attachment figures. What is tragic and dangerous is that they often achieve internal security at a cost that is paid by their victims as well as they themselves.

ATTACHMENT THEORY AND OTHER PSYCHOANALYTIC ACCOUNTS

This need to protect the attachment figures in mind also accounts for the idealisation phenomena which we encounter so often in forensic practice. It seems fairly clear that a dismissing representation of attachment is extremely common in forensic populations. Fonagy *et al.* (1997) link this with a failure to develop the capacity for empathy, which seems intuitively correct: a person who dismisses their own distress is not likely to be able to take others' distress seriously either. But psychoanalytic forensic psychotherapists have also understood idealisation to be a manifestation of perversion: a state of mind, linked with Klein's paranoid-schizoid position, in which attachment figures (although not described as such) are either idealised or denigrated in a way which is at the same time rigid and unstable. A perverse state of mind is a defence against feelings of hatred for the attachment figure (Stoller 1975), perhaps also against intolerable grief. There is an important link here between the two theories: both posit the existence of unstable mental states which involve the conscious disavowal of distress, conscious idealisation of others, and unconscious disavowal of feelings of rage, distress, grief and fear. Attachment theory is a theory of object relations, and in that sense is no different to other psychoanalytic theories that influence the practice of psychotherapy with forensic patients.

Of course, there has been debate and dissent within psychoanalytic circles about attachment theory, which has turned on the relevance of external world events to the internal world, and about the importance that attachment theory attributes to real world experience. Interestingly, this debate is paralleled in psychiatry more generally in the debates about the concept of Post-Traumatic Stress Disorder and the effects of traumatic stress and fear on the mind. This debate about the interaction of external and internal world events and experiences is important and relevant to forensic psychiatry because forensic patients make things happen in the external world; they are living examples of how the dynamics of the internal world are acted out (literally) in a bodily fashion in the external world. Shakespeare, as usual, puts it best, in *Julius Caesar*, when Brutus acts on his murderous desire and says, 'Speak, hands, for me!'

RESEARCH IMPLICATIONS: RISK AND TREATMENT

What we do not know is exactly how, and in what circumstances, the capacity to contain cruelty and destructiveness is overwhelmed; and where insecure attachment representations fit into this failure to contain. It is clear that insecure states of mind are risk factors for violence in some populations at certain times, but perhaps no more than any other risk factor. The research published here provides evidence of highly disturbed states of mind with regard to attachment in offender patients, but then raises further questions. To what extent would this be true of all offenders and social rule-breakers? Didn't we know that anyway, given the levels and types of violence they have exhibited? It seems that insecurity of mind, as a category, is too non-specific to be useful for risk prediction (although this is true of most individual personality characteristics). What can this information be used for?

There are research projects that have looked at the implications of insecure states of mind for therapy, and its effectiveness. Fonagy *et al.* (1996) found that individuals with dismissing states of mind did well with in-patient psychotherapy in a specialised psychotherapeutic setting, although, as the authors note, this group made more gains because they had most to make. Dozier (1990) and Dozier *et al.* (2001) describe how insecure states of mind affect treatment compliance in patients with severe mental illness, and how dismissing states of mind can make it difficult for patients to engage in therapy. Colleagues at Broadmoor Hospital are currently studying how attachment representations affect staff–patient relationships and behaviour on the ward (including violence), and the extent to which these representations can and do change over time.

It certainly seems sensible to extend the attachment research paradigm to therapeutic relationships between staff and patients, since theoretically we can expect re-enactments of previous attachment relationships with professional carers (Adshead 1998, 2001). Several attachment researchers have begun work in this area. Such work is likely to be of particular importance in those forensic settings where staff and patients may literally spend years together. In prisons and high security hospitals, where patients spend the 'life' sentences passed upon them, it is possible for young patients and staff to literally grow up together, and for older staff to act like parents to both groups. There are forensic institutions where several generations of family have worked as members of staff. In such circumstances, we may expect toxic attachments to form and be enacted. We need to understand much more about the capacity for caregiving: what makes caring difficult, and especially how to care for people who mistrust care.

ATTACHMENT AND MORALITY

Even more fascinating research questions arise if we think about the meaning of attachment relationships in the context of making or acquiring the capacity to make moral choices. Fonagy *et al.* (1997) offer a broad (and ambitious) account of how the capacity to make moral choices might be linked to the capacity for self-reflection, and how this might apply to violent offenders. If we are not real to ourselves, reason Fonagy and colleagues, can others be real to us? Can we then even begin to take part in the complex moral discourses that give us both personal and social identities?

Certainly, the value that we place on our different attachment relationships has meaning, both emotionally and ethically. I care for my friend, Jim; I am attached to him. Because I am attached to him, I have some emotional investment in his welfare and happiness, and I want good things for him. I will avoid hurting him or doing him wrong, because this also hurts and wrongs me; I will therefore hold conscious ethical intentions towards Jim: namely, that I should not hurt him or wrong him. There are of course many other ethical reasons why I should not hurt him (he is human, it is generally wrong to do so, regardless of relationships, etc.); we suggest here only (as did the philosopher David Hume) that emotional attachments influence ethical choices about those attachments.

What attachment theory would also posit (like any other analytic theory) is that there are *unconscious* attachments that may influence our ethical choices towards others we are close to; and these unconscious attachment feelings may be as powerful and as negative as the conscious ones are powerful and positive. To put it another way, negative transference affects the way we relate to people; but if that is so, it will also affect our ethical choices about others, since these are also part of the relating process. Perhaps the key issue about self-reflective capacity, as described by Fonagy, is that it is an essential component of the capacity for metacognitive thinking (Main 1991); and further, perhaps ethical reasoning itself is a type of metacognition, in which we acquire the capacity to reason about our feelings, rather than act them out. The link between the ways people talk about ethical choices and the ways they talk about attachments would be of real interest to study.

AND FINALLY…

It is a truism to say that more research is necessary; and like many truisms, it is only partly true. At the time of writing, when it seems inevitable that some of the world's great powers will go to war, it might be useful to know more about how attachment theory applies to groups and communities, especially when the communities are close in geography and culture. It would also be useful to know more about the long-term consequences of disrupted attachments in children in traumatised communities.

We think there is also more to know about language and how attachment experiences influence how we talk about ourselves. As one AAI subject said in an interview: 'I guess it's not so much what happened to me, but what I make of it.' This is crucial for the forensic patient, who has to learn to speak about the unspeakable, past and present; and for the therapist, who has to listen.

REFERENCES

Adshead, G. (1998) 'Psychiatric staff as attachment figures.' *British Journal of Psychiatry 172*, 64–69.

Adshead, G. (2001) 'Attachment in mental health institutions: A commentary.' *Attachment and Human Development 3*, 324–329.

Dozier, M. (1990) 'Attachment organisation and treatment use in adults with serious psychopathological disorders.' *Development and Psychopathology 2*, 47–60.

Dozier, M., Lomax, L., Tyrell, C. And Lee, S. (2001) 'The challenge of treatment for clients with dismissing states of mind.' *Attachment and Human Development 3*, 62–76.

Fonagy, P., Leigh, T., Steele, M., Steele, H., Kennedy, R., Mattoon, G., Target, M. And Gerber, A. (1996) 'The relation of attachment status, psychiatric classification and response to psychotherapy.' *Journal of Consulting and Clinical Psychology 64*, 22–31.

Fonagy, P., Target, M., Steele, M., Steele, H., Leigh, T., Levinson, A. and Kennedy, R. (1997) 'Morality, disruptive behaviour, borderline personality disorder, crime and their relationships to security and attachment.' In Atkinson and K.J. Zucker (eds) *Attachment and Psychopathology*. New York: Guilford.

Freud, S. (1957) 'Some character-types met with in psychoanalytic work.' In *Collected Papers Vol. IV*. Trs. Joan Riviere. London: Hogarth Press. First published in 1912.

Main, M. (1991) 'Metacognition knowledge, metacognitive monitoring and singular (coherent) vs multiple (incoherent) model of attachment: findings and directions for future research.' In C.M. Parkes, J. Stevenson-Hinde and P. Marris (eds) *Attachment Across the Life Cycle*. London: Routledge.

Sarkar, S. (2002) 'The other 23 hours: Problems of psychotherapy in a "special" hospital.' Paper presented at International Association for Forensic Psychotherapy, Stuttgart.

Stoller, R. (1975) *Perversion: The Erotic Form of Hatred*. London: Maresfield.

The Contributors

Gwen Adshead is a forensic psychiatrist and psychotherapist working at Broadmoor Hospital. After her forensic training, she carried out research into post-traumatic stress disorder at the Institute of Psychiatry, and also trained as a group analyst. She is involved in a research study about the assessment of caring capacity in maltreating mothers, using an attachment paradigm, with Professors Lynne Murray and Peter Cooper at the University of Reading. Gwen's other main academic interest is ethical dilemmas in forensic psychiatry, and she is currently working on a book on this topic with Dr Sameer Sarkar.

Anne Aiyegbusi is a consultant nurse at Broadmoor Hospital. She has worked in medium and high secure mental health services for over 20 years and is trained in the use of the Adult Attachment Interview. Anne is interested in the psychodynamics of forensic mental health care and the application of attachment theory to nursing practice in forensic mental health care.

Kerry Bluglass is Consultant Psychiatrist at Woodbourne Priory Hospital, and Senior Clinical Lecturer at the Department of Psychiatry, University of Birmingham She trained in Birmingham and for several years was Director of Studies at St Christopher's Hospice. She is a member of the GMC's health Committee and the Mental Health Review Tribunal. She is a Member of and Psychiatric Advisor to the Information and Support Committee for the Foundation for the Sudden Infant Death and Member of the Psycho Social group of the European Society for the Prevention of Infant Death (ESPID). Kerry has a particular interest in bereavement reactions and mother-child relationships. Recently, she has specialised in the assessment of mothers who have demonstrated Munchausen Syndrome by proxy behaviour, and she has written and co-authored several papers on this subject. She is shortly to publish a book about experiences of children hidden during the Holocaust.

Peter Fonagy is Freud Memorial Professor of Psychoanalysis and Director of the Sub-Department of Clinical Health Psychology at University College London. He is Director of the Child and Family Centre at the Menninger Foundation, Kansas and also Director of Research at the Anna Freud Centre, London. He is a clinical psychologist and a training and supervising analyst in the British Psycho-Analytical Society in child and adult analysis. Peter's clinical interests centre around issues of borderline psychopathology, violence and early attachment relationships. His work attempts to integrate empirical research with psychoanalytic theory. He has published over 200 chapters and articles and has authored and edited several books.

Elisabeth Fremmer-Bombik is a clinical psychologist. For many years she worked with professor Klaus Grossmann at the Institute of Developmental Psychology at the University of Regensburg. Klaus Grossmann and his wife Karin Grossmann were the pioneers in introducing attachment research in Germany, conducting longitudinal studies of attachment prototypes and the consequent attachment representations, and Elisabeth coauthored some of their research and does own research in the field. She is now working as a clinical psychologist and psychotherapist at the hospital for Child and Youth Psychiatry in Regensburg.

Franziska Lamott, completed her Ph.D in Sociology at the University of Munich and trained as a group analyst. She has worked in criminology at the universities of Bielefeld and Munich, Germany, and as assistant professor in social psychology at the university of Klagenfurt, Austria. Since 1995, she has been an assistant professor in the department of Forensic Psychotherapy at the University of Ulm. Franziska has published widely in the fields of criminology, psychotherapy research, gender-, and cultural studies.

Mark Morris trained in Medicine and Psychiatry in Glasgow, moving to London to work in the Cassel Hospital in Richmond. His first consultant post was in St Bernards Hospital, along with a spell in the Charing Cross Gender Clinic while he completed his training with the British Psychoanalytic Society. He then worked as the Director of Therapy in HMP Grendon for four years. Mark's current appointment is as a Consultant Psychiatrist in Psychotherapy in the Portman Clinic, London and has an attachment to the Prison Services Close Supervision Centres. He contributes to the work of the Association of Psychoanalytic Psychotherapists in the NHS, and the British Confederation of Psychotherapists.

Michael Parker has extensive experience in therapeutic communities and qualified as a group analyst in 1995. In 1998 he joined the prison service as a Wing Therapist on A-Wing, HMP Grendon. This has now become the first accredited therapeutic community prison wing in the world to receive official home office accreditation as a 24-hour-a-day regime helping to reduce re-offending. He has an increasing interest in combining aspects of management with psychotherapy and in the process of continually transferring skills and competencies within the staff group and into the inmate group: the heart of the Foulksian group-analytic tradition.

Friedemann Pfäfflin is professor of Psychotherapy and head of the department of Forensic Psychotherapy at the University of Ulm. He trained as a psychiatrist and psychoanalyst at the University Clinic of Hamburg, Germany, and has been working in Ulm since 1992. Friedemann Pfäfflin is former president of the International Association of Forensic Psychotherapy (IAFP) and the president of The International Association for the Treatment of Sexual Offenders (IATSO) and has published widely on forensic psychiatry and psychotherapy, the history of psychiatry during Nazi times, and on transgenderism and transsexualism.

Paul Renn is a psychoanalytic psychotherapist in private practice in west London. He is a member of the Centre for Attachment-based Psychoanalytic Psychotherapy (CAPP) and also works as a probation officer in London, supervising high risk offenders in a community-based public protection team. He has a particular interest in and experience of assessing and working with violent men from an attachment theory and research perspective. Paul is a member of the International Attachment Network and the International Association for Forensic Psychotherapy. He has contributed papers to *Violent Children and Adolescents: Asking the Question Why*, edited by G. Boswell, and to the *Journal of Attachment and Human Development*.

Thomas Ross studied psychology and clinical psychology at the Universities of Freiburg, Germany, and Edinburgh, Scotland. Since 1997 he has been a researcher in Forensic Psychotherapy at the University of Ulm, Germany. In addition to conducting attachment research, he works on the development of research instruments for the study of the psychotherapy process in offender groups and the prediction of violence within the thematic network Study COMSKILLS, funded by the European Union. He has also carried out research on crime as it relates to mental disorders in migrants.

Natalie Sammet is a former staff member in the department of Forensic Psychotherapy at the University of Ulm. She is now working in private practice as a cognitive behavioral psychotherapist in Ulm, Germany.

Subject Index

Author Index

Lightning Source UK Ltd.
Milton Keynes UK
UKOW030603190312

189198UK00001B/2/A